P9-AON-535

MOBOCRACY

HOW THE MEDIA'S OBSESSION WITH POLLING TWISTS THE NEWS, ALTERS ELECTIONS, AND UNDERMINES DEMOCRACY

MATTHEW ROBINSON

FORUM

An Imprint of Prima Publishing

Copyright © 2002 by Matthew Robinson

All rights reserved. No part of this book may be reproduced or transmitted in any form or by any means, electronic or mechanical, including photocopying, recording, or by any information storage or retrieval system, without written permission from Random House, Inc., except for the inclusion of brief quotations in a review.

Published by Prima Publishing, Roseville, California. Member of the Crown Publishing Group, a division of Random House, Inc.

FORUM and colophon are trademarks of Random House, Inc.
PRIMA PUBLISHING and colophon are trademarks of Random House, Inc., registered with the United States Patent and Trademark Office.

Library of Congress Cataloging-in-Publication Data
Robinson, Matthew.
   Mobocracy : how the media's obsession with polling twists the news, alters elections, and undermines democracy / Matthew Robinson.
      p.   cm.
   Includes bibliographical referencs and index.
   ISBN 0-7615-3582-9
   1. Mass media and public opinion—United States. 2. Mass media—Political aspects—United States. 3. Election monitoring—United States. 4. Public opinion—United States. I. Title.
P96.P832 U668   2002
302.23'0973—dc21   2002133032

02 03 04 05 HH 10 9 8 7 6 5 4 3 2
Printed in the United States of America

First Edition

Visit us online at www.primapublishing.com

CONTENTS

For Alice Moore Robinson,
whose friendship and giving
continue to bless me.

ACKNOWLEDGMENTS

THIS BOOK would not have been possible without the gracious support of Tom Phillips, president of the Phillips Foundation. The Phillips Foundation gave a California surfer the opportunity to leave the harried life of daily writing and editing to focus all of his energies on one project. I owe him my deepest thanks.

In the course of working on the book, I learned that becoming a Phillips Foundation Fellow means far more than financial resources. Starting with the interview process, Tom Phillips, Don Hodel, Robert Novak, Al Regnery, and John Farley asked questions that showed that my work struck a chord and that my research would inform and aid my fellow citizens.

As the process progressed John Farley was of great assistance in everything from helping ease my move from California to reading the manuscript. He began as the consummate professional and ends a valued friend.

I hasten to add, however, that I would have never been considered for the Phillips honor if it were not for the kind mentoring, advice, and recommendations of Mark Cunningham, Tom Gray, and John Merline. They are all amazing writers and were among the many reasons I learned so much at *Investor's Business Daily*.

I'd also like to thank those who discussed and read the manuscript as it evolved. Special thanks go to Owen Brennan Rounds, who proved repeatedly not just a skillful editor, but also a man unmatched in creativity, humor, and insight about political questions, from polling to the defense of liberty. I also owe special gratitude to James Bovard, whose experience writing books and whose conversational gifts were the source of invaluable counsel through the protean struggle of producing a work such as this.

I'd also like to thank Mark Hemingway, Josh London, Ben Boychuk, and, in the final press of deadlines, Susan Hensley. Their insights and conversations helped press the book and my spirit forward.

Political scientists and pollsters Paul Lavrakas and Michael Traugott were especially gracious early in the process, taking time to speak with me about their careful studies.

At Prima Publishing, I'd like to thank Tara Mead, David Richardson, and Steven K. Martin—all of whom handled every step of the process with professional skill and a shared dedication to excellence.

If there are any mistakes, let me assure the reader, they are my own.

CHAPTER ONE

Media Lifeblood

THE ROAR FROM THE WHITE HOUSE had finally come to an end and an uneasy quiet followed. Congress gratefully buried themselves in the business of legislation. The news anchors were returning to more prosaic headlines. The scramble of journalists had broken up and moved on. The political debate shows on cable television searched for new scandals to keep their audiences. The lawyers closed their leather briefcases and withdrew into air-conditioned splendor. The private investigators went back to mundane divorce cases for juicy details. And the public sighed with genuine relief that it was all over.

One year after the impeachment and Senate acquittal of the president of the United States, the nation barely reflected on the legal case against William Jefferson Clinton. But the pollsters remembered. How could they forget their moment of greatest glory, their days of triumph? In late 1998, in the thick of the impeachment crisis, a CNN/*USA Today*/Gallup poll confidently announced that only 35 percent of adults said they backed the House of Representatives, impeachment of

Clinton. Like so many media outlets, this poll, which seemed to expose the "vast right-wing conspiracy," suggested political doom for the politician who crossed Clinton and the public. But one year later, with the crisis nearly forgotten and Monica Lewinsky adorning cute weight-loss ads, Americans did a strange thing. They began to back the House of Representatives' vote to impeach. Some 50 percent of Americans favored the action,[1] while just a year earlier, only 29 percent thought the Senate should remove Clinton. By 1999 that number rose to a dramatic 42 percent. Like the passions they measured at the time, the polls had changed. As *USA Today* declared, it was "a major shift in public attitude against the president." And that sentiment would continue to grow. By the time of the election in 2000, Bill Clinton, president during the most productive and long-lasting economic expansion in the twentieth century, would become the secret weapon of his rival.

What had saved the president from removal?

On a cool Washington evening in February 1998 at a White House reception, CNN's senior political analyst William Schneider, the very man who had masterminded the Clinton-backing poll, walked up to the president and claimed that title of savior. "I think I saved you," he told Clinton. Schneider was convinced that quick polling after news of Clinton's affair with a twenty-two-year-old intern kept elite opinion and Democratic disgust from demanding the resignation of Clinton. According to Schneider, "The polls showed that even though people weren't ready to demonstrate to keep Clinton in office, they still opposed his removal."[2]

> "The polls showed that even though people weren't ready to demonstrate to keep Clinton in office, they still opposed his removal."

For the next year, poll after poll would crash on the populace. The case, which according to Clinton defenders was "all about sex," would pit spin, popularity, and retribution against the rule of law. Whoever held the upper hand in the trial-by-media found favor in the polls. In this gladiatorial spectacle, the dramatic slashes of the partisan attack and the political thrusts of the unscrupulous details garnered attention and the public's thumb's up or down—not the quiet of reflection or reasoned discussion. In this arena, were the people informed? Were the sides equal?

Was Bill Clinton saved at the price of democratic deliberation and the rule of law?

In a 1965 article, polling pioneer George Gallup linked the pollster's measure of public sentiment directly to the future of democracy:

> As students, scholars, and the general public gain a better understanding of polls, they will have a greater appreciation of the service polls can perform in a democracy. In my opinion, modern polls are the chief hope of lifting government to a higher level, by showing that the public supports reforms that will make this possible, by providing a *modus operandi* for testing new ideas. . . . Polls can help make government more efficient and responsive; they can improve the quality of candidates for public office; they can make this a truer democracy.[3]

It is hard to imagine a more optimistic prophecy than that. Unfortunately the reality is vastly different. Since Gallup penned his words a generation ago, America has seen an explosion in the number, variety, and coverage of polls. There are polls on politics, celebrities, and sex. They are conducted by telephone and on the Internet. Pollsters ask for public opinion about candidates, actors, movies, and government policy—even people's opinions about cats and dogs. Men are interviewed for women's magazines. Women are interviewed for men's magazines. Networks and news shows instantly canvass citizens about massacres, chemical spills, gun violence, nutrition, and what they think about such hoaxes as the existence of aliens and the future solvency of Social Security. Newspapers base whole series of articles on a single survey, follow up with editorials, ultimately to finish with the musings of columnists. Meanwhile, Web sites for almost every major publication have Internet pseudo-polls, asking an unscientific sample to give their opinion, just to attract viewers.

The media are enthralled to polling. But was Gallup right? Are polls technical measures deepening the American understanding of politics, history, and the Constitution? Is the rule of law defended by ubiquitous random-digit-dialed surveys? Is the Bill of Rights protected by the instant scientific measures of sentiment and passion? Has the poll empowered the voice of the individual citizen? Is this Age of Polling and the advent of impression democracy more sophisticated, more scientific, a step forward in the name of Progress?

Or are polls something else entirely?

Medieval foot soldiers armed themselves with a relatively straightforward weapon called a poleax. It was simply a long staff, topped with an ax, which was used to unseat enemy knights from their warhorses. Once down, the dregs of the army would swarm over the armored foe and finish him off with daggers and clubs, slitting his throat and breaking his bones. Yet that crude strategy of the Dark Ages seems rather sophisticated when compared with the style in which the media wield polling data. Coupled with plenty of chest thumping, polls are used not only to find the majority blocs in public opinion, but also to cleave opinion and bludgeon political figures.

Citizens got a good example of such "poll axing" when President-elect George W. Bush announced he would nominate former Senator John Ashcroft to be his attorney general. The nomination of Ashcroft, a born-again Christian and conservative Republican, was instantly interpreted as confirmation of Bush's conservative core. And the liberal establishment—from abortion rights groups to the American Bar Association—banded together to try to stop Ashcroft. The polls were right behind them.

On January 13, 2000, *Newsweek* magazine, the weekly owned by the *Washington Post,* ran a Web article entitled *"Newsweek* Poll: Reject John Ashcroft." As the headline indicated, it was hardly a piece of balanced reportage. To start, the headline was misleading: It failed to reflect the true opinion of the majority of people polled. The article begins, "By a 41 percent to 37 percent margin, Americans say the U.S. Senate should reject President-elect George W. Bush's choice of John Ashcroft for Attorney General, a new *Newsweek* poll says." Media pundits followed, of course, piling on. Reuters joined in with a cleverly worded interpretation: "[M]ore than 40 percent of Americans said the Senate should reject Ashcroft because he is too far right on issues like abortion, drugs, and gun control to be effective." Time.com and CNN picked up the results, as well.

What few people knew was just how misleading the results were. The poll questions were framed to pummel Ashcroft, raise doubts, and, most of all, exploit citizen ignorance. In an evenly split electorate with a new president seeking to unite the country, the Ashcroft nomination was a convenient way for the media to signal that Bush was outside the mainstream. As we shall see, such uses of polls are most common in times of controversy—just when polls should be most helpful. In fact, it seems to be a law of media polling: You can always expect the most underhanded and irresponsible tactics from the media when polls will augment their agenda and frame the issues that favor their allies in times of crisis and controversy.

Here is the exact question as posed by *Newsweek* to a random sampling of Americans that elicited such doubt about Ashcroft:

Do you think Congress should approve Bush's choice of John Ashcroft for Attorney General, or reject Ashcroft as too far to the right on issues like abortion, drugs, and gun control to be an effective Attorney General?

With that kind of wording, it's a wonder only 41 percent opposed Ashcroft.

Polling advocates like to talk about polls as the consummate instruments of democracy. But while media organs and their polling units brag about how their polls contribute to the open discussion of ideas in the name of the people, they obfuscate their information with all the skill of an Eastern Bloc police state.

For instance, *Newsweek* singled out the poll's most damaging question about Ashcroft, then wrote the story to emphasize the public's supposed anti-Ashcroft response. *Newsweek* wielded its own poll-ax, which was only the first blow against Ashcroft. Partisans on the left were eager to finish him off with a sustained attack of accusations and bombast. Because the public tends to be uninformed, as discussed in chapter 5, most citizens only pay attention to politics when outrage and controversy demand it. Create that controversy and doubt, and the media have the ability to push opinion.

You can always expect the most underhanded and irresponsible tactics from the media when polls will augment their agenda and frame the issues that favor their allies in times of crisis and controversy.

Skeptics may view these comments as unfair in the way they focus on a poll that singled out one question. So it is helpful to look at how *Newsweek* tried to slant the other questions, while at the same time managing to miss the real news about the overwhelming popularity and approval of President-elect Bush when conventional wisdom in the media described the nation as starkly divided. *Newsweek* asked:

> Do you think Bush should scale back his political agenda because he lost the popular vote nationwide and has such a narrow margin in the Electoral College, OR that he should go ahead and pursue his plans for the country regardless of these factors?

An amazing 68 percent thought Bush should pursue his plans. Here is a *super*-majority, favoring Bush's leadership and judgment, craving an elected leader to deliver on his campaign promises. Yet Newsweek editors chose to emphasize the trumped-up anti-Ashcroft angle of their results. Their editorial decision reveals further their belief that the real news was about 41 percent of Americans who were opposed to the nomination of a man "too far to the right on issues like abortion, drugs, and gun control."

Newsweek also sat on polling results that revealed the public's heightened criticism of Democrats. Forty-two percent of adults thought that "the Democrats in Washington have been too partisan in their early opposition to Bush appointments." Forty percent disagreed. They thought that Democrats "have been correctly representing the views of half the public that did NOT support Bush for president."

As we shall see, in chapter 4, such biased wording is evidence of a sloppy, if not overt, attempt to manipulate the response of the person being polled.

In this capacity, the *Newsweek* poll goes beyond the art of medieval poleaxing; it illustrates how the media manipulate ignorance and how polls are employed to give a faulty sense of disgust (or occasionally support) to a controversial issue or figure on the public stage. For Newt Gingrich, Kenneth Starr, even on occasion Bill Clinton, media strikes were measured not just in negative stories, but in skeptical poll questions as well.

In the midst of the controversy over the Ashcroft nomination, polls reported various levels of support. But they also revealed something very interesting: massive ignorance. A large segment of Americans had no idea what the pollsters were talking about. To wit: An NBC News/*Wall Street Journal* poll from almost the exact same time (January 13–15) asked:

> I'm going to read you the names of several public figures and I'd like you to rate your feelings toward each one as either very positive, somewhat positive, neutral, somewhat negative, or very negative. If you don't know the name, please just say so. John Ashcroft . . .

With this wording, 8 percent of voters had a "somewhat negative" view and another 14 percent a "a very negative view." Just 22 percent were negative: a stark difference from *Newsweek*'s ominous results. Eight percent were "very positive" and 12 percent "somewhat positive" about the Ashcroft nomination. But where the NBC News/*Wall Street Journal* results are most telling is that 32 percent didn't know Ashcroft's name or weren't sure, and another 26 percent were neutral (which could very well be those who knew nothing but didn't admit it).

Newsweek could not plead to not knowing that it was push polling ignorant voters. Earlier in the week, a *Time*/CNN poll (January 10–11, two days prior to the release of *Newsweek*'s scathing poll) found that a majority of Americans didn't even know who John Ashcroft was. The media giants asked:

> I'm going to read you the names of some people in the news today. Please tell me whether you have generally favorable or generally unfavorable impressions of each, or whether you are not familiar enough to say one way or another. . . . Attorney General nominee John Ashcroft . . .

Fully 51 percent said they were "not familiar" with Ashcroft. And another 7 percent were "not sure." (Note the wording of the question and how the *Time*/CNN poll made it far more acceptable for the respondent not to know who Ashcroft was.)

CBS News also found on January 15 that 58 percent of 1,086 adults didn't know or weren't sure about Ashcroft. For Gallup/*USA Today*/CNN (January 15–17), it was the same: 34 percent saw Ashcroft favorably; 28 percent unfavorably. *But 17 percent admitted they'd never heard of him, and 21 percent had no opinion.*

> The media can manipulate ignorance and polls can be used to give a faulty sense of disgust (or occasionally support) to a controversial issue or figure on the public stage.

More damning, polls that put the issue in context produced results that were radically different from *Newsweek*'s activist poll. In their poll, ABC News and the *Washington Post* (January 11–15) drew attention to Ashcroft as the president's choice:

[George W.] Bush has nominated John Ashcroft for Attorney General. Do you think the U.S. Senate should or should not confirm Ashcroft as Attorney General?

Fifty-four percent said the Senate "should confirm" Ashcroft. Just 26 percent said that the Senate "should not confirm" him. Finally, to emphasize how selective results can be, the ABC News/*Washington Post* poll found that voters took a different view of Ashcroft when they saw what he was up against and what he was for. They asked:

[George W.] Bush has nominated John Ashcroft for Attorney General. This nomination is opposed by organized labor and by some groups that advocate women's rights, legal abortion, civil rights, and gun control. Do you think the U.S. Senate should or should not confirm Ashcroft as Attorney General?

With left-wing advocacy groups singled out (yet still without the "too far right" label or connotations of extremism), 47 percent said Ashcroft should be confirmed. (Forty-three percent came down against him).

The problem with all these varied results is that only by reading the questions from the *Newsweek* poll could a voter know the bias in the reportage and the headline. This bias is something all too common in media polls. In addition, the other results did not get the same headline attention in wire stories and pundit discussion precisely because they showed little controversy or else revealed the far more problematic issue of voter ignorance and apathy. The point of polling is to judge public opinion, so it is no surprise that when polling results are ginned up, the media pundits become drunk on controversy and attention.

The Senate eventually confirmed Ashcroft, ending one round of poll manipulation, and looked toward an even bigger debate early in their 2001 term: campaign finance reform. Hoards of journalists crusade for campaign finance reform, which is designed, in theory, to equalize the balance of power in political campaigns. Yet public opinion polls, instead of giving the public a voice, arm the media with a crude but very effective weapon. When armed with carefully worded polls, journalists can recklessly knock down politicians, giving the dregs of the Sunday morning talk shows and advocacy groups the scent of fresh blood and the opportunity to finish the kill.

For most citizens, the bias of media polling is unknown. It takes in-depth analysis of all the questions surrounding a controversial subject to find what is ignored and what is emphasized by the press. Was this analysis unfair? Was John Ashcroft's treatment in the press just a fluke?

Tax Cuts: The Eternal Debate

Not long after the Ashcroft battle, President George W. Bush ignited the eternal debate in modern-day Washington: the benefit of cutting taxes. For careful observers, the debate that followed in the papers and on television provided yet another example of how selective, even harmful, poll questions and media coverage can be. Even when a media poll is timely, it is possible that journalists can shape opinion by *not* reporting the results, or by selectively focusing on certain results. On February 27, 2001, President George W. Bush appealed to Congress "on behalf of the American people" for a modest across-the-board income tax cut that totaled $1.6 trillion over ten years.

> The point of polling is to judge public opinion, so it is no surprise that when polling results are ginned up, the media pundits become drunk on controversy and attention.

It was Bush's first address before both houses of Congress and the American people. Like other media outlets, CBS News polled on Bush's performance and persuasive skills. The organization found that 67 percent of Americans supported the president's tax cut, with 31 percent opposing it. Nevertheless this overwhelming support for an idea the media had at one time declared a scheme and little more than a campaign gimmick wasn't reported by CBS. Instead CBS anchorman Dan Rather introduced a story by John Roberts, saying, "President Bush insists what the economy really needs is his major tax cut. Democrats and some independent economists believe the Bush plan is risky business." Failing to mention CBS's own poll, Roberts interviewed two women in Omaha, Nebraska, where Bush was pushing his tax cut case. In the words of Roberts, both women thought the tax cut was too big, and one "fears the president is rolling the dice on eight years of success just for political gain."

What's interesting is that the CBS Web site described tax cuts as Bush's most popular idea: "Given a choice of four of the proposals offered by Bush, the viewing public is most interested in his proposal to cut income taxes. Thirty-eight percent of viewers say they would like to see it happen in the coming year."[4]

Like the *Newsweek* poll questions that seemed to be worded to emphasize Ashcroft's conservatism, CBS and others simply focused their reportage on those parts of the polls that found weakness in the Bush plan or presidency. An ABC News/*Washington Post* poll at the time found that 58 percent of voters agreed that Bush's tax plan was either "about right" or "too small." In the middle of a debate in which both Democrats and Republicans claimed to have the support of the American people, reporter Terry Moran looked at ABC's numbers and highlighted how Bush had an "anemic rating" for his stewardship of the economy. Moran also reiterated what is one of the most effective partisan attacks on Republicans: "[B]y a margin of two to one, 61 to 31 percent, Americans polled in our polls say that the president favors large business corporations over the interests of ordinary working people." Why? It is difficult to understand why this was a relevant question when Bush openly rejected any business tax subsidies, loopholes, or add-ons to his income tax cutting plan. The Bush plan favored lower income groups and added more progressivity to the tax code by shifting a greater tax burden onto those who earn more.

But little of this mattered to media pollsters. In impression democracy, ideas and policies are rarely debated clearly, because prejudice, spin, and smear are far more valuable—whether plied by pundits, party hacks, or political reporters. ABC and CBS weren't the only media outlets to emphasize economic doubt. Their print partners consistently found the real story to be economic doubt, skepticism about Bush, and concern with his plans. The *Washington Post* blared in a front-page headline: "Poll Shows New Doubts On Economy: President's Tax Cut, Policy Are Questioned."

"In the poll, Americans express mixed views about the president's proposals to avert a recession and question key assumptions that undergird the administration's economic recovery plans," wrote Richard Morin and Dana Milbank. The sense of journalistic misgiving gained momentum as the article went on: "A majority gives qualified support for Bush's plan to cut an estimated $1.6 trillion in federal taxes over the next ten years. About half—48 percent—say the tax cut is 'about the right size,' and 10 percent say it is too small. More than a third—36 percent—say the tax cut is too generous."[5] Note how the poll reportage is massaged to give the appearance of weaker support—using words such as "qualified" with support, "about half" instead of nearly half, and then sidelining the additional 10 percent at the end of the sentence while adding the appearance of greater opposition to the plan by using the words "more than a third."

The *New York Times* showed far more balance in the headline: "60 Percent Favor Bush, But Economy Is Major Concern."[6] But the Gray Lady also noted in the subhead that "50 Percent Don't See the New President as in Charge," choosing to follow another skeptical media narrative that Bush wasn't in charge; Vice President Dick Cheney was. In a broad measure of public impression, George W. Bush succeeded in making tax cuts a top public priority—and this was the real news, at least by the standards of previous *New York Times*/CBS News polls. For the first time since Bush started running for the presidency in 1999, Americans ranked tax cuts the number one priority, even ahead of education.[7]

But the *Times*/CBS poll is useful for another reason: The general structure of the poll and the story shows just how easily the seemingly objective measurement of polls can be manipulated or selectively used to give a new impression to political debate. In the article, the questions on taxes begin with an almost useless inquiry: "How much have you heard or read about George W. Bush's proposed tax cut?" Such questions serve little purpose because they ask voters to evaluate their own knowledge with no way of proving how correct their rosy-eyed view might be. (As we shall see in chapter 5, like a high school class, people claim they do their homework, but when the teacher hands out a real quiz with real questions, the result is almost invariably a D–.) Still, such questions are popular in media polls. They give the appearance of an informed electorate, papering over the substantial and nagging problem of voter ignorance. They lend credibility to the poll and hide the manipulation of opinion.

> In impression democracy, ideas and policies are rarely debated clearly, because prejudice, spin, and smear are far more valuable—whether plied by pundits, party hacks, or political reporters.

In fact, the only time a report on poll results touches on a lack of knowledge is when the results tend to show support for a right-leaning idea. Thus, the *Times* story, based on the CBS News/ *New York Times* poll, hints at the problem of ignorance when it comes to support for Bush's tax cut plan: "[T]he public doesn't know much about either plan . . . but both plans gain support" as voters learn more about them.

Bush's plan, described as using "one-third of the budget surplus to cut taxes, about a third to reduce the debt, and the rest for other purposes, including government spending," garnered the support of 57 percent of those polled. The Democratic plan got 49 percent support when it was described as using "more than half of the budget surplus to reduce the debt, and divide the rest among a tax cut, other government spending, and a reserve fund." Forty-three percent said they had not read or heard much about the Democratic plan, yet on learning more, support surged to 49 percent—clearly help for the minority. But the absurdity of the CBS News/*New York Times* poll reaches new levels when the journalists write, "Mr. Bush should be encouraged that most Americans endorse his signature blueprint to cut taxes. Yet they do not seem enthusiastic. Most see the plan as favoring the rich and doing little, if anything, to help average, middle-income people or to stimulate the economy."

The poll questions reveal that 58 percent of those polled said "the rich" would benefit the most from a Bush tax cut, with just 24 percent saying those in the middle income areas will get the most help. Meanwhile, 47 percent say the Democratic plan would go to those in the middle class. This last is a remarkable number given that 43 percent admitted they had not read much about the Democratic plan and only 16 percent could say they read "a lot." As we shall see in chapter 5, in either case, it is difficult to believe that voters had enough information to make such a call. The question left unanswered: Was the poll measuring fact-based opinion or just reinforcing years of impression and party prejudices?

CBS, ABC, the *Washington Post,* and the *New York Times* weren't the only ones to focus on select left-leaning questions in the polling smorgasbord. The Associated Press found much weaker support for the Bush tax plan according to an April 10 article: "Poll: Bush Tax Plan Lacks Support."[8] AP writer Will Lester wrote, "President Bush has not yet persuaded a majority of Americans to support his tax cut plan after months of trying, says an Associated Press poll taken in the days leading up to this year's tax deadline." The AP story did not reveal any of the questions, nor did it present the order of the questions. But the reader was told, "Just under half, 48 percent, said they support Bush's plan, while 32 percent oppose it. Almost one in five said they don't yet know what they think about it—and both sides in the tax debate will be working hard to win them over in the coming weeks." Once again, the uninformed are singled out.

Despite the polling results, nearly every anecdotal quote in the story criticized the Bush plan in some way:

- Retiree Mary Litty of Lavalle, Wisconsin, said she supports the president's tax cut plan, but would prefer that the tax cuts be targeted toward those with less money. "I could use all the help I can get," the Republican said, adding that the wealthy always seem to benefit from tax cuts. "It seems to me they've had theirs in the past. Now it's our turn."

- "I really don't think it's going to do a heck of a lot for the economy," said Rhett Harrelson, a thirty-four-year-old car salesman and political independent from Andalusia, Alabama.

- "I think it's a bad idea," said Vanessa Wooten, a thirty-nine-year-old Democrat from Hollywood, Florida. "I don't think everyone will see the discounts. . . . The small fellow keeps giving, and the people in control keep taking."

Only one of the quotes in the story reflected a wholly positive view of the Bush cut. The story took 48 percent support and whittled it down to just one person out of four who could endorse the cuts with simple and clear support. The last item in the story to get Lester's focus was that "six in ten think taxes are too high."

In contrast, Fox News Channel took the same poll and found a different focus—the very numbers relegated to the end of Lester's eight hundred words of skepticism: "Poll: Over 60 Percent Think Taxes Too High." FNC reported, "The Associated Press conducted a recent poll on taxes, which found the public is still behind President Bush's tax cut proposal. The poll also found a strong majority of Americans believes they are taxed too heavily."[9] Neither side cited an earlier question that proved growing or falling support—although

Fox could point to earlier polls by others that showed substantial growth in support for Bush's plan. Still, the example shows that polls aren't always objective measures. The frame of interpretation used by reporters is rarely objective, and few readers have access to all the public opinion polls, which can provide needed nuance.

Reporting or Manipulating Public Opinion?

In a nation in which the public is nearly equally divided between the parties, polls exercise extraordinary power. And the media know this. To be successful, a pollster must learn what words, phrases, and sentence constructions push or pull public opinion one way or another. And in a nation where the media are overwhelmingly left-leaning, media pollsters can find majorities when majorities are hard to find.

The ease with which polls can be manipulated for stories is all too clear. Returning to the CBS News/*New York Times* poll on Bush's tax cut plan, it is easy to see the journalistic discomfort with Bush's popularity. For instance, by retooling a few questions, the *Times* was able to produce results that fit in nicely under the headline: "Policies That Sound Good at First, But Less So on Second Thought." The implication being that Bush *is* popular, but take heart Democrats, as people think about his ideas, their opinion of him will decline.

To anyone familiar with the plasticity of public opinion and the limitations of polling, the *New York Times* assertion is both ridiculous and all too accurate. What the CBS/*New York Times* pollsters did was ask follow-up questions that emphasized the cost of various courses of action and belief. Typically Americans will say yes to ideas that sound good. But give them the cost of the idea, and they hesitate. Emphasize cost and consequences, and support inevitably slides. Yet note how the pollsters framed the first question on missile defense: "Do you favor the United States continuing to try to build a missile defense system in light of the fact that $60 billion has already been spent on it?" This is a powerful example of media bias and poll manipulation.

The reader should take a close look at the question and see all the insidious ways the pollsters tried to edge support away from missile defense. The phrase "continuing to try to" hints at failure and stresses skepticism. As if that was not enough, the two media giants added "in light of the fact that $60 billion has already been spent on it," leaving the citizen with the sense that he's been hoodwinked and the program is going nowhere. Miraculously, 67 percent of adults still back research for threats against rogue missiles from belligerent nations.

> To be successful, a pollster must learn what words, phrases, and sentence constructions push or pull public opinion one way or another.

But the *Times* and CBS weren't finished. They then asked: "Do you favor continuing to build such a system even if it means breaking the arms control treaty we now have with Russia?" Support plunges to 33 percent as the pollsters stress the ideas of breaking a promise, angering Russia, and bringing instability to foreign relations. But the fact is, the *Times* and CBS manipulated public ignorance. There is no arms control treaty with Russia. And you only believe there is one if you are a hardened liberal who opposes any missile defense research. The Antiballistic Missile Treaty was signed with the communist regime of the Soviet Union, thankfully dead now for over a decade. But such information is ignored and other more damaging information emphasized.

On school vouchers, a key component of the Bush education plan, the CBS News/*New York Times* showed similar bias at a critical juncture of public debate. The media giants asked:

> Should parents get tax-funded vouchers they can use to help pay for tuition for their children to attend private or religious schools instead of public schools?

Under the frame of ideas presented by George W. Bush and other education reformers, school choice (or vouchers) is intended to help those in the nation's worst schools. But CBS and the *New York Times* chose the loaded term "vouchers" and then added the far more damaging wording of "tax funded." By using the word "instead," the question also emphasized that under such a plan private and religious schools would sap money from government schools, as if the trade-off would inarguably hurt the education of public school children—another arguable premise. Amazingly, this idea also pulls a majority of public support (49 percent). So it is left to the media pollsters to finish the job they started and eliminate all signs of apparent support for the conservative, Bush-related idea. They ask:

> Should parents get tax-funded vouchers even if that means public schools would receive less money?

In this scenario, in which "public schools" are clearly demarcated as losers in school choice, it is not surprising to see that support plunges to just 30 percent. "Even if" signals a huge trade-off, and one that does not give the other side of the equation: that such a reform would spur schools to serve the very low-income students being ignored by the establishment in the current system.

Media giants, such as CBS News and the *New York Times,* understand all too well just what prejudices, impressions, and "hot buttons" to press, as this poll showed. One of

Bush's most innovative ideas was to give private charities and social service programs run by religious groups an equal opportunity to solve problems unmet by government-run public welfare agencies. Many of these groups have proven to be the best anti-crime, anti-drug rehabilitation programs, but were unable to get public resources. The *New York Times* asked:

> Is it a good idea for the federal government to give money to religious organizations to provide social services like job training and drug treatment counseling?

An overwhelming 66 percent of Americans liked the idea. But in the follow-up question, or "on second thought" to put it in the *New York Times'* terms, the pollsters invoked a series of prejudices and worst-case scenarios to undermine support:

> Is it a good idea if that meant the government would be giving money to religious organizations like the Nation of Islam, the Church of Scientology, and the Hare Krishnas?

Of course, in this "objective" measure of support, just 29 percent favored federal help to these groups—even as the question elided any reference to the fact that the programs work and they are nondenominational.

Of course, polls like these that veer from objectivity yet are absorbed in political dialogue and policy debate present us with a problem. From the very beginning, America was a nation built on public opinion. The men and women of the American Revolution filled pamphlets and broadsides, sermons and newspapers; they wrote plays and composed poems to appeal to their fellow citizens to join in the principled resistance to unjust rule and unjust taxes. Political discussions took place in taverns over beers and ciders, in ornate homes over glasses of fine Madeira, and in hot state houses over angry Tory objections. American liberty and resistance began with the education and persuasion of the public. Our interest in public opinion ran so deep, our desire to compel and persuade was so far reaching, that Americans declared their love for freedom in a beautiful document that signaled to the world the reasons for the final and decisive break with the tyrannical rule.

Public opinion—whether as public resistance or citizen involvement—has always played an important part in American society. Abraham Lincoln knew this better than most: "In this and like communities, public opinion is everything. Without it, nothing can succeed. With it, nothing can fail." In a free society, he stressed, "[T]he first task of statesmanship is not legislation but the molding of that opinion from which all legislation flows."

Today, after a contentious election marked by an evenly split electorate and two parties opposed (in theory) on the role of government and whether to increase the power of government, public opinion plays a critical role. The party that can claim the backing of the people possesses a special confidence in debate, wielding the threat of electoral consequences when facing opponents. In 1998, President Bill Clinton was able to survive impeachment almost solely due to his support in public opinion polls. All this might seem as it should be. Public opinion—that is, the public—appears to rule.

Unfortunately there is a dark side to the American trust in public opinion. Although our desire for truth, knowledge, and a free marketplace of ideas has made the First Amendment unassailable and rightfully integral to the cause of freedom, our trust in public opinion has left the citizenry and the television viewer vulnerable to the manipulation and creation of majorities. Our love for peaceful and reasoned deliberation has blinded us to the continued and clever manipulation of public opinion. Nowhere is this more dangerous or noticeable than in the proliferation and abuse of media polling.

Polling has become the high-octane fuel of American political debate. It powers television, radio, and press coverage. It influences how candidates interact with the public and with each other. It has ignited a never-ending effort to find out what the people think and how they see the candidates and issues. In the past, discussions and deliberations, from dinner tables and town meetings to party gatherings and political speeches, enabled the candidates and elected leaders to meet with private minds to synthesize new ideas and explain new facts.

> From the very beginning, America was a nation built on public opinion. American liberty and resistance began with the education and persuasion of the public.

But with the rise of media polling and its unreflective use, the Fourth Estate has been given a powerful weapon to push and mold the perception of public opinion and thereby affect political destiny—eliminating the deliberation of ideas between public servant and private citizen. Few people understand just how easily press biases can affect the measurement of public opinion and how difficult they can be to detect.

At first glance, polls appear to be an information-gathering device designed to plumb public opinion. Pollsters routinely say that they give us a "snapshot in time" of how our fellow citizens feel. They sample the opinions of the American people, giving politicians a sense of where voters stand. Modern proponents consider polls valuable because they provide, with apparent scientific precision, an insight into what voters think. For the supporter of polls, they are a communication conduit and a leveling device—a way for the public to be part of elite debate.

"There are two distinct dimensions to polls," as polling expert Michael Traugott puts it. "One is the horizontal: Polls provide for communication among citizens. That also has an entertainment aspect. The second is vertical: Polls allow for communication with government."[10] In other words, through the polls, the people tell those in power what they want and the polls tell citizens what their fellow voters think and believe. Politicians, our elected "leaders," have used polls for decades. And the press has used polls to cover politics for years. What has changed most dramatically is the frequency and demand for polling. Consider the more modest use of polls in administrations past. In the first hundred days of President John F. Kennedy's term, there was only one poll asking the public what they thought of the new president and his policies. In the twenty months leading up to President Nixon's resignation, the media conducted 128 polls. By 1992, there was one poll every 2.7 days asking how Clinton was doing in his first hundred days. In just nine months after the Monica Lewinsky scandal broke in January 1998, the media conducted more than 325 polls. The number of presidential "horse-race" polls during the first seven months of each election year, a period marked by voter ignorance and inattention, has surged.

According to the Roper Center for Public Opinion Research, in 1980 there were 26 such polls; in 1984, 42; in 1988, 50; in 1992, 86; and in 1996, 99. By September in the 2000 presidential race, voters had already been pummeled by 136 horse-race polls—an increase of 400 percent.[11]

But it wasn't just the proliferation of polls that has changed. The real difference is the strength of polling in the hands of the Fourth Estate. As *Washington Post* polling expert Richard Morin says, "[P]olling has never been so risky—or so in demand."[12] There is no shortage of academics or media experts to talk about the importance of polls. Political scientists Paul J. Lavrakas and Michael W. Traugott state simply, "[P]olitical polls are being used more and having greater effects than ever in history."[13] In the Age of Proliferating Polls, pollsters, especially in the media, see this impact as largely positive. Polling is regarded as a natural extension of democracy. News polls do two things, says Kathleen Frankovic, director of surveys at CBS News. "They keep the government honest, by not allowing misrepresentations of public opinion to be presented to the public," she said in 1999.[14] More importantly, they "inform and therefore elevate the public." She continues:

> News polls are a mirror to the public, permitting individuals to understand where they fit into the political system. Reporting public opinion polls tells readers and viewers that their opinions are important, and can be even sometimes more important than the opinions of the elite. In other words, that democracy matters and their opinion counts.

But do these polls "inform and therefore elevate"? In the thirty years since television and newspaper alliances began polling, interest in politics has waned. Voters have more information than ever about what goes on inside campaigns, in party meetings, and in strategy sessions. They hear more than ever about what motivates candidates, their supporters, special interest backers, and the collected strategies the political elite use to move the public. In the midst of all this, media polling has come to drive journalism, thus truncating issue debates.

In fact, a measure of the power of polls is that they haven't simply become more important to the political process. Pollsters themselves have been given a privileged position as diviners of public opinion, commentators on the political scene, and even shapers of our shared political vocabulary. Pollsters are now celebrities who dominate talk programs and issue debates once reserved for elected leaders and party officials who were responsible to their supporters. Kellyanne Fitzpatrick, Frank Luntz, Stanley Greenburg, Dick Morris, and others have all made television careers from their jobs as pollsters and consultants. This change has been so fast that it is easy to forget how deep it is. Reflecting on Watergate, Harry O'Neill, a pollster for President Nixon, noted that pollsters lacked real influence:

> You've got to remember that in those days the pollster was really an outside, third party, objective individual who was not in Washington and was not in the inner circle, as you see today. Today you see the pollsters for presidents on Sunday morning talk shows and they're partisans and apologists and everything else as well as pollsters. We did not see the president and his aides discuss the data or really know how they used the data. We had telephone conversations by and large. We would discuss the question wordings. And the differences in wordings would be based on what they thought they might be able to do with respect to changing public opinion.[15]

At first glance, it might seem tempting to accept the media view that Americans need their polls, their reportage on polls, and their interpretations of public opinion. After all, it is hard to reject the claim of polling without seeming to reject the importance of the people and the deliberative importance of working out public opinion.

Yet at the same time that polling has metastasized, voter disconnect has surged. In the 1960s, more than 60 percent of registered voters turned out for national elections. In 1998, that number was just 36.4 percent. Voters have also grown to distrust

Pollsters are now celebrities who dominate talk programs and issue debates once reserved for elected leaders and party officials who were responsible to their supporters.

government. In 1999, just 29 percent of respondents said they trusted government to do the right thing, according to a poll by the Council for Excellence in Government. And 64 percent of

Americans said they felt "disconnected" from government, even though that government was bigger and more involved in their daily lives than ever.

The media blame politicians. Politicians blame the media. But could it be that in playing to polls designed by the media, politicians have had to become less substantive, and their debates, less educational? Could the Age of Spin be a necessary aftermath of the Proliferation of Polls? The answer is almost assuredly, Yes.

It is not hard to believe that the illusion of public input and the media obsession to use polling as judge, jury, and executioner have killed interest in the political process. The very form of political coverage today—with its focus on the future, conflict, and the spoils of victory—robs citizens of the deliberation. In such a universe in which media polling questions mirror media coverage, polls subtly distort (and sometimes outright mislead) the deliberative process.

The repeated samples from polling may give us a representation of the state of the body politic, but the likely effect of sample after sample will be to drain the health and vitality out of the nation as Americans tune out, the media frenzy is heightened to attract some modicum of attention, and politicians are left to issue debates defined in advance by media organizations. The cost is clear to some. Sander Vanocur, former presidential debate moderator and CBS News correspondent, notes, "My own elementary theory [about declining turnout]: With all television, with ads on television, with the polls, by the time November rolls around, the American people think they've already been part of a plebiscitary process. Therefore, why go to the polls?"[16]

While media pollsters sell their wares as the objective measurement of public opinion, the civil disconnect, apathy, and disinterest rising over the past three decades hardly indicate the empowerment or voice of the people. In fact, most voters are indifferent to the very polls that occupy the front pages.

Does the Public Care About Public Opinion Polls?

Most Americans, even those loyal to a political party or ideology, are poorly informed about politics. So for them, the struggle is the acquisition of knowledge, not absorption of the latest poll results. Not so for the political elite. For most Americans, polls are largely irrelevant to their lives—according to those same polls. A survey by the Joan Shorenstein Center on the Press, Politics, and Public Policy found that most voters are ignorant of the splashy data and charts that regularly appear on the front page or that headline the network news. The Shorenstein Center poll found that 71 percent of Americans claimed to be unaware of *any* news stories about the candidates' standings in the 2000 presidential polls.[17] Of the 29 percent who did say they heard or read something about recent polls, three-fifths claimed that Governor George W. Bush held a lead over Vice President Al Gore. In this they were correct. But another one out of five believed incorrectly that *Al Gore* was leading, and the other one-fifth thought the two were tied. Even among those who could rightly put Bush in the lead, most were wrong about the *size* of that lead. A majority put Bush's lead in double digits, when it was closer to five to seven points. That leaves fewer than 9 percent who knew where poll numbers actually stood.

And yet the political elite use polls to gauge every aspect of the political debate. Polling has become the most dominant and powerful player in politics by driving the media coverage that influences the frames and impressions that many voters use to judge events, policies, and candidates. In addition, polling measures have become more important as media organs vie to increase the impact of their own measures.

Unfortunately, in the avalanche of numbers and measurements, there is one thing that polling doesn't measure: its effect on public discourse. Journalists and pollsters are quick to turn away criticism about the consequences of machine-gun polling. For the media, polls are an important insight into the political process that allows them to write about how the people see our political actors. Polling may be decades old, but the effect of the media-pollster alliance has gone relatively unstudied.

Yet there is more and more evidence that there *are* consequences to our American obsession with measuring public opinion. There is evidence that polls cut off debate and undermine new ideas. Campaign consultants from both sides of the aisle complain that they are hemmed in by political consultants. In everyday political exchanges, candidates carefully denude their language of anything controversial for fear that a single slip will feed the media-polling threshing machine, which converts errors into a deadly news cycle. In response, campaigns focus on soft, warm-and-fuzzy "themes;" pundits comment on the horse race; and reporters track the conflict of people and parties. Indeed, it is the media obsession with the so-called hard data of polls that calls into question whether polls are a boon or bane to American freedom. The media's Cult of Strategy has made polls the ultimate currency in public debate. Should a politician step outside the boundaries demarcated by media polls, the hammer of press justice comes down mercilessly. Even before a candidate can introduce and make his or her case for new ideas, polls are taken and headlines are created.

Whether the proliferation of polls is a good thing depends on how one views our representative democracy. If you see public opinion as sentiment at a given moment in time, then there is nothing to fear. But if you believe that debate and persuasion are part of the American system, then the proliferation of polls may be a premature measure of often ill-formed ideas that are recklessly used to undermine our republican institutions.

The importance of communication and the free exchange of ideas should be self-evident to anyone who supports free government. The "vertical-horizontal" theory of polling plays such an important role in the minds of many pollsters, they believe that polling actually forces politicians to look at the issues. The idea of polls as a communication device has become the justification for their widespread and still growing use. Polling has reached far beyond mere interesting trivia or media-generated news. One need look no further than the trial of President Bill Clinton, a man who by all accounts—whether party official, media pundit, or political leader—was fated to be forced from office after allegations of an affair with a young White House intern.

> In everyday political exchanges, candidates carefully denude their language of anything controversial for fear that a single slip will feed the media-polling threshing machine.

That is, until the polls spoke.

The relentless wave of polls that broke proved the power of the poll and its new position in the political debate. Instead of debating the actual provisions of important questions, such as welfare reform, Medicare reform, or the evidence in the Lewinsky scandal, pundits and politicians are now locked in a "meta-debate" about the polls on these subjects. Like postmodern literary criticism, the subject of debate is often lost in the rancor of the debate about the debate.

Rarely questioned, however, is the effect of how polls are covered and what that coverage does to public deliberation and meditation on national affairs. The almost monomaniacal infatuation with polling comes at a cost. It ignores what citizens know or don't know and undercuts the way in which voters are educated. Media polls especially fail to note the limitations of polling and even the vagaries of public sentiment. The unreflective use of polls has become a danger to the public debate that ought to characterize a republic.

There are many reasons for the proliferation of polls, and there are many methodological reasons to take poll results with a grain of salt. But as we shall see, the combined shortcomings of polls make it almost undeniable to conclude that the process of public deliberation and education has taken a backseat to results of the poll lottery. Journalists, in particular, are drawn to use polls and explain the numbers, working within the constraints of time and space. As those limited resources are given over to the story of polls and where candidates stand in relation to one another, the time and space given to debate, candidate statements, and civic education must decline.

One of the worst aspects of the constant focus on polls and instant response is the tendency to transform elections into horse races and create an atmosphere of the perpetual campaign, exacerbating the negativity, spin, and attack politics so hated by American voters. President Clinton is credited (or blamed) for inventing the year-round campaign. But he did not create a new way of thinking. He merely recognized and adapted to the reality of media polls and instant news judgments. The fact is, polling is the ultimate currency in Washington. Clinton's enthusiasm for polling can only be seen as an all-too-comfortable realism.

There is a backlash emerging against the ways polls function. It so happens that some of the most trenchant critics of the prevailing polling mania are pollsters themselves. A growing public outcry against the ubiquity of polls has struck a nerve in the polling industry. At the 1999 gathering of the American Association for Public Opinion Research, pollsters expressed their concern with a new phenomena: the plummeting response rates from the public. More and more, Americans are tuning pollsters out.

Pollsters tend to be nuanced and careful in their appraisal of any poll. Their bread-and-butter is the interpretation of the subtleties of polls. They are attentive to how questions are asked. They want to know what a poll *doesn't* say, as well as what the numbers are. A pollster almost invariably fires off a barrage of questions when asked by a reporter to evaluate poll results from another organization. *What's the sample group and when was the poll taken? How were the questions worded? Were there any news events that would affect the results? How were the questions asked and in what order?*

Kellyanne Fitzpatrick, president of The Polling Company, warns, "Polls have become a substitute for thought, for reporting, and for principles."[18] John Zogby, president of Zogby International, has expressed his own discomfort with the use of overnight media polls, one of the chief enablers of the proliferation of inaccurate or deceptive polls. "A combination of public demand and media demand requires that we get results immediately the next day," said Zogby.[19] He gives two reasons for concern. The first is that such polls break many of the rules of random probability sampling. The second is that such polls distort opinion before citizens can digest events or new ideas.

American culture is of two minds on the subject. Obviously, polls generate news and attract curiosity. They make good copy. But the rank and file are annoyed, often angered, by the instant measure of public opinion. Their criticisms range from the lighthearted to the nearly savage. The conservative Web magazine Federalist.com took Ted Turner to task for his remarks that the Catholic Church was backward-looking on the issue of adultery. "People who think like us may be in the minority, but we're the smart ones. . . . [The Ten Commandments] are a little out of date. If you're only going to have ten rules, I don't know if [prohibiting] adultery should be one of them." One Internet 'zine responded with a defense of the divine origin of a moral code, adding "had moral principles been poll tested and focus grouped, they'd likely be the Three Advisements—eat, drink, and be merry." Polling is a source of humor, which is a measure of its common currency in political debate.

The television show *The Simpsons* made fun of the absurdity of polls. When millionaire C. Montgomery Burns, owner of a polluting nuclear facility, runs for governor, he hires a battery of handlers, consultants, and pollsters. As one consultant puts it, "Now, here's the problem as I see it. While Governor Bailey is beloved by all, 98 percent of the voters rate you as despicable or worse."[20] Through emotive commercials and saccharine campaign stops, Burns rises in the polls until the headlines read, "Burns Nukes Bailey in Latest Poll." His advisor once again pulls him aside to deliver the polling results:

> **Advisor:** The voters now see you as imperial and god-like.
>
> **Burns:** Hot dog!
>
> **Advisor:** But there's a downside to it. The latest polls indicate you're in danger of losing touch with the common man.

Through polling and pandering, even a despised Monty Burns can gain the attention and support of the people if his campaign team and pollsters are skilled enough. When a reporter asks about Burn's campaign momentum, rival Mary Bailey says, "My worthy opponent thinks that the voters of this state are gullible fools. I, however, prefer to rely on their intelligence and good judgment." The reporter responds, "Interesting strategy."

Others lack such *levitas.* One *Wall Street Journal* editorial from December 1998 simply declared, "Polls have become the crack cocaine of national politics." Looking at the wild swings of the CNN/*USA Today*/Gallup Poll and others during the 2000 election season, former Nixon speechwriter William Safire wrote, "Are you getting the feeling, as I am, that we are being jerked around by wildly swinging poll numbers?" The *New York Times* columnist continued: "The reasons for the unprecedented swings, and for the reporting that further exaggerates the swings, are (1) the pressured pollution of the public opinion polls, and (2) the horse-race media's hyping of polls as predictors of voting behavior."[21] Hal Bruno, reflecting on his twenty years as ABC political news director, told CNN, "My complaint about polls was, though, that they were overused, misused, and abused, and there was too much reliance by the media in general on polling. And television, in particular, does not do a very good job of explaining polls; the print media does it much better, they analyze the polls in much more detail."[22]

Some pundits have even encouraged people to lie to pollsters. "Alas, it seems that as long as pollsters exist, politicians are going to consult them," syndicated columnist Arianna Huffington wrote in 1998. "So in order to wean our political leaders off their daily numbers habit, what we need to do is make the numbers themselves completely unreliable. That's as easy as hanging up your phone."[23]

What kind of effect would this have? Huffington sees far-reaching benefits. "Once this fad sweeps the nation, the pollsters' sample will consist only of very bored, very lonely Americans who want somebody to talk to. This will mean that polling data will become so polluted it will be useless to politicians." Huffington isn't the first columnist to call for such conscious deception in the cause of the public. The late *Chicago Tribune* columnist Mike Royko similarly flogged the issue in the 1980s and told voters to lie to exit pollsters. Alison

Mitchell, writing in the *New York Times* Sunday Week in Review, was even more brutal in the midst of 2000's wildly gyrating polls: "And now for a modest proposal: Ban all political polling between now and Election Day."[24]

ABC News anchorman Peter Jennings also has criticized the effect of polls on the media. "[I]t seems to me that politicians are looking at the polls every day, and I confess that we in the news business are as well," he said. "Polls [have] become a substitute for actual journalism."[25] Tom Rosenstiel, director of the Project for Excellence in Journalism, agrees: "We use polls as a crutch, and it's weakening other skills we have."[26]

"Polls have become the crack cocaine of national politics."

Some critics might dismiss the objections of editorial pages and columnists. Their objections, one might say, are really anti-democratic sentiments. But even principled representatives of the people inside the political establishment—conservative and liberal, Democrat and Republican—have become disillusioned with the hypnotic attention given to what the polls say.

New York Democratic Senator Daniel Patrick Moynihan told *Civilization* magazine that the pressure of polls and lobbyists were undermining our constitutional system. "We have lost our sense of ideas that we stand by, principles that are important to us," he said. "We've got very near to becoming careless with the Constitution." Moynihan believes that polls have put Congress in the position of responding reflexively to popular ideas, even when those ideas aren't lawful or good. He cites the example of the line-item veto that Congress passed in 1995. The idea of letting the president strike individual items from the federal budget remains popular with a public that believes government spending is out of control. Although local constituents favor pork-barrel projects, the general sense is that the federal government spends too much on frivolous projects best handled by state and local authorities. The Republican-controlled Congress, anxious to address this issue after years of debate, passed legislation.

Less than three years later, the Supreme Court held the law unconstitutional and a violation of the separation of powers. The president was being given a legislative function, the High Court declared. Moynihan concluded that such a law wouldn't have passed before the Age of Polls: "[L]eft alone without these polls, the Congress, the Court, the executive will read the Constitution before they do something. . . . Now given the overwhelming popularity of doing something wrong, we go ahead and do it anyway."

Of course, some people see the bright side in all this. It is, in their view, part of the further democratization of America. More polls are just another stage of that process, akin to extending the right to vote to those whites without property, then to blacks, then to women, then to voters aged 18 and up.

But if polling is the final decisive measure, then it leads to another question. As Senator Moynihan has said of the people's representatives, "Are we really necessary? Couldn't the polls just report our vote?" Moynihan is not keen on the idea, but other political actors have suggested as much. Reform Party founder Ross Perot made the national plebiscite a cornerstone of his 1992 campaign for president.

In the rush to define public opinion and polling as one, the media has distorted the results and deformed the institutions of representative democracy. America is more than simple democracy and instantaneous majority rule. The Athenian experience with direct democracy was well known to America's Founding Fathers. At the time of the constitutional convention in 1787 and at the time of the writing of the state constitutions, the founders could have easily constructed direct democracy. But they did not, often explaining that they openly distrusted such regimes. And this is exactly Moynihan's point:

"[W]e have to watch out for something primal in our constitutional republic. We are not a plebiscitary democracy, in which everyone gets together in a stadium and decides then and there, and everybody has an equal vote. We are a representative democracy."

In the midst of the Lewinsky scandal, House Judiciary Chairman Henry Hyde stated categorically, if defensively, polling is "an art, not a science." And House Majority Whip Tom DeLay complained, "Polls are a snapshot in time," implying that they are subject to momentary pressures and prejudices. For both of those Republicans, their objections seemed to be directed at the overemphasis on polls by the media. But they aren't the only ones voicing such opinions.

At a youth rally for Democrats in August 2000, Bill Clinton told young loyalists: "We can't pay any attention to polls or anything else." Clinton urged his audience to "get up and saddle up and fight" for their future. "If we do, we win," he added.[27] When Al Gore trailed George W. Bush, many Gore followers would try to mute the drumbeat of defeat coming from media commentators. "I know enough about politics and enough about polls to take all this with a heavy grain of salt, if not the entire saltshaker," said Andrew Cuomo, then secretary of housing and urban development in the Clinton administration. "I really do believe that sometimes it is as simple as people have not yet focused [on the campaign]."[28] Gore repeatedly emphasized, "I don't really put much stock in the polls."

Polls, politicians understand, may grab the front page and move journalistic coverage, but they do not deserve attention when the public isn't paying attention. At the ideological antipodes, Steve Forbes agreed. Three months before the 2000 primaries began, the GOP presidential hopeful said, "Polls right now are like writing in the sand. When people start to really focus on this race, this campaign that you see here today has the grass-roots and committed people who want to make positive things happen."[29] Forbes did not win, of course, but his open appeals returned the issue of high taxes to the arena of political debate.

Most media pollsters and their journalistic defenders are quick to charge that the protests over polling represent nothing more than the carping of losers and laggards in the polls. But Americans sense something else. Rhetorically there isn't a politician in this nation who would stand up and cite polling results as a reason to take a certain action. Public opinion? Maybe. But as politicians perfect their technical ability to pander and market policies to specific constituencies, a growing backlash against polling is making the word no longer synonymous with democracy but rather with all that is wrong in politics: wan and feckless leadership, meaningless debate, and fuzzy, blurred lines between the parties.

> In the rush to define public opinion and polling as one, the media has distorted the results and deformed the institutions of representative democracy.

Without taking a poll, more and more politicians have gone on the offensive. They aren't just indifferent or agnostic about polls, they are openly defiant, even contemptuous. In 1998 future Republican presidential candidate Governor George W. Bush of Texas attacked the culture of polling in a speech to the National Center for Policy Analysis:

> We live in an age of up-to-the-minute news, beyond-the-limits talk shows, and a steady barrage of information that bombards our senses. Every day it's: "Answer me this. Respond to that." The media are always pressing for instant reactions to some trend or scandal or fill-in-the-blank event of the day. And we're always pressing to capture the mood of the moment. There are polls for everything—to tell us who's ahead, who's behind, what's popular, what's not.

Everything from which foods we hate to which *Baywatch* stars we love. Unfortunately there is a strong temptation for some in public life to find their compass in the latest poll. But all they wind up doing is sacrificing principle for the sake of expediency. Good, long-term public policy cannot come from sticking your finger in the wind to make up your mind.[30]

Such speeches often garner the most enthusiastic applause. Many of the House members who managed the impeachment case against Bill Clinton say they wear their experience of standing against the polls as "a badge of honor." Senator John McCain scored roaring applause during the Republican debates when he told the audience, "Let me talk about Dean Acheson a second. When Dean Acheson walked into Harry Truman's office in June of 1950 and said, North Korea has attacked South Korea, Harry Truman didn't take a poll."[31]

Politicians are, of course, the closest students of public opinion: Their jobs are dependent upon their understanding of it. Are these politicians, from the left and the right, onto something? Polls are not the only way elected officials gauge public opinion. Our representatives get letters and calls from constituents, they attend town meetings, and they often take questions after public speeches. They understand that there are other, often better, sources of public opinion than the poll, which, as we shall see, is marked by limitations of all kinds. Ask any politician, and it is clear that polls aren't necessarily the measures of the people's voice. The people don't commission the poll. The respondents rarely use their own words, and they rarely determine the subject of the poll. Polls are poor measures of the intensity of individual Americans' interests to work, fight, or educate others to take up a political position.

America's founders understood the need to hone and channel the intense debates that flow from public opinion in a free nation. Instead of giving feeling, impression, ignorance, and prejudice free reign, they wanted a republic, or representative democracy, that educated elected and electorate alike. They appreciated the problems posed by relying on public opinion too much or too little. James Madison wrote in 1788 about the two critical differences between a republic and a democracy. The first is that in a republic, governmental powers are delegated to a small number of citizens elected by the rest. The second is that a republic can govern a greater number of citizens and a larger territory. For our purposes, however, it is the former that bears on polling and public debate. Madison writes in *The Federalist* that:

> The effect of the first difference is, on the one hand, to refine and enlarge the public views, by passing them through the medium of a chosen body of citizens, whose wisdom may best discern the true interest of their country, and whose patriotism and love of justice will be least likely to sacrifice it to temporary or partial considerations. Under such a regulation, it may well happen that the public voice, pronounced by the representatives of the people, will be more consonant to the public good than if pronounced by the people themselves, convened for the purpose. On the other hand, the effect may be inverted. Men of factious tempers, of local prejudices, or of sinister designs, may by intrigue, by corruption, or by other means, first obtain the suffrages, and then betray the interests of the people.[32]

For the founders, history provided a warning to those who believed in direct democracy or poll-driven impression democracy. Specifically, the founders were fascinated by the fates of ancient Rome and ancient Greece. That great republic of Rome had fallen because of demagogues who sought to live above the law. The fork-tongued seekers of popularity pandered to the people, who then backed unscrupulous leaders in their self-serving efforts to undermine the rule of law. The challenge in free nations, then, is to find a balance between the demands of the people for reform (sometimes expressed by polls and popularity) and the preservation of wise deliberation in the context of the rule of law. For public opinion to be useful, we need something more than instant media polls declaring winners and losers. We must recognize the disconnect and ignorance of the public and the corresponding need to "refine and enlarge" public debate in the framework of the Constitution.

We must understand that constitutional mechanisms, House procedures, Senate filibuster, and the presidential veto may all serve to give the citizenry the time to fully weigh the full costs of legislative action.

Understanding Public Opinion in the Context of the Constitution

For many of America's early leaders, the defense of the people often meant temporarily opposing popular ideas or standing up for principle and law against political vilification. Leadership required the protection of liberty, even if at the peril of one's job. Alexander Hamilton defined the "true patriot" as one "who never fears to sacrifice popularity to what he believes to be the cause of the public good."[33] In the American heart, we still respect and value such moral courage. A deeper understanding of public opinion requires us to look beyond and even be critical of polling.

The founders built institutions with these concerns in mind. They wanted members of the Senate to be chosen by state legislatures. The upper chamber was meant to protect the people "against their own temporary errors and delusions." Senators were to "withstand the temporary delusion, in order to give them time and opportunity for more cool and sedate reflections." Hamilton then hoped the people would have "courage and magnanimity enough to serve them at the peril of their displeasure."[34]

Any critique of polling should then remind us of the need for debate and education as part of developing and enacting public opinion. The media's Cult of Strategy and Polls does not do this.

"Polls purporting to be *vox populi* almost dare public officials to do something different than the public opinion polls suggest they ought to do," said

> The challenge in free nations is to find a balance between the demands of the people for reform and the preservation of wise deliberation in the context of the rule of law.

University of Virginia professor Larry Sabato.[35] Too often the media exacerbate this environment by using polls as levers of action when it fits in with their political beliefs.

The thesis of this book is that polling is undermining America's republican form of government. The frenetic use of polls to judge tragedy and express outrage has created a climate of "temporary error and delusion." The way polls are used forces politicians to respond instantly to tragedy, often with little thought or consideration. Polling creates a bandwagon effect in the media and has become a way for the media to ratify their saturation coverage of issues—issues that attract their attention and appeal to their political leanings. Polls in the era of the short news cycle and twenty-four-hour cable have become a way for elite organs to drive political discourse and to dictate the agenda of debate. As pervasive as public opinion measures are, it is important to remember that representative democracy is only part of the equation for the preservation of liberty.

The American republic isn't built on polls. The first words of the *Federalist* focus on the founding of a constitutional government based on "reflection and choice." America is a nation built on the idea of individual liberty, limited government, and the rule of law. Popular sovereignty is the basis. But media polling has started to inhibit free and open debate. Americans have a variety of institutions and principles that are meant to encourage deliberation and even to run contrary to, and indeed discourage, the herd-mentality quick-government fixes and simplistic solutions advocated in polling by a progressive journalistic elite. *This* is mobocracy: The reducing of a constitutional republic to destructive and unreflective mobs stoked by selective polling and reportage.

The Constitution and Bill of Rights are, of course, the most visible banners of rule of law and the ideals of measured debate as well as the defense of minority rights. Through the separation of powers, frequent elections, and a deliberative legislature, Americans diffuse power and thereby protect freedom. The founders were dedicated to the idea of limiting the power of the government, and our institutions reflect that. Democracy—whether direct Athenian style, poll-driven, or focus-group impression democracy—was never viewed as the sole guarantor of freedom. Nor should it be. In fact, as conscious of history as they were, the founders saw as much danger in democracy as they did in autocratic control. For this reason, they sought a virtuous, intelligent citizenry—one informed by knowledge and moderated by reason and reflection. To quote Madison again:

A republic involves the idea of popular rights. A representative *chuses* the wisdom, of which hereditary aristocracy has the *chance;* whilst it excludes the oppression of that form. And a confederated republic attains the force of monarchy, whilst it equally avoids the ignorance of a good prince, and the oppression of a bad one. To secure all the advantages of such a system, every good citizen will be once a centinel over the rights of the people; over the authorities of the confederal government; and over both the rights and the authorities of the intermediate governments.[36]

That is a grave task. And in today's poll-happy America, those citizens who wish to be sentinels of the people's rights and the guardians of the cause of freedom would do well to understand the limits of polls, their manipulation by the media, and their negative effect on the public square.

CHAPTER TWO

The Mirage of Democratic Debate

Polling has become the haunting, dark side of practical politics—the antithesis of thoughtful idealism or soaring, daring leadership.

■ ■ ■

POLITICIANS ARE COMMON TARGETS of scorn. One of their weak points, in voters' minds, is their tendency to do whatever will sustain their tenures in office, as exemplified by the Washington fat cat who sacrifices and trades on his principles to secure popularity and reelection. This stereotype has become so ubiquitous that politicians who wish to separate themselves from it openly promise to ignore the polls and "do what is right."

From the very beginning, Americans have been distrustful of politicians and have regarded them as a suspect class. Now in this Age of Polling, opinion surveys, consultants, and spin have done little to alleviate suspicions about candidates and officeholders. The technological sophistication of polling has made it all too easy for the greasy politician to pander. Polling has become the haunting, dark side of practical politics—the antithesis of thoughtful idealism or soaring, daring leadership. Because it is the strange echo of what the people want to hear but often not what *ought* to be done, it has deepened cynicism and made Americans more suspicious of those in power.

Yet as much as polling has transformed the lives of the candidates and our conceptions of officeholders, it has had just as radical and far-reaching an impact on American journalism. The proliferation of polls has changed the focus, depth, and number of stories about the political process, a fact that is rarely noted. In turn, the media have dumbed down polling questions, emphasized their narratives, and sped the deployment of thousands of polls. The media-polling relationship has not been, on balance, a mutually beneficial one for the nation or for pollsters. The explanation of why this has happened illustrates the power of polls in our lives and why they have become so destructive to our national dialogue about politics.

Fiat Flux—Let There Be Media Polls!

Media polls first developed as a way for journalists to evaluate independently what was going on inside the minds of citizens. Candidates and parties had used polls for years, but they would release only data that helped their interests or hurt their opposition. Damaging information was carefully hidden from the Fourth Estate, leaving journalists dependent on other sources or on the whims of parties and candidates. Before the 1970s, the media often had to rely upon the polls provided by the parties and their candidates. Another option was to use subscription services like those of The Gallup Organization. Unfortunately, these polls could not be tailored with the speed demanded by news editors and producers. In an effort to maintain their objectivity and develop their own stream of information, the media began to deploy their own polling units and sought to perfect their own survey techniques. Beginning in 1976, with a historic partnership between CBS News and the *New York Times,* media polling steadily increased, from a few polls a year to the more than 300 public opinion surveys conducted in the last two months of the 1996 presidential election alone.

Polling data have graduated from being a mere source (just part of a news story) to the front-page focus of a newspaper (often garnering their own headline). For many organizations the poll is—barring the most extraordinary news events—a top story. As Peter Jennings notes, "[I]t seems to me that politicians are looking at the polls every day, and I confess that we in the news business are as well. Polls [have] become a substitute for actual journalism."[1] The temptation to use polls is almost irresistible to a media that value speed, breaking stories, and original content.

While social scientists and statisticians have studied the accuracy of polls for years, very few have examined the aggregate effect of polling and media coverage. But exactly how is public opinion affected when polls are piled upon one another and reinforced by continual, nearly relentless coverage of a single news event? Despite the possibility of such an unacknowledged side effect, the media are one of the chief cheerleaders for polling results. From the sideline, the nation's top anchors triumphantly announce the "score" as embodied in polling results. The pundits then crunch the numbers like Monday morning quarterbacks, noting errors in strategy and political execution.

> Polling data have graduated from being a mere source (just part of a news story) to the front-page focus of a newspaper (often garnering their own headline).

It's easy, though, to see why polling has so seduced journalists. Surrounded by politicians and their handlers, lobbyists, activist groups, and even the chatter of other reporters, the individual journalist is bombarded by opinions, ideas, studies, spin, clever propaganda, and a lot of white noise. All these forces vie for prominence in news stories. Polls, with their numbers, trend lines, and instant deployment, give the appearance of being the only truly reliable facts in the hall of mirrors that is politics.

Polls also tempt journalists in another way. They can bring closure or present an endpoint to political debate. When campaigns run commercials, when candidates make accusations, or when political leaders speak, polling units roll into action to test whether the attacks, the charges, or the speeches work. As journalists search for the narrative of tomorrow's piece—the dramatic plot that will undergird their stories— polling numbers enable them to add a data-loaded denouement. Polling makes it possible for journalists to declare who wins and who loses when the vortex of a controversy finally passes through the public consciousness.

How Poll-Driven Journalism Distorts Debate

Just because polling suits the needs of the media does not mean that representative democracy is better off for it. Just as we must be careful of the wording and methodology in any poll, so too must we be vigilant about how poll results are reported and portrayed in news reports. We must also question how and when polls are deployed, because the questions they ask are as important as the results they obtain.

The effect of polling and the strange relationship it has with the twenty-four-hour media culture should make any poll consumer wary. As Susan Herbst writes, the "precise character of numbers has not created a more rational political sphere ruled by instrumental reason. On the contrary, instead of becoming the tools for the *resolution* of ideological or policy conflicts, quantitative data have often been the *source* of such struggles through American political history."[2] Many methodological factors can bias a poll or affect the results in subtle ways. In this section, we look at how polls affect and are affected by their symbiosis with the media.

USING POLLS, JOURNALISTS REASON FROM EFFECT TO CAUSE

In the current state of affairs, we are left with this absurdity: Polls determine the success or failure of campaign tactics for journalists and then provide the cause. For instance, in the fall of 2000, journalists focused on trivial issues such as whether Democratic presidential candidate Al Gore could remake himself into an "alpha male" or whether a change of wardrobe emphasizing earth tones could attract women. During the primaries, journalists asked whether Governor George W. Bush smiled or "smirked" and whether this would turn off voters.

The same journalists who provide such coverage then explain what is making public opinion tick. They see a candidate rising in the polls and then explain that his bigger crowds and sunnier disposition come from his better wardrobe, his more relaxed demeanor, or his health care, education, or tax policy. On the other side, a candidate doing poorly is "struggling" because he isn't communicating well, he is evasive, he is failing to talk "specifics," or one of his policy proposals is sour. But what exactly is the connection between the cause (new poll numbers) and the effect (any number of untested factors)?

This problem of polling and journalistic bias is much more difficult for readers and voters to detect. Readers must look at the size of the sample, who was asked, what was asked. Small samples or the use of registered voters can cast doubt on results when it comes to close political questions. The wording of polling questions can influence public opinion results in one direction or another. When the basic information of a poll is provided in a story or on the Internet, a vigilant reader can ferret out the errors or the sloppiness. Yet journalists are apt to extrapolate causes that seem logical to them but that have no basis in the polls.

Journalistic coverage of campaigns often closely mirrors what journalists see in polls. A social science researcher or an academic pollster is usually reluctant to draw conclusions about why respondents believe what they do until having specifically asked respondents themselves. Journalists rarely show such restraint, and media polls rarely are so specific. Journalists are apt to extrapolate causes that seem logical to them but that have no basis in the polls.

In philosophy, this is known as a problem of causality: Does X cause Y? As poll experts Sandra L. Bauman and Paul J. Lavrakas warn:

> Causal analysis involves linking observable behaviors or events to unobservable causes. This is exactly what journalists do when they present causal attributions to explain the findings of a public opinion poll. The poll result is an observable entity—it has been measured and represents opinion within its methodological constraints (i.e., sample selection, sampling error, etc.). However, journalists almost never can directly observe why public opinion has changed or observe *why* public opinion has changed or why it exists in the distributions it does.[3]

Unfortunately, few reporters and fewer pundits seem to understand this. Media polls rarely test the hypotheses put forward by journalists, anchors, and pundits, yet these individuals speak with confidence about what is pushing the polling numbers.

The reason the media can't speak with authority about what's causing polling effects is that they aren't asking. To facilitate the phone-questions format, polls about candidates are usually simple and straightforward. But this simplicity makes it almost impossible for a pollster to ask exactly why voters may or may not be changing their support and opinions about candidates or issues. To put it another way: Even though a polling story quotes the results of a poll, the explanations for movements or new trends do not have the same methodological strength as the polling results unless the same respondents have been queried about what's going on in their heads.

This is not entirely unfamiliar territory for some journalists. Howard Kurtz, media critic for the *Washington Post,* mocked a *USA Today* columnist who declared Al Gore's August 2000 convention acceptance speech a success. "How could reporter Richard Benedetto be so sure?" asked Kurtz. "Ah here's the answer [according to Benedetto]: 'A *USA Today/* CNN/Gallup poll found that [Gore] made himself more likable, increased support among Democratic supporters, and made big gains among two key groups he must have in his corner to win: women and independents."[4]

That same day, *Washington Post* polling specialist Richard Morin wrote, "Vice President Gore has climbed to a narrow lead following the Democratic National Convention by easing doubts about his leadership ability and personal style while establishing himself with voters as the candidate best able to deal with the economy, education, and health care reform, according to a new *Washington Post/*ABC News poll."[5]

> The reason the media can't speak with authority about what's causing polling effects is that they aren't asking.

The measure of the public's opinion is only as good as the depth and quality of the questions asked. According to Bauman and Lavrakas, this leads to a danger zone worthy of caution, because journalists must rely on "nonexperimental correlations" in polling data and "observation of change over time to infer these unobservable causes"—that is, journalists must rely on unscientific or anecdotal support for their hypotheses about why the polling data say what they do. It's rare for any media analyst or news story to warn readers about this kind of gray area because few journalists or pundits are humble enough to recognize the limitations of their perspective. After all, *they* are the experts.

Many papers have polling directors who try to "soften" the language used to report and speculate on why one candidate may be gaining or losing support. But it is rare for the media to honestly grapple with this serious problem. The use of words such as "seems to show" or "indicate" doesn't remove the problem. For unsophisticated readers, such words merely bury the problem. Polling itself seems to argue against the ability of such language to militate against readers drawing the wrong conclusions from polling data. But the critical reading abilities of most Americans hover at a level far below what's needed to pick up such nuances. This is one of the reasons the wording of polling questions can have such far-reaching effects on public opinion.

This problem of "substantive interpretation" is a serious one and not something to be dismissed lightly. A methodologically sound poll can suffer in the hands of an unreflective media forced to report only some of the results, usually without reference to the words, and then to give an explanation for *why* voters are supporting a measure. One pundit's theory is as good as another's, *unless* the poll asks specifically why and what a voter is thinking. The lesson goes beyond simply waving a cautionary flag over any polling result. It tells us that polls may be giving us a false sense of confidence about media reportage. The media present the work of social science and statistical research without any of the humility of professionals in those disciplines.

In 1994, many in the media were stunned by the Republican congressional victory—and not just because nearly every pundit's predictions were proven wrong. The GOP takeover of Congress was predicated on the GOP's "Contract with America," a document, signed by nearly every Republican House candidate, that promised key reforms in ten areas, including a balanced budget amendment, a line-item veto, tort reform, and a daring tax cut—all in the first 100 days.

Frank Luntz, the GOP pollster for the Contract, claimed that every item on the list was supported by more than 60 percent of the American people. At first the media took Luntz at his word, and in the weeks following the election, the GOP's claim of having a mandate seemed almost unassailable. Media stories stressed the popularity of the Republican agenda. Meanwhile pollsters expressed fear that journalists too readily accepted the data as an explanation for the smashing Republican victory. In subsequent polling it was discovered that less than one in five voters even knew what the Contract was.

The temptation to bow before the perceived power of polls isn't limited to politicians. Journalists are especially defenseless because they value conflict and crave controversy; they are particularly prone to poor explanations because time compresses research and their own comrades create a rush toward convenient, pleasing explanations. It wasn't until almost a year later that Luntz was proven wrong and publicly censured by the American Association for Public Opinion Research.

Officials from the 1,400-member AAPOR asked Luntz to provide his research, but he refused. When he finally complied, the materials he submitted were only a partial record. AAPOR's president at the time, Diane Colasanto, said, "When researchers make public arguments based on their research data, then refuse to say how their research was conducted, that harms the public debate on issues and reduces the credibility of all survey and public opinion research."

Journalists are guilty of a similar sin when they fail to note clearly and decisively the limitations of their polls when drawing conclusions and offering explanations. In such cases, the effect is just what Colasanto describes: Doing so reduces the credibility of all survey and public opinion research. The only difference is that the media rarely police themselves and almost never acknowledge their own errors or mistakes with the same banner headlines given to front-page stories of the latest poll.

GENDER GAP ASSUMPTIONS

Polling produces numbers, statistics, and colorful graphs, but these do nothing to alleviate the basic problems that stem from analytical error. Take one recurring theme in media coverage of presidential campaigns: For the past three election cycles, one of the most common stories coursing through the collective mind-set of the press corps has been the "gender gap," or the difference between a candidate's share of the votes from men and from women. Since the election of Ronald Reagan, more women have backed Democrats and more men have sided with Republicans. But in the media's coverage, this issue is typically portrayed as a problem for the Republican Party.

The problem started in 1980, when Ronald Reagan beat President Jimmy Carter. According to exit polls, the two pulled in approximately the same number of women (47 percent versus 45 percent). Reagan's dominance flowed from his popularity with men. He led among male voters by 55 percent to 36 percent. In 1984, Reagan increased his lead with women, beating Walter Mondale, 56 percent to 44 percent. Among men, Reagan crushed Mondale by 25 percentage points (62 percent to 37 percent).

In 1988, Vice President George Bush beat former Governor Michael S. Dukakis with numbers similar to those of Reagan's 1984 victory. But that summer, the media began to develop their obsession with the GOP's "gender gap." In a typical example, CBS devoted an entire piece to Bush's perceived weakness with women. Reporter Bob Schieffer declared that women are "a big problem for George Bush because [they] don't seem to like him very much." Schieffer quoted a CBS News/*New York Times* poll showing that "women favor Dukakis overwhelmingly, 53 to 35 percentage points, what some call a 'gender gulch.'" (Schieffer didn't cite the source of the "gulch" descriptor.) As George Bush began to climb in the polls, though, the gender gap began to decline as a media theme.[6] Eventually Bush would close the gap completely: He beat Dukakis by 1 percentage point among women (50 percent to 49 percent). He also held Reagan's strength among men, beating Dukakis by 16 percentage points (57 percent to 41 percent).

> The media rarely police themselves and almost never acknowledge their own errors or mistakes with the same banner headlines given to front-page stories of the latest poll.

In 1992, Arkansas Governor Bill Clinton began to reverse the trend, drawing women just as Reagan drew men. He and Bush drew almost equally among men (41 percent to 38 percent). Clinton's real strength came from women, where he beat Bush by 8 percentage points (45 percent to 37 percent).

In 1996, the gender gap became a full-fledged national journalistic obsession. The question of how Bob Dole would surmount the gender gap and attract the "soccer moms" became a subject of intense and burning interest to every journalist interviewing a Republican player. New poll results were cast under the rubric of this GOP dilemma. The horse-race mentality handicapped different ways for Republicans to bridge the gap and, more conspicuously, questioned those conservative policies that were scaring off soccer moms.

The issue of the gender gap doesn't just suggest how the media can abuse polling and numbers when it suits them. It also illustrates how the national dialogue can then be corrupted by an almost complete lack of reference to any polls that test the pet theories of the media machine. The soccer mom theory was never substantiated and was in fact called into question by some pollsters; for instance, Republican strategist and pollster Donald Devine wrote in April 1996 that the GOP's electoral woes weren't with soccer moms or even with feminists. The real flight to Clinton came from elderly women who felt Clinton was a better protector of Medicare. Devine recommended a Republican drive to pass legislation on Medicare, but instead the media fixation on the gender gap and soccer moms led to debates among the punditry and even efforts by Republicans to solve the soccer mom "problem."

It wasn't enough to move the incoherent and chaotic Dole candidacy. Still, Dole actually beat Clinton among men (44 percent to 43 percent). But Clinton proved dominant among women, winning over female voters 54 percent to Dole's 38 percent.

Is the gender gap a Republican problem? Media reports would lead the average American to think so, but the evidence seems to point to the exact opposite conclusion. Republican strength in national contests has slowly grown *because* of the exodus of men from the Democratic Party. As feminist author Barbara Ehrenreich wrote in a 1996 essay for *Time*, "The reason for the gender gap is not that women are different . . . but that men have [been] drifting off."[7] Had the media investigated the issue from a more objective viewpoint, they would have found a far more provocative and interesting story. As reporter Steven Stark writes, "Although many media accounts still give the impression that the gap is greatest on 'women's issues' such as abortion and an Equal Rights Amendment, men and women do not differ much on these issues. Rather the gulf today tends to be on issues involving the existence and expansion of the social welfare state."[8]

JOURNALISTIC NEEDS
INCREASE BIAS IN POLLS

Readers of *USA Today* got a quick and decisive lesson in just how ridiculous the media drive for poll numbers can be. On Monday, August 7, 2000, the paper blared in block letters: "Bush Lead on Gore Grows to 17 points." The *USA Today/* CNN/Gallup poll followed on the heels of the Republicans' very successful convention—so it was easy to understand why Bush might be doing well. But the very next day, another front-page story reported that Bush's lead had *shrunk* to just two points after Democratic presidential candidate Al Gore chose Senator Joseph Lieberman of Connecticut as his running mate.[9]

Why the discrepancies in the numbers? Was Lieberman that popular? Was Lieberman's condemnation of Bill Clinton decisive, as some pundits reported? Hardly. Given the level of ignorance of the average voter, there is little chance voters had even heard of him: Fewer than 50 percent of Americans can name their own member of Congress, and barely one in ten can identify him or her with a specific policy. Overall, more than half (53 percent) of all registered voters said they did not know enough about Lieberman to rate him, including 24 percent who had never heard of him at all. These numbers didn't make it into the story.

The reason there are huge opinion swings during election campaigns isn't just because people haven't made up their minds. A pollster's methods and the media's own journalistic imperatives can combine to undermine the accuracy of polling.

The reason for the huge drop in Bush's lead was methodological. In the survey that showed a 17-point lead, the Gallup polling firm interviewed *likely* voters. In the second poll, Gallup interviewed registered voters, who tend to be more volatile. In its press release, Gallup noted: "Typically, although not always, likely voters tend to be more Republican than registered voters are, giving Bush about a 4- to 5-point larger lead."[10] Another reason for the differences in the two polls is that Gallup interviewed over two days in the first poll, while the second poll was conducted overnight. Finally, the *USA Today* numbers tapped only 667 people in their overnight poll, far fewer than the 1,000-person "loose" standard. When Gallup went back to the more accurate likely voters at the end of the week, it found a 16-point lead for Bush among likely voters and a 10-point lead among registered voters.[11]

Richard Morin, polling specialist for the *Washington Post,* warned readers of such phenomena during election years:

> This year, many of us [i.e., pollsters] are contributing to volatility by cutting corners and taking unprecedented risks to meet the needs of the Internet- and cable TV–driven twenty-four-hour news day. To meet these frenzied demands for content, polls have been downsized. CBS, for example, reported a survey of 503 registered voters over the weekend. These tiny samples come with correspondingly larger margins of sampling error, which about guarantees more survey-to-survey variation in the horse race that has exactly nothing to do with actual changes in the race.[12]

Just as the media force their issues and interests on campaigns, they also force their standards on polling. Polling has inherent limitations that must be handled with care. Question wording, issue framing, samples, response rates, and voter knowledge can subtly influence polling numbers. When probing and interpreting public opinion, the results are only as good as the questions asked.

The journalistic competition and the battle for ratings conspire to produce media-generated polls that are done more quickly and with less care than those conducted in the academic community. "There's a joke that goes around that academic polls really do the best job covering public opinion—the problem is they come out a year later," says Murray Edelman, president of the AAPOR. Edelman isn't attacking media polls; he just acknowledges that "the media are simply more focused on what is happening right now."[13]

> A pollster's methods and the media's own journalistic imperatives can combine to undermine the accuracy of polling.

Thanks to the telephone, random-digit dialers, and computer banks, media polls can be conducted more quickly than ever. When tragedy or crisis strike, media polls can be deployed almost as quickly as the cameraperson and reporter driving the news van to get to the story, whether it be a school shooting, a court judgment, a candidate speech, or a toxic spill. The imperative of speed is rarely acknowledged as a source of error in public opinion surveys, and journalists are more likely to turn their attention to their next story than to dwell on their past record during a major news period.

But this lack of reflection carries costs. As academic pollsters Paul J. Lavrakas and Michael W. Traugott write, "Unfortunately, the . . . methods that nowadays are used to conduct most pre-election polls that are meant for public dissemination too often are linked primarily to news deadlines rather than to confident knowledge that the chosen methods are adequate to the task of producing accurate findings."[14]

From the very beginning, academic pollsters approach their subject with a different mind-set than the journalist.

While the social or political scientist tries to find the inconsistencies or contradictions in public opinion, the media pollster strives to ask quick, decisive questions. The academic researcher has the luxury of demanding "trade-offs" from voters by asking the same question in different ways to expose how wording may be affecting results—or, in polling parlance, generating "response effects." Media polls often don't test how much the public believes in an idea or how soft opinion may be. A thorough poll asks what voters are willing to trade or give up when their ideas are in conflict. These techniques prevent the respondent from "going along to get along" by juxtaposing competing values and then asking for the respondent's opinion.

Media polls often fail to do any of this. Instead, questions exist in a vacuum where alternatives aren't always clear. Journalists want an immediate answer to the question of where public opinion stands in moments of political controversy, national crisis, or partisan debate. As pollster Daniel Yankelovich laments:

> For subtle and complex responses, one needs subtle and complex opinion surveys. These demand time, money, and skill. Today, the trend is toward oversimplified, cheap, crude public opinion polls, not subtle, complex ones. This is not because the profession wants it that way: Opinion research professionals have never been more alert to the dangers of superficial polls. The villains are the mass media who increasingly commission, pay for, and themselves conduct public opinion polls. [15]

Media polls aren't just a shallower measure of opinion; they also often create the false impression that public opinion is settled. The framers of the Constitution sought an informed and watchful citizenry. But not only do polls cut short thoughtful consideration, they also accelerate the policy debate. Polling today is technologically advanced enough that polling results can actually be rushed into the public eye before all the facts are in or all the ideas considered. The problem with such a scenario is that, by necessity, the pollster reduces a complex debate to a few short statements that purport to represent all sides. In the real world of tough choices, such reductions usually carry an implied *ad absurdum*.

In the wake of an airline crash, school shooting, or similar tragedy, polling is now one of the hallmarks of the media feeding frenzy. In this context, polls make public opinion as much as they observe it. It is an elementary polling error to conduct a poll immediately after a major news event, because such an event can lead to artificial surges or bounces in opinion. Are the media being responsible when their pollsters question Americans about tighter airline regulations or increased gun controls after a tragedy?

Following the 1999 massacre at Columbine High School, when two students went on a gun-toting rampage and killed twelve students, one teacher, and then themselves, media attention turned to gun control. The tragedy also provoked its share of polls, which were published alongside cover stories and emotive pieces. *Newsweek, USA Today,* and other media asked Americans about gun control measures. The *New York Times* headline blared, "The Politics of Guns: Tilting Toward the Democrats," with Republicans doing an "about-face" to offer their own gun controls, while Democrats stayed "determinedly on the offensive" in the wake of the tragedy.[16] As the *Times* put it, "Five years ago, when the Democrats lost their majority in Congress, they felt they had paid dearly for backing a ban on many kinds of assault weapons. But that was before a series of school shootings culminated in the massacre at Columbine High School. And today there were strong signs that both parties sense that the politics of guns and violence are shifting."

The *Washington Post:* "Littleton Alters the Landscape of Debate on Guns."[17] The *Dallas Morning News:* "Gun Lobby Faces First Congressional Test After Littleton."[18] As one *Dallas Morning News* reporter put it: "The gun lobby, on the defensive even before the Colorado high school shootings, now faces its first congressional test in the post-Littleton political world."

Newsday declared: "Gun Control Bolstered: Americans Want Tougher Laws, Poll Shows."[19] The Associated Press–authored story led with: "Support for gun control jumped in the week after the high school shootings in Colorado, according to an Associated Press poll, with a majority of Americans saying tougher gun laws are the most effective way to stem violence." But only a careful reader would notice that gun control advocates weren't the big winner.

> Media polls aren't just a shallower measure of opinion; they also often create the false impression that public opinion is settled.

AP's pollster, ICR Media, had actually tested the issue of gun control in a more stable framework—before the tragedy, without the emotional fuel of media sensationalism feeding the bonfire of hyperbole. According to that poll, only 42 percent of Americans thought stricter gun control would be "more effective." Forty-seven percent said that the key was stricter enforcement of the laws on the books. But in the days after the tragedy, that 42 percent increased to a bare majority of 51 percent who believed that tougher gun laws would be more effective. Another 39 percent advocated better enforcement.

Is it fair to test public sentiment in such circumstances and then claim growing support? What if a woman defended herself from rape by brandishing a legally owned handgun? Would polling after a heroic incident fairly test opinion on concealed-weapon permits? Media coverage is manifestly biased against this scenario. According to a two-year study by the Media Research Center, the network newscasts are overwhelmingly in favor of gun control. Of the 635 stories on gun policy carried on the evening news during that period, stories advocating gun control outnumbered those opposing such measures by ten to one. (There were 357 gun-control advocacy stories, 36 with a Second Amendment bias, and 260 that were neutral.) The Center also noted that evening news stories tended to play off emotion and rarely focused on crime-reduction programs that worked, favoring the gun control angle instead.[20] The themes are as familiar as they are one-sided: "Access to guns leads to shootings"; "Concealed weapon laws will only increase the carnage"; "Gun makers are responsible for the violence"; and "Will Congress waste the momentum we created toward gun control?"

In 1999, *Time* magazine columnist Roger Rosenblatt expressed the outrage and anger of left-oriented journalists:

> [A]s terrible as all the gun killings of the past few months have been, one has the almost satisfying feeling that the country is going through the literal death throes of a barbaric era. . . . My guess, in fact, is that the hour has come and gone—that the great majority of Americans are saying they favor gun control when they really mean gun banishment.[21]

A few months later, *NBC Nightly News* reporter Gwen Ifill showed the typical left-leaning media impatience with Congress for failing to march to the tune of media polls: "Four weeks after the Columbine High School shooting, a month of public outrage, and yet the Senate remains tangled up in finger-pointing over gun control."[22]

Rosenblatt claimed, "Polls indicate that more people favor stronger gun control and that more are willing to make it a voting issue in the coming elections. But the atmosphere in the Republican Congress remains inhospitable to any effective bill."[23] Was this statement accurate and factual?

Polling and media furor combined to make it seem as if there was greater support than ever for stricter controls on firearms. Rosenblatt's misleading conclusions were based on instant polls that showed gun control majorities in the wake of tragedy. As happens in so many cases of tragedy or scandal, polling acts as a ratifying device, expressing the public's backing of media sentiments. But even by the standards of media polling, the public support wasn't higher than ever. In 1990, 78 percent of those polled favored stricter gun laws, according to the Gallup Organization. A decade later, that number had fallen to 61 percent.

Media coverage and polling questions often inspire fear and foment insecurity. At the time of the Columbine High School tragedy, for instance, school violence was actually on the decline, but few news organizations provided this context. To their credit, *Newsweek*'s Jerry Adler and a team of reporters did so spectacularly: "Out of powerlessness [to protect their kids at school] comes fear: 64 percent of adults surveyed in the *Newsweek* poll considered a shooting incident at their local schools either very likely or somewhat likely. In fact, in 1996 only 10 percent of schools registered even one serious violent crime; on average a high-school senior is 200 times as likely to be admitted to Harvard as to be killed in his school."[24]

What is most amazing is that Columbine and the two perpetrators of that tragedy opened a new debate around parental responsibility and cultural decay. When gun control was included in a more nuanced list of ways to prevent similar tragedies—that is, when a poll was taken that didn't just ask about well-intentioned and unspecified gun control measures—the results weren't as stark as the media coverage at first claimed. The Gallup Organization asked 1,025 adults on May 7–9, 1999, a week after the shooting:

Next we have some questions about the shooting at the Littleton, Colorado, high school (April 20, 1999) where 2 students killed 12 of their classmates and one teacher. In your opinion, what is the single most important thing that could be done to prevent another incidence of school shootings by students, like the one in Littleton?

The responses were divided into thirteen possible answers. The most popular response was "parental involvement/responsibility," getting the nod from 32 percent of those polled. "Better gun control/law/issues" garnered just 12 percent of the support. Even though support for broader cultural and moral solutions was divided among several other responses, the results clearly told a different story on how to stop rogue shooting. Here are the complete results of this poll on how to prevent school violence:

Parental involvement/responsibility: 32 percent

More security at schools: 16 percent

Better gun control/laws/issues: 12 percent

More counselors/counseling/teachers: 6 percent

Lift laws on disciplining children: 6 percent

Control media violence/video games/Internet: 4 percent

Better communication students/parents/teachers:
3 percent

Raise morals/people's standards: 3 percent

Better education/students/parents: 3 percent

Put prayer back in school/home: 3 percent

Stricter punishment on children/laws: 2 percent

Dress codes/uniforms: 1 percent

Other: 4 percent

Not only did some polls cast doubt on the typical media coverage, but also few people believed that gun controls would work, hinting at a suspicion that the causes of crime were deeper than the "availability of guns." An ABC News/*Washington Post* poll in April 2000 asked whether "stricter gun control laws would reduce the amount of violent crime in this country, or not?" A bare majority (51 percent) said yes. A nearly equal number (48 percent) did not think stricter measures would have an impact on crime.

> **Media coverage and polling questions often inspire fear and foment insecurity.**

Typically gun polls pit new gun laws *and* better enforcement against no new laws and enforcement. This throws significantly more support to the gun control camp. Asking Americans if the laws should be enforced is a "gimme" question. That's why questions that ask whether voters favor "stricter" gun laws are deceptive. They lack content. (What kind of laws?) In addition, use of the word "stricter" implies enforcement and common-sense effectiveness, throwing support to gun control advocates. Yet in recent years especially, when the question pits better enforcement against more laws, enforcement wins. Perhaps one of the most carefully worded polls was the NBC News/*Wall Street Journal* poll of April 29–May 1, 2000:

> Which do you think would be more effective in reducing gun violence: passing new restrictions on the sale of handguns, such as requiring trigger locks and registration; or ensuring stricter enforcement of existing laws on gun sales and ownership; or do you feel that both new restrictions and stricter enforcement would be best?

Only 11 percent backed "new restrictions." More than three times as many (35 percent) wanted "stricter enforcement." And 45 percent said both. An ABC News/*Washington Post* poll, taken at about the same time, had similar results. Fifty-three percent believed that the "best way to reduce gun violence in this country" was by "stricter enforcement of existing laws." Just 33 percent thought it was "by passing stricter gun control laws."

What's interesting is that polls did not always ask such questions. In fact, according to the Roper Center at the University of Connecticut, only since 1998 have respondents had a choice on gun control polls that included "stricter" or "better" enforcement of *existing* gun laws. A Nexis database search shows that the first such poll to ask the question was a 1998 Fox News and Opinion Dynamics poll. Before that, questions tended to focus on the availability of weapons in order to push the issue of stricter controls. But testing the proposition in such a one-sided manner ignored other public policy alternatives. Yet as support for "stricter enforcement of current laws" grows, the popularity of "more gun control laws" diminishes.

The fact that the cultural/moral aspects of the story received some attention made Columbine different from most shooting stories. But again, the Columbine case showed not only the power of media slant, but also the bias of the media. As journalist James Bovard points out, Columbine was notable for how little scrutiny was given to the conduct of the police, whose failures to act may have given the perpetrators free rein to turn a shooting into a slaughter. With the assistance of instant polls and one-sided ideological reporting, mass shootings are all too conveniently converted into public policy events that support the position of gun control advocates, regardless of the facts of the shooting or the nuances of public opinion. The cycle is the same: Stories focus on the outrage. Journalists criticize the National Rifle Association. And editorial boards and pundits bully politicians who oppose yet more legislation, threatening Election Day consequences for those who don't read the polls their way.

Even though some polls cast serious doubts on the media coverage of Columbine, the media still singled out polls that purported to show new support for more gun laws. Yet the same *New York Times* that declared "The Politics of Guns: Tilting Toward the Democrats" just after Columbine would recant a year later after an election in which supporters of the Second Amendment had a decisive impact on the election. "[M]any centrist and conservative Democrats have also concluded that gun control has become their party's albatross, costing it crucial votes among white, male, rural voters in key states across the South and Midwest."[25] And former President Bill Clinton noted that the National Rifle Association "probably had more to do than anyone else in the fact we didn't win the House this time, and they hurt Al Gore." Measuring public opinion by the ballot box and the membership rolls of the NRA (a citizens' organization seeking to persuade voters) revealed a far different story, and one that belied the polls used so cleverly for so many years by the media.

Polls Cater to, Rather Than Challenge, Media Stories

Instead of challenging media stories or operating as just another source, polls are deployed after the shock troops of political accusation or media exposé have hit the public conscience. Then, in a kind of self-ratification of their own coverage, media polls lend the air of public support to journalists' often one-sided and biased take on a national debate.

The very act of asking a question about public opinion raises the public's consciousness about an idea. This phenomenon by itself fits in with the media's role as public agenda setters. The media play a powerful role in campaigns and public policy debates. But the core of their influence on the public debate doesn't come from their ability to affect the mind of voters and citizens; rather, it comes from their ability to set the agenda for the news.

"Polls are newsworthy because they provide a new piece of information," said S. Robert Lichter, director of the Center for Media and Public Affairs. "They're instantaneous, and they have numbers which seem to lend credibility. They're news by definition, so there is a temptation to abuse them."[26]

After the 1994 election, the Republican Congress sought changes in the Medicare system that included reducing the rate of growth in future spending. The idea was a politically costly one. For President Clinton, it proved to be high-quality political ammunition for blasting Republican "extremism" and reviving his own relevance in national dialogue. For the media, coverage tended to focus almost exclusively on the "cuts" and even "slashes" proposed by the GOP reformers.

> Instead of challenging media stories or operating as just another source, polls are deployed after the shock troops of political accusation or media exposé have hit the public conscience.

According to a content study by the Media Research Center, reporters writing for the *New York Times,* the *Washington Post, USA Today,* and the newsmagazines *Time, Newsweek,* and *U.S. News & World Report* were far more likely to emphasize the word "cuts," even though the term did not apply. In 1,134 Medicare stories from January 1995 to July 1996, reporters used the words "cut," "reduce," "scale back," "savings," and "slash" 1,060 times. At the same time, President Clinton was airing ads throughout America that portrayed the Republican plan as dangerous to the elderly. The controversy generated a great deal of attention from media and political opponents of the plan, and ultimately proved to be just the kind of sensational story that can be reinforced by pollsters' questions, convincing journalists they rightly punish the GOP.

On October 26, 1995, days before the congressional vote, a *New York Times*/CBS News poll was released that showed little support for the GOP plan. Here is how the question was worded: "If you had to choose, would you prefer balancing the budget, or preventing Medicare from being significantly cut?" At this point the reader should see the red flags waving over the wording. The question subtly softens and moderates the idea of balancing the budget through the use of the verb "prefer," while the emphasis in the alternative falls on "preventing" Medicare from being "significantly cut." What is the "significance" of that cut? The question doesn't say. But in the context of the reportage at the time, most voters would presumably think that the plan was "savage" or that it meant "deep cuts." Few understood that it amounted to $12 a month by the year 2002. Add to this the fact that the poll drew from the least accurate sample—American adults—a far less politically aware and far more Democrat-leaning source of opinion. (We will look at this more closely in chapter 3.) It should not be surprising, then, that opposition to the GOP plan was more than two to one (67 percent to 27 percent).

The question's slant was compounded by the coverage of the poll in the *Times*. The headline blared: "Americans Reject Big Medicare Cuts, New Poll Finds."[27] Reporter Adam Clymer's lead for the article declared, "As Congress takes up the budget, the American public fears plans of the Republicans to curb Medicare spending, scoffs at their tax cut, and flatly does not believe that the plan would produce a balanced budget by 2002, the latest *New York Times*/CBS News poll shows."

The wording was so biased that it drew protests from Republicans. House Speaker Newt Gingrich called it a "disgraceful example of disinformation."[28] Gingrich charged that the *Times* used "deliberately rigged questions that are totally phony that come out the morning of the vote." The *Times* defended the wording as "balanced." The paper's executive editor, Joseph Lelyveld, called the poll "straightforward honest journalism," adding that "[a]s for the timing[,] what better time could there be from a news point of view than the eve of the vote?"[29]

It's up to the reader to decide whether this is news or advocacy. But it is worthwhile to note that Lelyveld bragged that the *Times* poll asked more than ninety-six questions, all of which followed "long-established polling techniques." It is a phenomenon of the polling industry, as we shall explore more fully in chapter 4, that a simple change of language and emphasis can have vast consequences. But what the media choose to report can distort polling and give citizens cause to doubt the accuracy of numbers unreflectively reported.

For instance, among the ninety-six questions in the poll, the *Times* did not report the responses to the following:

> Would it be acceptable or not acceptable to you if Congress raised the monthly amount people on Medicare have to pay in order to keep Medicare services at their present level?
> *More than four in ten (42 percent) found such a plan acceptable, and less than a majority (49 percent) opposed it.*

> Would it be acceptable or not acceptable to you if Congress changed Medicare so that people with higher incomes pay a greater share of their own medical cost than people with lower incomes?
> *Fully 82 percent of adults thought this plan was acceptable, with only 14 percent demurring.*

The *Times* asked, and reported in passing, the following question, which assessed the level of respondents' actual knowledge about the bill:

> How much do you feel you know about the Republican Medicare plan—a lot, a little, or do you feel you know almost nothing about it?

> *Only 12 percent said they knew "a lot" about the Medicare plan. Just more than half (56 percent) admitted they knew "a little." Yet the* Times *felt confident in reporting that the public feared the Republican plan, even though one of its own polling questions found that 31 percent said they knew "almost nothing" about it.*

Of the ninety-six questions asked, the one most damaging to Republican efforts was the only one highlighted by the *New York Times.* There's no doubt that a focus on the other questions would have shown that support or opposition to the various reform plans wasn't as stark as the media portrayed, especially in light of such manifest ignorance. In fact, the unpublished results argued for better reportage on the substance of the rival plans and the need for education on the most basic issues. Such journalistic selectivity about what results should be reported to the public can undermine the credibility of public opinion polling and the press, if they are known. But the ultimate losers are the American people, the very people whose interests pollsters and the media claim to represent. When polls undermine the marketplace of ideas, democracy can only suffer.

It is interesting to note that in the end, the media's own taste for conflict resulted in a victory for Clinton, a costly defeat for Republicans, and the successful passage of the reforms. In 1997, Clinton signed legislation that mirrored the very reforms proposed by Republicans in 1995. As John Merline pointed out in *Slate* magazine, the spending "cuts" were nearly the same: $119 billion in the 1995 package versus $114 billion for the Clinton-backed bill. The new bill reduced payments to Medicare providers by $36.5 billion; the original plan, which Democrats had said would force hospitals to close, would have shuffled away $36.7 billion. And the bipartisan plan made seniors pay higher monthly premiums, too: $82.40, as compared with $84.60 in the 1995 reform—a "slashing" difference of

$2.40 a month.[30] But few Americans ever learned of these facts because the horse-race polls subsumed issue reportage. If journalists weren't interested in substance in Round One of the controversy, we shouldn't be surprised if the actual details were just too boring to be reported in Round Two.

WHEN IDEOLOGUES ATTACK: JOURNALISTS AND POLLING LANGUAGE

When it comes to polling, wording can play a decisive role in the results. Because Americans are often ignorant of policy facts or simply inconsistent in their political beliefs, they can be easily manipulated by the way a question is presented and the way issues are framed.

A good example of this occurred in November 1999, when the *Miami Herald* ran a series of articles based on a survey conducted by Washington pollster Schroth & Associates. The poll probed how Floridians viewed affirmative action, immigration, the embargo against Cuba, and school vouchers. The *Herald* covered each issue in separate articles. It interviewed people on both sides of the issues. And on all the questions

> The ultimate losers of journalistic selectivity are the American people, the very people whose interests pollsters and the media claim to represent.

except one—the question on school choice—the paper published the wording of the question it asked voters.

And there's the rub. Whether the term "school choice" or "voucher" is used in a question can radically alter the response. The *Herald* didn't warn readers of this fact, however. The front-page headline announced: "Majority of Voters Flunk Idea of School Vouchers."[31]

The story stated that 55 percent of voters opposed vouchers and only 38 percent supported the idea. But was support really that low? The actual wording of the question makes the reason for the results quite apparent. The pollster asked: "Do you favor or oppose providing vouchers paid for by taxpayers for those parents who want to send their children to private schools?" As Randy Lewis, spokesman of Floridians for School Choice, said at the time, "You just asked voters if they want to give taxpayer money to rich people to reimburse them for sending their kids to private schools."[32]

By adding the notion of "paid for by taxpayers," the question stresses the idea of waste and undeserved entitlement. What's more, the wording "those parents" subtly hints that vouchers will go to *other* people. If the pollster had asked voters if they would like vouchers to send *their* kids to a school of their choice, the results would have been very different. These are elementary red flags for anyone familiar with the dicey issue of vouchers.

Floridians for School Choice conducted their own poll in 1998. Nearly 65 percent of voters statewide agreed with the statement "Education dollars should follow the child to whatever school the family selects." Of course, this question stresses the notion of freedom and accountability. But voucher supporters could very well argue that it is an accurate representation of the actual mechanics of the voucher system.

Wording is not the issue here, however. What is at issue is media misuse of polling data and distortion of the polling process. Even the American Federation of Teachers admits that there is little difference among the words "vouchers," "choice," and "opportunity scholarship;" they all explain the same concept, but some words carry less baggage. The AFT warns reporters: "A voucher by any other name is still a voucher—public dollars leaving public schools for private schools."

The reporter covering the results of the Schroth & Associates study, Analisa Nazareno, must have taken a lesson from the AFT. In her lead, she defined vouchers as "taxpayer-funded private schooling." Such media bias gives us yet another angle on the limitations that polling brings to political debate. Instead of an open debate about the terms and mechanics of vouchers, school choice backers had to argue with the wording in the poll. This submerges political debate under the arcana of debate about polling.

When some school choice backers protested the poll's wording, they were forced to take their case to the pollster, Schroth & Associates, in Washington. Ostensibly a detached and objective observer of the political process, the pollster became part of the political struggle. Rob Schroth, head of Schroth & Associates, just shrugged off the complaint: "Vouchers have never been popular among voters, either in Florida or throughout the nation," he told the *Herald*. Such a claim is manifestly false; coming from a pollster, it is almost unbelievable. But the end result was that *Herald* readers were left with a pollster and a reporter who saw no nuances to the issue and seemed unaware of the effect of wording on how voters think about this issue.

Such cases exemplify the peculiar mixture of media and polling that afflicts the political process. The shallow reportage, the biased choice of words, the pollsters' own slant, and the article's omission of the question wording gave ammunition to the opponents of school choice in a debate that is filled with fiery public opinion broadsides from both reformers and advocates for the status quo. Polling plays a larger and more important role in American democracy than ever before, and as the *Miami Herald* experience shows, bias can creep into a story in subtle ways. The shifting results of polls are a reminder that voters need to hear substantive debate and read stories that aren't just about the political horse race.

When it suits its purpose, the elite community of national journalists is quite capable of ignoring the polls it so adamantly presses in its own stories. For instance, in the twenty-seven months leading up to the Senate debate about "campaign finance reform," the *Washington Post* and the *New York Times* ran editorials on the subject an average of once every six days. It was a perfect example of the media driving the national agenda, because according to those same polls that are considered so critical to our national dialogue, the issue of "campaign finance reform" was a nonstarter. In fact, support for the idea seemed to be slipping. Yet the power of the media could not have been better illustrated. Over a span of two weeks in March 2001, Senator John McCain, R-Ariz., was able to throw aside all consideration of the new president's tax cuts, the budget, and any measure to help an ailing economy so he could debate an issue of critical import to a journalistic press corps that had made him a modern-day Teddy Roosevelt.

Media stories hailed McCain as "courageous," a "rock star," a "maverick," a "crusader," and the "skunk at the Republican picnic" for taking on his own party. But what did the media polls say? When asked to rank the importance of "campaign finance reform," respondents inevitably put the idea in the basement. *Newsweek* asked on December 14–15, 2000:

> As George W. Bush begins his presidency, which ONE of the following do you think should be his top priority: [rotate] education, Social Security reform, prescription drugs for seniors, tax relief, upgrading the military, or campaign finance reform?

Education ranked number one, with 29 percent backing the idea. Social Security came next (18 percent). Third was drugs for seniors at 17 percent. Tax cuts was fourth at 16 percent. Upgrading the military notched fifth with 10-percent support. Dead last: campaign finance reform, with only 6-percent support. In fact, the longer the list, the worse the issue fared. During the election, when stories continued to percolate on campaign finance reform and the high costs of elections, an ABC News/

Washington Post poll from September 4–6 asked voters what issues were "very important." Campaign finance reform came in just after education, the economy, Social Security, health care, morals/values, budget, crime, the middle class, taxes, drug benefits, defense, environment, foreign affairs, gun control, abortion, and partisanship. In other words, it ranked last. Even as months ticked by, the results were the same. A Gallup poll from January 23, 2001, once again put "improving the way campaigns are financed" last. Higher up: education, American prosperity, Social Security reform, prescription drugs for seniors, balancing the federal budget, Medicare reform, improving health care, building the military, improving conditions for minorities and the poor, fighting illegal drugs, the environment, race relations, and cutting federal income taxes.

> When it suits its purpose, the elite community of national journalists is quite capable of ignoring the polls it so adamantly presses in its own stories.

Six months later, an ABC News/*Washington Post* poll (March 25, 2001) asked the question in a different way but with similar results:

> We'd like to know what kind of priority you want to see George W. Bush and the Congress give to some issues. For each one, please tell me if it should receive the highest priority, a high priority but not the highest, a middle priority, or a lower priority.

Under such a rubric, campaign finance reform ranked last, with just 45 percent saying it should be given the highest priority. Other concerns, such as the economy, saving Social Security, protecting the environment, and cutting taxes, were all given higher rankings, meriting anywhere from 73- to 89-percent support as a "highest priority."

The polls had a definite slant. Stories focused on the need to "get money out of politics." At first glance, the questions seem balanced. They merely asked about whether people favor "stricter laws." But in every case, there was little reference or attention given to *why* special interests, lobbyists, and others seek to influence the process. In other words, voters weren't presented with another frame of values (such as the First Amendment), the costs of one course of action over another (the empowering of incumbents), the failure of past legislation (the consequences of the 1974 laws), nor were they asked questions that cast a skeptical eye on the constitutionality of eliminating private groups (the parties) from taking part fully in elections. The polls tapped into the American dread of corruption with little reference to fact or possible consequences. (Compare this with the lead-in questions in chapter 1 used by the *New York Times* and CBS news to note that support for Bush's plan wasn't as high on "second thought.")

It might appear that the low priorities given to campaign finance reform show that there are limitations to the media's manipulation of polls. But the proliferation of polls showed campaign finance reform was an issue of passion to the media and could cost politicians dearly if they voted against the "reform." And that sentiment mirrored reporter's stories.

Journalists used sneer-quotes to describe "sham issue ads"—campaign commercials that focused on the record of a politician, usually on a single issue. Stories used "soft money" to describe "unregulated contributions," with the not-so-subtle hint that such money goes to a system out of control. But such private contributions go from citizens to private political associations, such as the Democratic and Republican parties. Yet story after story parroted select numbers, such as the rising amounts being given to soft and hard money, totaling $1 billion in the 2000 election. It seems like an impressive number except when it was compared with the magnitude of government spending on entitlement, pork, and subsidies at issue: $1.9 trillion a year. In fact, the very words "campaign finance *reform*" biased the debate against those who, as they saw it, were defending the citizen's right to free speech and the integrity of election as instruments to educate citizens and hold politicians accountable. How different the debate would have been if McCain's crusade were described even modestly as a "campaign finance restriction bill" because it reigned in the rights of private citizen groups to use television to reward or punish incumbent politicians.

Nevertheless, the bottom-rung ranking of campaign finance made little difference. In the end, the media got their way. McCain's bill passed in the senate. It banned so-called soft money. It outlawed commercials thirty days before Election Day that were produced by outside groups and political parties. It doubled hard money limits so incumbents wouldn't have to work so hard when raising money. And it eliminated limits when an incumbent faced a millionaire challenger spending his own money, stopping the last people who can unseat a sitting politician once the parties were taken out of the political process.

Media Polling Undermines Democratic Debate

The journalistic need for speed and passion for drama isn't just in conflict with the social science imperatives of depth and nuance. The media's drive to push overnight polling and to constantly survey public opinion also runs counter to the need for mature deliberation in the political process. Many institutions and interests go into the formation of public opinion in a representative democracy. Individual citizens, special interest groups, and elected leaders all play a role in working out public opinion, but they are also legitimate voices in themselves.

The competitive media drive that produces poll after poll doesn't simply engage public policy questions in shorter and shallower bursts. Polling can actually truncate public debate. In the hands of the media, polls are too often presented as the final word on a subject. In a time of crisis, controversy, or tragedy, the media will blitzkrieg a new story, deploying every manner of commentary, coverage, and explanation. But this rarely results in a substantive discussion of public policy issues.

Among the many weapons for bombarding the viewer with news is the "overnight poll," which is less accurate than other surveys because of sample error. Random sampling, the key to methodologically sound polling, decreases in accuracy when pollsters can't interview all those selected for questioning. Because of the compressed time frame, there is less chance that pollsters will be able to reach those selected with callbacks. This can lead to methodological errors. But overnight polls have a negative side beyond possible sample inaccuracy. They can be probing for a public opinion that may not even be formed. For this reason, many pollsters oppose overnight polls as detrimental to true measurement of the public's views on a matter. Pollster Daniel Yankelovich warns, almost bitterly, "Many of these opinion polls [overnights and quickie polls] are worthless because they ignore every trap and pitfall the profession has uncovered, at great pains and cost, in its more than half century of analyzing poll results."[33]

> The media's drive to push overnight polling and to constantly survey public opinion runs counter to the need for mature deliberation in the political process.

For John Zogby of Zogby International, the problem goes even deeper. Instant polls don't just measure shaky opinion, they undermine the deliberation that leads to public opinion. "There is a very interesting symbiosis in public opinion," he told an audience at the National Press Club. "On the one hand, the public needs to see and hear the talking heads. They need to see and hear considered opinion from them as well as their co-workers before they form their final judgments."[34] Instant polling, especially overnight polls, can undermine this dialogue. The proliferation of polls has heightened the competition to be the first to do a poll. With giant media players battling for a limited audience, the incentive to jump the gun and assemble polls as quickly as possible grows. It is also one reason the campaign season seems to begin earlier and earlier, with every unscientific state straw poll gaining power.

But media competition doesn't just lead to shallower polls; it actually undercuts debate. Keying off an event, these polls will be one-sided policy tests, designed for the moment, with little reference to context or inconsistencies in respondents' minds. And because politicians are judged on the basis of these polls, with little reference to the limitations of public opinion measures, political leaders are pummeled by the results. Thus a news event that proves worthy of front-page coverage can instantly ignite a conflagration of polls.

"The principal problem with polling today is that there are too many polls," says Arnold Steinberg, founder of California's political polling firm of Steinberg and Associates. "What's happening is too many news media are trying to compete by being different. And there's way too much focus on horse-race questions such as 'Is Smith ahead of Jones?' The results change radically from time to time because such great emphasis is put on selling the poll in terms of media coverage."[35]

The paradox is that, as media has increased horse-race and strategy reportage, the public has become more disconnected. Even more disturbing, the public alienation from politics has resulted in a citizenry quite ignorant of the issues. Thus shallow reportage is followed by shallow polling questions of a shallow populace—a vicious circle if there ever was one.

Journalists are often so eager to cover who's up and who's down that the only source of information for many voters on policy questions becomes the media pollsters' questions. And those questions come from the same groups caught up in the glitzy coverage of the political tug-o'-war. In the few words it takes to set up the question, poll respondents are asked to judge a complex policy issue. They must track and decide the issue—one that should be debated in the public square, not synthesized for the first time over the phone.

Democratic theory does not require that voters should understand the full import of their decisions. Full consciousness or total awareness is not possible. But when voter responses are reported as representative of the people at large, it is important to understand how strong their political beliefs and foundation of knowledge are. The framers' hopes (whatever their views of the franchise) were that institutions of society would educate voters and leaders. The friend of democracy ought to seek increased competition in the marketplace of ideas—not a grunting exchange of thoughts based on a multiple-choice test.

It is beyond argument that poll results can have long-term consequences and can profoundly influence political parties and democratic institutions. Their power stems directly from the presumed power of the polls as a surrogate for debate. We consider polling results to be the purest expression of public opinion. But if the media's quick-fix mentality alters the political landscape because their questions are shallow or fail to present the full ramifications of a policy, then the media poll ceases to be informative and the media begin to threaten the institutions they purport to protect.

Jumping the Gun: Polls Undermine New Ideas

The media's use of polls is a double-edged sword. Overnight polling often tests an idea long before the public has had a chance to think about it. For instance, when presidential candidate Steve Forbes announced his support for the flat tax in 1996, much of the media considered the issue dead on arrival. For months, the polls of Iowans ranked tax issues far below the social issues that were supposed to be of prime interest to Republicans in the Buckeye State. Pundits and journalists cited poll numbers to explain how Forbes's ideas did not resonate. But as Forbes pushed his message and explained how the plan would work, he was able to make tax reform and tax cuts a subject of interest. The media, however, seemed surprised as Forbes surged forward as a presidential contender based primarily on his call to institute a 17-percent tax rate across the board. For the media, the early signal from the polls caused a cursory and dismissive evaluation of Forbes's tax plan even before journalists reported the details.

Conversely, while big ideas can suffer because of premature and incessant polls, media polling can give a false sense of support for small-scale ideas. Daniel Yankelovich writes about a polling phenomenon that often goes unreported: "In opinion polling, one constantly encounters the say-yes-to-everything phenomenon when people are asked whether they agree or disagree with various proposals," he writes. "If the proposals sound appealing, people will say that they agree with them, even though they may be incompatible with other proposals that people also agree with."[36]

President Clinton exploited this oddity of polling in his re-election campaign. Clinton abandoned the message of far-reaching change he had preached in 1992 for a more subtle and cautious program outlined by pollster Dick Morris. Morris sought to grab headlines with daily policy measures that were modest and poll-tested. The result was a popular program that pushed cosmetic reforms—such as school uniforms and the V-chip—that were symbolic measures rather than bold initiatives. These headline-grabbing stories attracted media attention and invariably polled well, lending support to Clinton's re-election bid.

In this sense, the media's blitzkrieg use of polls must in some way reinforce the status quo because it contributes to the oversimplification of public debate itself. Bold, large-scale ideas such as Social Security, the reform of Medicare, the tax code, or public education tend to do poorly in polling. For the media, the debate of ideas is a gladiatorial spectacle where the policy proposal is subjected to an up-or-down gesture from the crowd. This tends to eliminate discussion of issues and time spent educating the public. The pros and cons of an idea are ignored, which may explain voters' startling ignorance on most issues.

The Effects of Media Polling on Political Candidates

Over the past three decades, the media's role in the political process has increased at nearly the rate of polling. As the power of political parties declined, candidates began appealing directly to the public. In response to the bizarre nomination of Hubert Humphrey in 1968 by party leaders, the McGovern-Fraser Commission sought to put the Democratic nomination process on a more democratic footing. The commission made popular participation—through either primaries or open party caucuses—the only way to secure the Democratic nomination for office. These reforms were meant to democratize the process and give the little guy a bigger say in the selection of candidates.

The reforms helped eliminate the "smoke-filled rooms" where elected and organizational leaders of the Democratic Party had selected candidates who were often different from what the rank-and-file sought. But the reforms had an unintended consequence as well. They weakened the political parties and severed the public from one of the free associations that worked toward producing an involved and informed democratic electorate. The parties had hitherto acted as intermediaries, helping to organize support and educate voters as well as elevate party loyalists. Under the new system (which Republicans soon adopted, too), candidates answered directly to the people in elections. This seemingly democratic reform required potential candidates to appeal directly to the citizenry for votes. To be elected, candidates had to get television time and newspaper ink, and this put the media in a powerful new (and often unfair) position as both the determiner of the news and the medium of deliberation, debate, and voter information.

> While big ideas can suffer because of premature and incessant polls, media polling can give a false sense of support for small-scale ideas.

Unfortunately, what a journalist considers news can be vastly different from the debate about issues and the basic information that voters seek. The problem with the media's agenda, writes political scientist Thomas E. Patterson of Syracuse University, is that "the game has overtaken substance, bad news overshadows good, controversies outrank policy matters, news images prevail over issues of leadership, and news attention is distributed unfairly."[37]

Journalistic values put a premium on controversy. Journalists prefer to report on conflict, accusations, and the political gamesmanship in campaigns. These values often demean and trivialize election contests, injecting heavy doses of personality analysis and journalistic cynicism. These aren't new observations. Alexis de Tocqueville wrote in *Democracy in America:* "The characteristics of the American journalist consist in an open and coarse appeal to the passions of the populace; and he habitually abandons the principles of political science to assail the characters of individuals, to track them into private life, and disclose all their weaknesses and errors."[38]

With the balancing force of the parties removed, television became the chief conduit to the mass audience of voters. Journalists' new position was strengthened by another development: the advent of media polling. The result has not just been more horse-race journalism with all the handicapping and strategic play-by-play, but also more shallow coverage.

The media's constant use of polls has created virtual primaries that winnow out candidates long before voters enter the booth on Election Day. The race for the White House in 2000 is perhaps the best example of this new phenomenon. Most voters don't think about elections until the final few weeks of a campaign. Yet in 1996, even before voters had officially re-elected Bill Clinton, pollsters were already in the field asking about the 2000 Republican nominee. The early choice: Republican scion George W. Bush. Bush was running for re-election as governor of Texas at the time, but this didn't stop pollsters from asking voters who their likely choice in 2000 would be. The absurdity of this proposition is apparent to all except those in the Greek chorus of the media. No wonder voters are often bored by election campaigns. The only reason voters don't view the political system as cynically as journalists do is because they are blessed with a willful ignorance of the process.

The media's imperative is to get the story as early as possible. Horse-race journalism has become such an obsession that stories focus on elections months, even years, before they happen. With the increase in polling data, we shouldn't be surprised when media pundits and reporters greet the seemingly inevitable victory of candidates with all the jejune detachment of world-weary European existentialists.

Bush was the ultimate winner of the "virtual primary" of public polling. His name recognition was no doubt helped by his father—especially when as many as one out of four voters thought they were voting for Bush *père*. Bush also secured the GOP establishment's support because he did well in the polls, attracting Hispanics and women, and seemed to have the Clintonian charisma and soft edges other Republicans lacked. In the early and decisive virtual primary, his strength in the polls became *the* story and overwhelmed almost every debate about ideas. Bush's image of success and his aura of invincibility promised a coronation, because in hypothetical matchups with the presumed Democratic candidate, Vice President Al Gore, Bush led by double digits. (Never mind that no one knew anything about his record.) In the battle of the polls, Bush was so dominant that he raised $70 million, a record-breaking sum that utterly destroyed any chance for a rival to beat him.

Some of the best-known Republicans—former Secretary of Transportation Elizabeth Dole, former Vice President Dan Quayle, and former Tennessee Governor Lamar Alexander—fell by the wayside early and hard because they could not show support in these polls. After her withdrawal from the race, Elizabeth Dole told reporters that candidates were constantly "answering questions not about guns in the classroom or China in the World Trade Organization, but about money in the bank account or ads on the airwaves."[39]

> The media's constant use of polls has created virtual primaries that winnow out candidates long before voters enter the booth on Election Day.

The virtual primary now determines more than which candidates journalists will cover. "In effect, preseason polls have become the surrogate for the traditional benchmarks of primary elections, which determine whether candidates meet the expectations that journalists set for them," write S. Robert Lichter and Jeremy Torobin for the Center for Media and Public Affairs.[40] The effect of these preseason polls is immense and goes far beyond mere grist for the pundits' mills, because how candidates fare in polls helps determine how they get covered.

In the race to handicap the next presidential race, media attention helps shape the ability of candidates to raise funds. Long before Americans are able to make their voices heard, the field of candidates can wax or wane based on the media's choice of who makes the A-list and who will appear in their early polls. This provides a new hurdle for the candidate who must succeed in getting the media plaudits necessary for getting his or her name on the polling ballot for the virtual primary. This gives the media a unique ability to shape the choices that ultimately come before voters.

In the case of Bush, the expectations generated by media polling seemed to have nominated him long before he announced any intention to run for the nation's highest office. It is interesting to note that Bush was already appearing on presidential polling surveys even though he sought to dismiss such questions while running for re-election as governor.

Pollsters are careful to point out that polls are *not* predictive, of course. Polls, as pollsters like to say, give "a snapshot in time." But for the media, such statistical niceties are irrelevant. Polling has become a predictor. New numbers generate thousands of scenarios and explanations of what the future holds. No sooner has a candidate secured a nomination than polls are used to identify weaknesses and feed the machinery with hypothetical running mates, issues, or vulnerabilities. In fact, the journalistic attention given to polls is so great that what surprises us are those times when the polls are wrong. As Charles W. Roll Jr. and Albert H. Cantril write:

> Victory or defeat in the electoral process is no longer absolute but often becomes relative with electoral showings being judged by standards of "what was accepted." Thus, it is not enough simply to win, a candidate must win big. And, to win big—even if the margin is modest or even nonexistent—is to indicate a degree of strength on Election Day that surpasses poll-ridden expectations. Thus,

narrow victories are turned into landslides and cold defeats into moral victories.[41]

Campaign coverage is so often exhausted by Election Day that even before the voter tunes in, pundits and journalists are already showing signs of fatigue. Races seem predictable to them, and their contempt spills over onto candidates who are "saying nothing new" or "fail to talk about issues." When the media focus on the horse race by constantly referring to the polls, the result is a tired insider report on the establishment candidate of each party. Polling data focus media coverage like a laser beam, giving the leading candidate a tremendous edge in fundraising from donors anxious to back the winner. Thus candidates leading in money and support early on can win a virtual primary and start running a general election campaign before citizens have even voted in the actual primary. And, of course, once a nomination is locked in, a new plot develops in the media about how the characters are tacking to the middle and "positioning" themselves for the general election.

POLLING FEEDS
HORSE-RACE REPORTAGE

At the same time that polls are gaining in influence and importance, the media are spending less time informing voters and more time handicapping the political horse race. As this occurs, the ability of politicians to educate and persuade voters is consequently falling. Since the 1960s, the power of the media (or at least their attention to themselves) has increased at the expense of candidates for public office and political leaders.

Political science professor Thomas E. Patterson sampled *New York Times* campaign stories from every presidential election year from 1960 to 1992.[42] He found that the share of articles about policy issues declined markedly: from more than half of all front-page stories in 1960 to less than one out of five in 1992. Stories about the horse race, in turn, rose from 40 percent of all stories to 80 percent of front-page coverage. Not only did the media increase their coverage of personalities and tactics, they have also steadily increased their own analysis of personality and tactical questions. Patterson found that more and more, journalists impose themselves on the campaign process, often at the expense of candidate outreach. Stories about campaign events fell from 90 percent to less than 20 percent. At the same time, reporter commentary skyrocketed from 10 percent of all stories in 1960 to more than 80 percent in 1992. Most Americans can see such coverage in the headlines that play up tactics, attacks, and campaign gambits.

According to the Center for Media and Public Affairs, the network evening news shows devoted 483 stories (13 hours and 8 minutes of airtime) to the 1996 presidential race from Labor Day to Election Day. That comes out to 12.3 minutes per night: 44 percent less than 1992 and 30 percent less than 1988. Such scant coverage tells only part of the story. Further analysis found that nearly *three-quarters* of that campaign airtime was given to anchors and reporters. Only 13 percent of the airtime was given to candidates presenting themselves in their own words. And no matter how eloquent the candidate, this meager sampling could do little to elevate public debate or energize supporters, because the average length of a candidate sound bite also shrank. In 1996 a presidential candidate was given an average of 8.2 seconds to make his case—down from 8.4 seconds in 1992 and 9.8 in 1988.

Although reporters and anchors were given far more time than candidates were given, policy debate did not improve. Just over one-third (37 percent) of the campaign stories on the evening news discussed policy issues: up from 32 percent in 1992 and down slightly from 39 percent in 1988. In lieu of policy discussion came a focus on the candidates' strategies and tactics. The evening news, all told, did 103 stories on Bob

Dole's tactics in 1996. Media coverage focused another sixty-eight stories on Clinton's campaign efforts, and the evening news shows ran another twenty-nine stories on the "tone" of the Dole campaign—that is, an analysis of Dole's criticisms of Clinton's policies. Where did issues figure into this picture? At the very bottom of the media's priorities. The top policy issue at the time was a debate about the burden of taxes and Dole's promise of a 15-percent across-the-board cut. That story, however, garnered only twenty-six stories. Such a scant number barely compares with the two hundred broadcasts about campaign maneuvering, tactics, and strategy.

Martin Plissner, former CBS news director, has charged that newspapers have similarly diminished the space and time given to candidates. According to Plissner, the size of the "ink bite" has declined in the same way as has the sound bite. Comments are more fragmentary and filled with more interpretation by journalists. In many cases, candidates for office or elected officials don't even get full sentences to express their thoughts. Key comments are pulled out to lend adjectives and color commentary to stories about political foes rather than to contrast policy ideas or objectives.

Polling is uniquely suited to aiding and abetting the media obsession with who's up and who's down in political races. It gives journalists a way to test their own theories. Instead of the hard work it takes to do careful issue-oriented reporting, the media can pass the buck and report on what they are talking about with their fellows on campaign trips. "Polls give a new level of sophistication to inside reporting," writes *Washington Post* columnist E. J. Dionne. "Looking at the numbers they generate and the statements and advertisements of the candidates, reporters can know *often even before they talk to insiders* why a candidate is doing what he is doing and what the insiders themselves are thinking."[43] Much of journalism, then, becomes the art of second-guessing or kibitzing: Journalists hint at what a candidate should or shouldn't do, how a strategy may hurt or help a candidate later, and where a candidate should go to rally voters.

Polls give journalists the inside-strategy scoop they crave. Indeed polls can let journalists know what motivates a candidate's public actions. Thus instead of deepening our knowledge, polls tend to drive journalists to play armchair strategist on Sunday morning talk shows, in news commentaries, and even in hotel bars after a day of following a candidate.[44]

More than any other tool, polling gives journalists the power to talk about tactics, personalities, and the public reaction to the spin and controversy. Every journalist is looking for a narrative. Polling gives journalists statistical denouement in their newspaper dramas. It allows them to be the perfect "objective" observer, dispassionately commenting on the actors and the crowd reaction.

The polling obsession also extends to policy issues, not just candidates. As *Washington Post* columnist William Raspberry writes about the flurry of polls on vouchers, "[Journalists] tend to report on the expert fights—the mutual name-calling, the oversimplifications, politicizations and, yes, the poll results. We seem more interested in who's winning than in the educational implications of victory."[45]

Polling is uniquely suited to aiding and abetting the media obsession with who's up and who's down in political races.

Polling doesn't just cap off the media's failure to inform, it has also led to increasingly shallow reportage about candidates. In a study of polling results and the media coverage that followed, Patterson discovered that coverage often mirrors the perceived political strength or weakness expressed in the polls. Candidates who were "up" in the polls and garnered public support were portrayed as "strong," "eloquent," "thoughtful," and "capable." Candidates who were "down" in the polls were "stiff," "hesitant," or just plain "weak."

A good example of how the media hammer can come smashing down was provided in August 2000 following the Democratic convention. Republican George W. Bush had been leading Democrat Al Gore. But after the Democratic convention, Gore moved into the lead in several polls. Just a day after a *Washington Post*/ABC News poll gave Gore a 50 percent to 45 percent advantage, the *Washington Post*'s front page declared "A Shift in Bush's Footing." The *Post* wrote that Bush "suddenly finds himself on the defensive, behind in the polls and struggling to fend off attacks on his policies."[46] The *New York Times*' headline stated: "Bush Stumbles, and Questions Are Raised Anew." "[I]n recent days on the trail," the *Times* said, "[Bush] found himself reaching for big numbers and defending his proposed tax cut in a manner that came across as reactive and not entirely coherent."[47]

A *Los Angeles Times* article, like others, resurrected the focus on Bush's verbal slips—a problem mostly ignored by the press since the primary. Bush "seriously taxed his rhetorical abilities" over two days of campaign stops. "But the more the Texas governor talked—sometimes confusing billions with trillions in a rambling speech—the more puzzled the audience looked."[48]

"It's gut-check time for George W. Bush," wrote the *Christian Science Monitor*. "Suddenly, Bush has been drawn into Gore's game plan, debating the details of policy proposals, and in particular, has been pushed into a defensive posture on one of his key policy proposals, a $1.3 trillion tax cut over 10 years."[49] What *was* sudden was the new success of Gore and his rallies, which only a week before were "desperate" efforts to inject "new life" in a "lagging" or "struggling" campaign (almost invariably in "disarray"). "Famously wooden, Al Gore never claimed he was Mr. Personality," AP wrote on the eve of Gore's most-important-in-his-career convention speech. "The goal: to persuade Americans he can be just as likable as George W. Bush—but has a lot more experience and substance."[50]

Gore was revitalized and refurbished by the post-convention bounce. With the new poll numbers, enthusiastic supporters sprang from the American soil like myrmidons sown from dragons' teeth. The *Boston Globe* wrote of a Gore rally: "The crowds are thicker and rowdier, the poll numbers are up, and Al Gore, his determined voice raspy from frenetic campaigning, is displaying a confidence and fieriness he hasn't shown since the hard-fought Democratic primary. The Gore campaign, at long last, appears to be gaining momentum, heading into what campaign aides say will be a consistently tight race until Election Day."[51] The Associated Press, in particular, showed how journalists view the zero-sum game of campaign rallies: "As Gore basked in the afterglow of his convention from the deck of a Mississippi riverboat, the Republican nominee had a ragged few days of campaigning."[52] One could almost see the shimmering sun playing on the surface of the water while the languorous current gently carried a triumphant Gore downriver. The "famously wooden" Gore had undergone a transformation. He "rewarded the crowd with an uncharacteristically peppy speech," wrote the *Washington Post*. The *Post* described a rally in Clinton, Iowa, in which the vice president "was almost, ironically, Clintonesque. The straining voice, the beaming spouse, and The Gaze, a sort of otherworldly stare that said, 'I'm in the zone.'" Gore was "easily drawing his largest crowds ever."[53]

POLLS CAN UNDERMINE POLITICAL LEADERSHIP

When the media conduct a poll that attacks a politician, they stop being simple observers and become active agents. Candidates can suffer greatly from polls' withering attacks. As S. Robert Lichter of the Center for Media and Public Affairs has observed, "If the media give someone bad coverage and commission a poll on the public's opinion and then cover the poll which shows the public's negative opinion, one can call this a media-generated phenomenon." [54]

Simply put, sound polling doesn't prevent the misinterpretation or poor reporting of data. Such media abuse of polls can include a shallow focus on horse-race journalism, the one-sided presentation of data, causal errors, overemphasis on the meaning of a particular poll, or an all-too-simple presentation of what Americans believe.

It's common for the media to use polls to judge political figures. But when do those polls become push polls? Just days after George W. Bush announced his running mate, the Texas governor found himself in a full-fledged media/partisan cross fire as Republican vice presidential candidate Dick Cheney met a media reception that reminded many Americans of what is wrong with the Washington press.

The Associated Press headline read, "Cheney Defends His Record." Reuters: "Cheney Defends Voting Record in Congress." The *New York Times*: "Voting Record Dogs Cheney as GOP Team Campaigns." The *Washington Post* headline was softer: "Bush-Cheney Debuts in Wyoming." But the *Post* made up for it in the subhead: "Running Mate Challenged on House Record."

Not only were the headlines similar, the stories were too. Every article was front-loaded with the same plot: archconservative under fire, forced to defend his record in Congress. But forced to defend it from whom, exactly? The stories hinted of a united outrage and a fusillade of questions hitting Cheney. But there were no hecklers or protesters in the audience asking the questions. Reporters were writing about themselves.

"Despite the campaign's efforts to keep a cheery face on the day's lone event," wrote the *Washington Post*, "the two men could not avoid questions about Cheney's votes." The reporter then passed along the colorful work of Democrats who "have characterized him [Cheney] as to the right ideologically of former House speaker Newt Gingrich and the

National Rifle Association." The *New York Times* was a bit more reserved, saying that "the Texas governor was quickly hit with questions." The AP reported that Cheney "defended his conservative record in interviews on three network morning television programs."

Quite unsurprisingly, while the media represented the Bush-Cheney campaign as if it were being bombarded by questions about Cheney's fitness for office, the handiwork of the Democrats and Gore was carefully concealed. The press could have easily taken a different tack. For instance, reporters could have written about how quick and nasty the Democratic response was to Bush naming Cheney. They could have asked why Democrats felt the need to smear Cheney so early.

> When the media conduct a poll that attacks a politician, they stop being simple observers and become active agents.

(Answer: To shape public perception while voters were still gathering information.) The press, in short, could have taken a more neutral position. Instead reporters took the path of least resistance by softening and cloaking Democratic Party opposition research and rhetoric. The *New York Times* said the Democrats "pointed to Mr. Cheney's conservative voting record." The *Post* called the Democratic attacks "efforts to portray" the two as the first "Big Oil" ticket. Mark Z. Barabak of the *Los Angeles Times* wrote that Democrats were "fairly bursting" at the chance to "highlight" Cheney's record. That record includes, Barabak reported, "numerous votes against abortion and gun control—issues of symbolic importance to many swing voters." Not only is this straight out of the Democratic playbook, it is also unsupported in the article and by fact. For anyone familiar with polls, gun control and abortion are not priorities for swing voters. Not even close.

Yet all of the stories had some version of the Democrats' spin, focusing on Cheney's votes against gun control, against

South African sanctions, against the ERA, and against a gaggle of favored liberal programs. For the mostly left-leaning journalistic corps, Cheney had to answer for such outrages.

Cheney answered in a measured way and helped explain some of his votes. But it didn't really matter what he said; the story was in motion. He was portrayed as defensive about his record as a Wyoming congressman, and, worse, his performance was graded by the same people who felt he had something to defend. (Journalists are hawks in spotting apparent conflicts of interest—unless it involves them, of course.) According to the *Washington Post,* Cheney "struggled to explain his votes" while Bush "jumped in," as if Cheney's record and performance were so poor he needed help. Even as Cheney argued for considering his votes in context, the *Post* wrote that he "suggested that he had softened some of his hard-line conservative positions." One doubts "hard-line" was the term the soft-spoken Cheney used to describe his record.

When Cheney "defended" the use of the surplus for Social Security, AP reporter Laurie Kellman said the Democrats "pounced on the remark," presumably after the brand-new candidate's words were passed on to interviewee Doug Hattaway, the spokesman for Gore. The Democrats set the agenda on Cheney, with journalists acting as their willing minions—a role that journalists are too often willing to play.

Compare Cheney's debut with what greeted Al Gore when he appeared side by side with candidate Bill Clinton in 1992: nothing but praise, even though Gore's views on the environment were as extreme from a GOP perspective as Cheney's were to a liberal Democrat. After all, Gore had just written *Earth in the Balance,* which conservatives saw as a textbook of environmental radicalism. But reporters never pressed Gore on the issue. Jim Hickey of ABC's *Good Morning America* saw only pluses with Gore: "One of the biggest advantages in choosing Gore as a political partner is the Senator's track record on the environment. He is a best-selling author on the subject. It's a track record the White House tries to paint as extremist. But Gore has already received the endorsement as an outstanding choice by the Sierra Club and other powerful conservation groups." Only one journalist, former CNN reporter Catherine Crier, pressed Gore about the radical ideas in *Earth in the Balance.*

What voters saw was a hit job on Bush-Cheney. But the media, loving conflict, went right along refracting the accusations and, if they were politically disposed, amplifying them. Cheney's votes, for most journalists, were simply "outside the mainstream." The coup de grace came after a series of reporting about the views of these reporters were given heft by the polling arm of the big papers. The media pollsters asked what the public thought about Cheney. On July 30, UPI announced, "Focus group raises concerns about Cheney."[55]

The same public that lacked almost any knowledge about candidates heard such sound and fury and got suspicious. The polling on Cheney failed to raise the hackles of a skeptical public, disappearing in the shadow of the Republican convention. But media reports lingered that Cheney and his views were a liability to Bush. Politicians from both parties counted on it. That's why the moment a poll appeared that showed some support for Cheney as vice presidential pick, the Bush campaign jumped on it. On July 28, a *USA Today*/CNN Gallup poll showed that Bush led Gore 54 to 40 percent after the Cheney nomination. Bush declared that Democrats "are doing their level best to tear people down, but they're not going to succeed."

In a strange twist, Bush and Cheney may have been helped by the *speed* of the polls during an election year. Before the Cheney attack was able to sink in, a *USA Today*/CNN/Gallup poll provided cover. GOP activists used it to declare the attacks a failure. Nevertheless, the weekend coverage continued the barrage. Cheney appeared on all the Sunday shows and answered the exact same questions as those put forward by the

Democratic critics. And still the polls were used to interpret the effectiveness of criticisms in the media. An ABC News/*Washington Post* poll found that Bush led Gore 53 percent to 42 percent among registered voters. The poll asked for voter impressions. Six in ten Americans approved the Cheney selection. (Then again, six in ten said they didn't know enough about Cheney to form an opinion.) ABC's Gary Langer wrote, "[A]s more people learn about Cheney, his negatives—particularly some of his more conservative votes in Congress—may outweigh his positives."[56] ABC asked how voters judged Cheney on the issues and his background:

- Voted against Older Americans Act. Favorable: 16 percent. Unfavorable: 77 percent.

- Voted against Head Start. Favorable: 19 percent. Unfavorable: 73 percent.

- Defense Secretary. Favorable: 68 percent. Unfavorable: 23 percent.

- Congressman. Favorable: 60 percent. Unfavorable: 23 percent.

- Head of Large Company. Favorable: 59 percent. Unfavorable: 27 percent.

- Head of Oil Company. Favorable: 36 percent. Unfavorable: 47 percent.

The list was nearly an exact echo of the complaints and concerns found on the Democratic National Committee Web site. Was this a case of push polling by the media?

Push polling is a heavily criticized campaign technique that uses the patina of public opinion surveys to spread negative information about rivals. Under the auspices of probing what a voter thinks, an interviewer calls homes to ask how certain positions or facts about a rival candidate affect a voter's views. Pollsters and journalists don't like push polls because they are propaganda campaigns hidden under the sheep's clothing of public opinion polling. The technique has fallen into such disrepute that it is reviled as much in editorials and in news stories as are negative television ads that foment division and resentment. Candidates can actually turn the tables on rivals if they can feed on outrage-producing media stories about how their opponents are using push polling. The Dole campaign used this clever weapon to undercut the momentum of the Forbes campaign in 1996.

In the 2000 GOP primaries, candidates George W. Bush and John McCain accused each other of using push polling. The Bush campaign reported that one of the Bush Iowa precinct captains had gotten a call asking, "Does it concern you that Bush will lie about taxes? Does it bother you that Bush is running a negative campaign?"[57] The *New York Times* reported that voters in South Carolina were being asked to give their opinions on John McCain after responding to a series of questions. As a front-page *Times* story put it: "In introducing the questions, the callers stated that Mr. McCain's tax plan would not cut rates for most people, that he had been reprimanded by the Senate Ethics Committee, and that his campaign finance proposals would give unions and the press more influence in deciding elections."[58]

Never mind that these were all factual, issue-oriented statements. (Only the last point is even slightly debatable.) The distinction between a legitimate poll and push polling, say pollsters, is that push polling is designed to *shape* voter perception, not measure it. But if that is really what makes the push poll objectionable, then we ought to give media polls better scrutiny. For instance, what is the difference between the issue-oriented "push poll" questions in the pro-Bush effort and the issue-oriented questions about Cheney in the ABC News/*Washington Post* poll? Both asked about real issues. Both were scant on context and exculpatory details. Neither allowed for a rival's response. Both polls contained predigested questions that any knowledgeable person would expect to yield a response unfavorable to the targeted candidate. Cheney skirted the worst of the onslaught because the poll concerning him was taken early, before most voters had much knowledge of him. Others weren't so lucky, among them some politicians, candidate Bill Clinton, new House Speaker Newt Gingrich, Lani Guinier (Clinton's unsuccessful nominee for assistant attorney general), and independent counsel Kenneth Starr. Their reputations were hurt significantly by the incessant regurgitation of negative information in poll questions and in stories about the poll results.

> Push polling is a heavily criticized campaign technique that uses the patina of public opinion surveys to spread negative information about rivals.

The pollster might interrupt at this point to say that the *intent* of the two polls was different. The anti-McCain effort was meant to hurt the McCain campaign, presumably by informing a selected sample of voters about issue positions they weren't likely to learn about from a press corps that writes 80 percent of its stories about the horse race. The journalistic poll ostensibly measures opinion; it does not intend to shape opinion. Yet one could argue that the ABC News/*Washington Post* poll probably reached far more voters than the few thousand contacted by the campaign poll. The intent may be pure, but the final result can be frighteningly similar. The ABC News/*Washington Post* poll got ink and airtime and conveniently followed a barrage of coverage that had a partisan edge originally honed by the Democratic National Committee.

Polling is not a perfectly objective process. The very act of observation affects the final results because the questions frame how respondents think, set the agenda for debate, and can shape the responses of ignorant or phlegmatic voters. Repeated and reinforcing polls, wording that echoes media stories, and negative questions taken from critics can all make the media poll look and, common sense says, function as a push poll. The difference is that the intent of political push polls raises our critical antennae, as it should. In the case of media polls, our naïveté about media objectivity and our fascination with the numbers dull our sensibilities and leave too many polls open to manipulative and misleading reportage.

Can Polls Be Reformed to Correct Journalistic Bias?

The quest to reform and improve the polls to prevent their abuse by the media is fraught with dangers. As long as the media lack humility in the use of poll results, the chances for reform are slight. Most researchers believe that polls aren't to blame for the current impasse. The problem is the media imperatives for speed and controversy—which, it should be clear to anyone who has observed a presidential election over the past twenty years, do not deepen, extend, or contribute to debate. For some academics, the way out of this polling dilemma is to focus polls on issues and not on the horse race.

But a little analysis soon creates a cloud of doubt over the possibility of reform. The results of issue polls are almost completely dependent on the way the question is asked. The sad fact is, the most accurate polling questions are those that are in the typical horse-race format—those that ask which candidate a voter prefers. These questions tend to be the most straightforward, with only slight response effects according to whose name is listed first.

Still, we would do well to consider the recommendations of thoughtful pollsters on how to rejigger polling for the issue-oriented story. Political scientists Paul J. Lavrakas and

Michael W. Traugott offer this thoughtful scenario: A "little known and underfunded candidate of good character" proposes a long-term vision for saving Social Security from bankruptcy. The policy doesn't provide any payoffs for incumbents, but it is sound. Journalists will write off such a candidate if he or she does not do well in the polls. Low poll numbers, in turn, will result in less coverage and even less ability to raise funds. In the "virtual primary," the candidate's future will be dismal indeed.

Lavrakas and Traugott, ever conscious of the promise and pitfalls of polling, ask this question: "What if the polls on this race focused more on the public's opinions toward the policy stances of the candidates rather than on trial heat type measures?"[59] Under this scenario, media coverage would have to follow the candidate whose ideas were most popular with the public in the polls. If the media's formula were reversed, issues would become the driving force once again. I must admit this is a tempting solution. With a focus on issue-oriented polls, so the argument goes, the "candidates of good character" would get coverage because their ideas are popular with the public.

But upon further reflection, it becomes clear that this practice would be unable to right the wrongs of an irresponsible media because of, once again, the problem of wording. After all, the person who "frames" the issue poll controls the debate. Because most Americans have a limited amount of knowledge and time to devote to politics, they come to public policy questions with a great deal of ignorance. Their opinions are ill formed and often incomplete. Horse-race questions, however repetitive, yield more accurate results because they are relatively simple and straightforward. Even so, they measure name recognition more than support for a candidate's stand on any policy positions. In 1992, fewer than one in five Americans knew where candidate Bill Clinton stood on the environment. Would the better candidate really be helped by the policy poll?

It's interesting that Lavrakas and Traugott use the example of Social Security. Probably no arena is more prone to ignorance than Social Security, and polling is the first line of defense for the opposition to new ideas. The media, because of their many competitors, love new stories; so once a reform is presented, it is often subjected to scrutiny long before the public has a chance to think about or even recognize the idea. Journalists who live and die by breaking stories are likely to assume that the public has already absorbed a new idea about Social Security, education, the budget, or whatever else political leaders offer up. The truth is, most Americans aren't just disconnected from government, they are disconnected from media coverage of news events as well.

> As long as the media lack humility in the use of poll results, the chances for reform are slight.

Americans don't come to politics with firm opinions. In their responses to pollsters, they are often reacting to the way the questions are asked as well as to the personalities and their impressions of candidates. Their lack of political interest isn't an entirely bad thing; American pragmatism is one of the reasons our political system has remained free and civil. Americans simply haven't had to contend with the strong ideological currents that have buffeted European democracies. We may not applaud the ignorance of the American voter, but it is still a fact of life—one too often ignored by the media.

Issue-oriented polling cannot correct the ills brought about by overpolling precisely because polling is a blunt instrument that forces opinion as much as it measures it. Media polling rarely deals in subtleties, and even when time and money are spent to explore the complexity of opinion, newspapers and certainly evening news programs lack the space to communicate the nuances of the public mind. Even the best issue poll can only approximate the ideas of a disconnected public. Public opinion is more than polling. It is also the debate, activism, and intensity, completely missed by polls, that make citizens get involved in politics. These citizens may be a minority, but media polling is essentially cheating the formation of public opinion by ignoring the other aspects of the public opinion dynamic.

Thus the most fatal flaw of polling is the fact that the media fail to caution readers, pundits, and politicians on the limitations of polls. Brief responses to short questions are but poor reflections of an ignorant public's sentiments. Testing bold new ideas in such a way is a crude exercise in futility. It guarantees mediocre politicians who are able to see only what has been, not what can be. Pollsters and pundits agree almost unanimously that reporters need to be "more skeptical about the numbers in public opinion polls" and "need to focus more intently on the actual questions being asked."[60] Evans Witt, president of Princeton Survey Research Associates, charges, "Too many journalists believe the number without going behind the numbers."[61]

Not only should the media ask deeper questions, but they should also use polls to challenge the orthodoxy, even if that means challenging the results found by other groups or media organs. In the final chapter of this book, we will look more closely at the specific measures needed to restrain the misuse of polls and to reinvigorate public deliberation.

CHAPTER THREE

Fixing the Game from the Start

Cheap, fast, and shallow. Media pollsters spend little on the "instruments of democracy," and it comes at a cost to America.

■ ■ ■

THE SIXTEEN AUGURS OF ANCIENT ROME shared a sacred duty to read the signs of the sky to tell the Roman Senate and the people whether the gods favored or opposed political action. The augurs' predictions and counsel might be based on the flight of birds, thunder, or the way sacred chickens ate their food. The *haruspices,* the soothsayers of ancient Rome, also advised political leaders about the state of public opinion on military action or political reform, usually by slicing open a bird or pig carcass and spilling the entrails or investigating the liver. It was left to these diviners to interpret the results by looking at the way the innards arrayed themselves once spilled outside the eviscerated creature. For many Romans, whether upper or lower class, these predictive methods were a mystery far beyond their ken.

Two thousand years later, the average American citizen finds media polling practices just as mysterious as the ancient Romans found their diviners. The priests in the Cult of Strategy bank on this ignorance. Whether the topic is spilled chicken guts and sacrificial doves or response rates and the margin of error, most citizens have little insight into how public opinion is measured or what subtle manipulations may be hidden in words. So, just like the ancient Roman, the average voter is left to the devices and scruples of the interpreters—the media pollster and the deadline-harried journalist.

Despite the media's seemingly careful attention to methodology and modern knowledge of statistics and sampling, polls today can be wildly misleading for a number of reasons, few of which are ever clearly explained to the public by the press.

Whether polling is better than splitting open fowl for directing lawmakers and the public to the right policies remains an open question. What is certain is that the power, even 2,200 years later, is still in the hands of the people who define what questions will be divined and how they will be interpreted. Despite the superficial covering of scientific certitude that pollsters lend to their craft, and despite the media's seemingly careful attention to methodology and modern knowledge of statistics and sampling, polls today can be wildly misleading for a number of reasons, few of which are ever clearly explained to the public by the press.

To see how inaccurate polls may be at gauging actual public opinion, look at the results of presidential polls in the run-up to the 1996 election. Even though all the major polls got the outcome of the election correct, their predictions of the spread in support between Bill Clinton and Bob Dole were wildly off the mark.

- The least accurate was the CBS News/*New York Times* poll, which heralded an 18-point election blowout. In this survey, Clinton drew 53 percent, Dole got 35 percent, and Ross Perot scored 9 percent.

- The Pew Research Center for the People and the Press predicted a 13-point margin of victory: Clinton 49 percent, Dole 36 percent, and Perot 8 percent.

- ABC News' final poll found similar results: a 12-point spread, with Clinton getting 51 percent; Dole, 39 percent; and Perot, 7 percent.

- Harris also projected a 12-point gap between Clinton and Dole: Clinton 51 percent, Dole 39 percent, and Perot 7 percent.

- The NBC News/*Wall Street Journal* poll projected a 12-point victory margin for Clinton: Clinton 49 percent, Dole 37 percent, and Perot 9 percent.

- *USA Today*/CNN/Gallup was in the same range, finding an 11-point Clinton advantage just before the election: Clinton 52 percent, Dole 41 percent, and Perot 7 percent.

- The HOTLINE/Battleground poll saw a 9-point difference, with Clinton showing as little as 45 percent support, Dole with just 36 percent, and Perot with 8 percent.

Only pollster Zogby International hit the mark. The Reuters/ Zogby poll wasn't just the most accurate, it also projected the lowest Clinton margin of victory—8 points. The final results after balloting were Clinton with 49 percent; Dole with 41 percent; and Perot with 8 percent.

Everett Carll Ladd, director of the Roper Center for Public Opinion Research at the University of Connecticut, called the polling results of 1996 worse than the misguided polls of 1948 that predicted Thomas Dewey would beat Harry Truman. Just weeks after the 1996 election, Ladd went so far as to recommend a blue-ribbon panel to investigate the results and methodologies used in media polling. The National Center for Public Polling tried to counter Ladd's claim by offering a study of forty-seven final pre-election presidential polls, beginning with 1936. NCPP's president declared triumphantly that the average error in 1996 "was low relative to historical experience" and "one of the better years for the national polls." For those with a bit more skepticism, it is scary to think that 1996 was a good year. One wonders what would qualify as a bad year once it was broadcast through the media megaphone.

Americans got their answer in 2000 when the media's relentless emphasis on polling confused even the most experienced political observers and left the public scratching its head. Over time, USA Today's polling with Gallup looked like an EKG for heart palpitations, the results surging and spiking wildly even when compared with other polls. Jim Norman, head of surveys, had to hold a special meeting in the middle of election season to calm USA Today journalists, who saw obvious problems with the data. Yet it wasn't until Election Night that Americans paid the full price for the media's obsession with polling and its unholy alliance with pollsters.

On that evening—November 7, 2000—the networks seesawed in their predictions of victory, giving the decisive state of Florida to Vice President Al Gore before the polls were even closed. Later they retracted the call, giving the state to Governor George W. Bush, only to discover in the end that the race was just too close to call. No one can say for sure what the consequences of these early predictions were across the nation and for voters in the northern part of the Sunshine

State. It is enough here to note that the methodologies once thought to be so sound placed the media in the middle of an electoral cross fire—one that, in the end, vindicated Ladd's concerns. The heads of the news divisions of all the major networks were forced to appear before Congress to apologize for their addiction to polling.

The Science of Polling

To understand how such blunders in polling can occur, it is necessary to understand the science of polling. This chapter traces a poll's development, from inception to release. Understanding the difficulties that pollsters face in getting an accurate gauge on public opinion is critical to understanding the weaknesses of polling, particularly because these difficulties are rarely, if ever, made clear. First, we'll look at sampling issues. Who should be sampled and why? And how does this affect a poll's outcome? What are some of the implications of using general samples, such as American adults or registered voters? We'll also look at the growing problem of rising refusal (or nonresponse) rates, and we'll look at the implications of subtle shifts in the methodology of a poll for what we think about American representative democracy and constitutional government. Finally, we'll look at the question of poll sponsorship. Who paid for the poll? Are private polls, or those conducted by advocacy groups, more or less reliable than those sponsored by major media organizations?

SAMPLING AMERICA— NOT ALL POLLS ARE CREATED EQUAL

The methodological challenge for pollsters isn't really one of getting a random sample. The challenge is *who* to sample. How that question is answered will have grave consequences for

American democracy. For polling to be statistically valid, every person in the target population must have the same chance of being contacted randomly. A pollster need not poll every person, but the exact number will affect the margin of error, which is really a measure of how confident public opinion researchers are in their data. But that confidence isn't 100 percent. In most cases, the "confidence interval" is 95 percent, meaning that if the polling question were asked 100 times, 95 times out of 100 the results would fall within the margin of error.

Thus if 1,000 voters were asked about the impeachment of Bill Clinton and 50 percent said they supported the House's action, the margin of error would be plus or minus 3 points (technically, 3.1 percent). Ask that same question 100 times, and in 95 cases out of 100 the results would fall somewhere between 53.1 percent and 46.9 percent. Of course, in those five other cases, the results of the poll would be entirely incorrect. At such times, no one knows which results are off base.

What's interesting to note here is that although journalists and political elites pay close attention to poll numbers and trends in opinion, a simple understanding of methodology casts doubt upon much of the reportage that purports to herald new voter trends. When the results from a 1,000-person poll can vary within a band of 3.1 percentage points, a "trend" that represents a shift of only 1 to 3 points is questionable.

A poll's sample can directly affect the results, and even seemingly unbiased samples can fundamentally change the measures of public opinion. Reputable pollsters usually survey between 800 and 1,000 people. More than this becomes

Table 3.1 Margin of error with 95-percent confidence interval

Sample Size	Tolerance
100	± 9.8 percentage points
200	± 6.9 percentage points
400	± 4.9 percentage points
750	± 3.6 percentage points
1,000	± 3.1 percentage points
1,500	± 2.5 percentage points
3,000	± 1.8 percentage points
5,000	± 1.4 percentage points

prohibitively expensive while adding only slightly more accuracy, as table 3.1 shows.

Unfortunately the margin of error is rarely reported in sufficient detail. Instead reporters refer to the margin of error in a way that gives readers a false sense of confidence in the polls—as if polls were always 100 percent accurate. But let's say we demand a 99-percent confidence interval. What happens to the margin of error then? As can be seen from table 3.2, the band of results, even on large polls, becomes as big as the largest shifts in voter sentiment during a tight presidential race or controversial policy poll.

Why do polls use a 95-percent confidence interval instead of 99 percent? It isn't hard to believe that if the media were to report a margin of error of 99 percent, they could undermine what they hope to be the appearance of 100-percent accuracy. Few stories, as we've seen, make even a 3-percent allowance for humility. The confidence interval may be 95 percent, but the hubris quotient is easily 100 percent.

As Harry W. O'Neill, vice chairman of the Roper Division of Roper Starch Worldwide, noted in a speech to fellow

Table 3.2 Margin of error with 99-percent confidence interval

Sample Size	Tolerance
100	± 12.9 percentage points
200	± 8.2 percentage points
400	± 6.5 percentage points
750	± 4.7 percentage points
1,000	± 4.1 percentage points
1,500	± 3.3 percentage points
3,000	± 2.4 percentage points
5,000	± 1.8 percentage points

pollsters, "Do we also mislead with the notion of sampling error, creating in the public's mind an image of being more scientific than is warranted? God forbid the public should ever find out that all 'margin of error' really says is that if you conduct the same biased survey among the same unrepresentative sample 100 times, you will get the same meaningless results 95 times within plus or minus some percentage points."[1]

O'Neill isn't the only critic of the misleading nature of margin of error. "When the media print sentences such as 'the margin of error is plus or minus three percentage points,' they strongly suggest that the results are accurate to within the percentage stated," writes Humphrey Taylor, chairman of Louis Harris & Associates. "That is completely untrue and grossly misleading."[2] The reason this is so, according to Taylor, is that "random sampling error" is the "least of our measurement problems."

Polling has many other difficulties, such as low response rates, biased wording, problems resulting from question order, lying by voters, and incorrect weighting of the initial results. Because the telephone is now present in almost every household, the challenge of getting a random sample has almost been resolved, at least at the theoretical level. At the practical level, however, there are still serious obstacles to getting a methodologically sound sample. Pollsters use a device called a random-digit dialer to contact potential respondents. RDDs are linked to computers that choose from phone numbers randomly selected from area codes for all the homes in the continental United States. Residents of Alaska and Hawaii are not polled because both states have populations so small that the effect of leaving them out is negligible. Alaska and Hawaii are also excluded because their residents live in different time zones, making interviews and timeliness more difficult. Their elimination tends to balance out, say pollsters, because Alaska leans right and Hawaii leans left.

After the computer selects the phone numbers, pollsters try to find a sample that best represents the U.S. population. Using U.S. Census Bureau data, they identify Americans based on sex, income, race, region, education, and age. What does that sample look like? A typical sample for a *New York Times*/CBS News poll looks like this:

- 47 percent men and 53 percent women

- 22 percent northeastern, 33 percent southern, 24 percent midwestern, and 21 percent western

- 80 percent white, 11 percent black, 1 percent Asian, and 6 percent "other"

- 24 percent college graduates, 27 percent with some college or trade school education, 37 percent high school graduates only, and 12 percent without a high school diploma

- 27 percent identify themselves as Republicans, 36 percent as Democrats, and 30 percent as Independents

- 32 percent call themselves "conservative," 42 percent consider themselves "moderate," and 20 percent consider themselves "liberal"[3]

Because methodology plays such an important role in pollsters' claims of scientific accuracy, the subject is worthy of attention. How can such a small sample represent the views of a nation?

Herbert Asher, professor of political science at The Ohio State University, uses a most helpful analogy. Just as a doctor takes only a sample of a person's blood, he writes, a pollster needs to draw only a small sample from the body politic.[4] Other pollsters liken sampling to a big pot of soup: To test how the soup tastes, you need only a spoonful. Of course, there are limitations to these analogies because of the structure of our government, the electoral system, the knowledge of citizens, and the fact that some voters are more likely to vote than are others. The sample must be representative of the people it purports to speak for.

REGISTERED VERSUS LIKELY VOTERS

To fill the sample, pollsters will often telephone roughly five to ten times the number of people actually questioned in the poll. Here all sorts of problems crop up. Most media pollsters tap registered voters. But with turnout rates at 55 percent for presidential elections and as low as 38 percent for off-year elections, the number of Americans actually making political decisions is much smaller than one might think, or than polls would suggest.

Polling only *likely* voters costs more, however. It requires additional time and effort to single out those Americans who are more conscientious about being involved and informed about politics. If you take the radically egalitarian position that polls are the aggregate of public opinion and that every person's voice should be heard regardless of knowledge or interest in issues, then polls should be constructed based on samples of all adults. Taking this position, however, guarantees that the polls will not resemble the results on Election

Day. Furthermore, the inaccuracy of polls will be amplified by the media and will probably provide a false sense of support for liberal, Democratic ideas and candidates.

The difference between likely and registered voters is stark. "Likely voters" are usually defined as people who have voted in the past two elections and say they are likely or somewhat likely to vote in the next election. Likely voters are older, more conservative on fiscal and social issues, and slightly more apt to come from the East. Thus a seemingly slight methodological shift from registered voters to likely voters can lead to radically different polling results. Likely voters also tend to be more educated. Only one in twenty likely voters lacks a basic high school education, compared with one in eight registered voters (12.6 percent). Twenty-five percent of likely voters have a high school education and another 31 percent have some college, compared with just over 34.8 percent of registered voters who are high school graduates and 29.3 percent who have some college. And just over 38 percent of likely voters have a college education, compared with 23.4 percent of registered voters. Democrats make up 38.7 percent of likely voters, Republicans make up 34.4 percent, and independent and third-party voters make up the other 26.9 percent.

Then there are the "unlikely voters:" registered voters who have not voted regularly in the past three elections. Independents tend to make up a plurality of this group—around 22.5 percent, according to Zogby International; Democrats make up 16.9 percent; and Republicans, 12.9 percent. Those who are "not sure" of their party affiliation and who do not vote regularly are 48.7 percent of those not likely to vote. Therefore any poll that turns to likely voters will naturally tap more informed and more partisan voters—not just those who reliably go to the polls.

When media stories focus on shifts in voter sentiment, the result can actually stem from changes in the sample population, not from changes of heart. The *Washington Post*'s director of polling Richard Morin writes in *The 1992 Election and the Polls* that the weekend before the 1992 election, Clinton's double-digit lead over George Bush dropped to just two points in a single Gallup poll. But the massive shift, although reported as a surge in Bush support, was, in fact, a byproduct of a Gallup effort to base its results in the final days of the race on likely voters, rather than registered voters as it had done in the preceding months. Thus Bush's number jumped as the proportion of Republicans and more conservative voters in the sample went up. Then Gallup did something truly confusing. The organization decided to perform yet another on-the-fly methodological change. That Monday, less than twenty-four hours before the election, Clinton's double-digit lead magically reappeared when the pollster gave the *entire* undecided vote to Clinton.

> Any poll that turns to likely voters will naturally tap more informed and more partisan voters—not just those who reliably go to the polls.

This wasn't the last time polling that methodology drove perceptions of support for a candidate. The decision about what sample to use can result in misleading perceptions about the strength and appeal of candidates. During the 1996 presidential campaign, a common refrain in campaign stories was the nearly insurmountable lead that President Clinton held over his Republican challenger, Senate Majority Leader Bob Dole. As early as that spring, some pollsters were reporting that Clinton had a 20 or even 30 percent lead over Dole. These numbers became so ubiquitous that media stories shifted from the Dole versus Clinton race to a discussion of whether Clinton's victory would be big enough to provide coattails that could drag other Democrats into office.

Writing more than six months before the election, William Kristol, editor of *The Weekly Standard,* titled one of his articles "A Dole Defeat and the Conservative Future." Kevin Phillips, writing in the Sunday *Washington Post,* declared that Dole had a chance of overcoming his 30-point deficit only if "one or two situations," such as Bosnia or the budget deficit, were to "go badly" for Clinton.[5] The dialogue continued in the ensuing months, with the controversy driving the chattering classes to one side or another. A few writers invoked the memory of Harry S Truman and defended the idea that anything could happen. But for many commentators, left and right, the election was over long before it started. What is strange is that repeated studies show that Americans don't really pay attention to a campaign until its final weeks. And even then, in primaries, as many as 40 percent don't decide until the weekend before Election Day.

The collective declaration that Dole's chances were poor was, in part, a methodological artifact. The early polls tapped the broadest possible population, American adults. As in almost every year, pollsters moved slowly from samples of American adults to registered voters to likely voters as Election Day approached. Such a cost-saving measure, as we've seen, tends to sample more left-leaning voters. Granted, Bob Dole's campaign was fumbling and he himself was a weak candidate known better for his insider connections than for any eloquence or strong conviction. But the consequences of the univocal polling coverage were still severe for him. The perception of a landslide was so strong that Clinton had to warn his supporters that the election wasn't over and that they still needed to go to the polls.

For many candidates, a large lead can be more problematic than a tight race. Get-out-the-vote drives are more difficult when a candidate holds a seemingly insurmountable lead. The Clinton-Gore team was genuinely worried about such a case because the stories on the TV news and in the papers promised a big victory. Although pollsters may be unsure about whether polls produce a bandwagon effect, political players fear that polls do. At one White House meeting, Senator Dale Bumpers, Democrat of Arkansas, savaged the Clinton White House for talking about a landslide. "Never, never say that word; never, never think that word between now and this election," a top Democrat quoted him as saying.[6]

In a study of every final election poll since 1956, Warren J. Mitofsky declared, "More than twice as many polls overstated the Democratic candidate's share of the vote than overstated the Republicans' share." Even more interesting, Mitofsky found that the Democratic-leaning polls also had a higher average error when compared with the final results at the polls.[7] Democrat-leaning polls had an average error of 4.4 percentage points versus 3.3 percentage points in Republican victories.[8]

So we must ask: Is the polling of likely voters as opposed to registered voters a bias or a move toward a wider canvas in our democracy? Polling likely voters is, by almost every measure, apt to produce results that more accurately represent the feelings and beliefs of those Americans who watch and participate in the political process.

> Polling likely voters is apt to produce results that more accurately represent the feelings and beliefs of those Americans who watch and participate in the political process.

Many media pollsters are loath to admit this because of the increased costs. But others, concerned with the proper use of polls, press for the use of the most representative sample: those who will actually vote. "We shouldn't rely on registered voters in predicting accuracy," says Ohio State University political science professor Paul J. Lavrakas, co-author of The Voter's Guide to Polling. "I think you have to go to likely voters when polling. You need to gather as much information as possible to 'squeeze' out exactly who is going to vote."[9]

Polling likely voters may yield a more accurate picture of what will happen on Election Day, but pollsters first have to find those voters. And this is difficult. "The worst way to determine whether or not someone is a likely voter is to ask them if they are likely to vote," says Kellyanne Fitzpatrick, director of The Polling Company. "Of course [respondents] are going to say 'yes.' They'll also tell you that they eat all their green beans, do their sit-ups every morning, and sit in the first pew of church every Sunday. But we know this just isn't true."[10]

In 1992, Gallup asked seven questions as part of a "turnout" scale for likely voters in the final weeks of the election. Respondents who met all seven (or sometimes six) of the criteria were counted as "likely voters." The criteria were routine but should give a sense of the challenge of finding people who are more likely to vote.

1. They said they had given "quite a lot" or "some" thought to the coming election.

2. They said they knew where their neighborhood polling place was located.

3. They reported having voted previously in the election district where they currently resided.

4. They said they voted "always" or "nearly always."

5. They said they planned to vote in the coming election.

6. They reported having voted in the 1988 presidential election.

7. They rated themselves between a 7 and a 10 on a 10-point scale where 10 represented someone who would definitely vote in the 1992 presidential election.

According to Gallup, these "likely voters" represented the top 55 percent of the sample of voting-age adults. Campaigns ask similar questions, because candidates and their election teams want to find out who is actually going to show up at the polls. A typical screen might ask:

> Some people have the time to vote in all elections, while other people don't have the time to vote at all. Which one of the following best describes how often you vote?
>
> 1. I ALWAYS vote in ALL ELECTIONS, including general elections and primaries.
>
> 2. I ALWAYS vote in GENERAL ELECTIONS, but sometimes miss primaries.
>
> 3. I SOMETIMES vote in general elections. (Thank and terminate.)
>
> 4. I RARELY vote in general elections. (Thank and terminate.)
>
> 5. DON'T KNOW/REFUSED (Do no read—thank and terminate.)

Campaigns will try to target voters who answer yes to numbers 1 and 2. Although screening voters in this way adds significantly to the cost and time spent on a survey, for campaigns, the cost is well worth it. Likely voters are that sliver of American adults who are more likely to respond and pay attention to political suasion and propaganda.

Bandwagon Effect on Polls

It isn't a radical notion to suspect that a continued barrage of stories about double-digit differences between the candidates would lead some people to turn away from a candidate who is predicted to lose or even to change their preference to the "winner." Social scientists call such a phenomenon a "bandwagon effect." The problem is that it is nearly impossible to prove whether this effect actually occurs; there are simply too many variables. In addition, an alternative theory suggests that voters may move in the direction of the candidate trailing in the polls. This is called the "underdog effect."

The fact that social scientists don't know definitively whether there is a bandwagon effect is reason enough to be wary about the results of polls and their effect on democracy. Polling has such far-reaching consequences in the way elections are covered by the media that we should stop to consider the implications of these gaps in professional pollsters' knowledge. If there is such a thing as a bandwagon effect, the proliferation of polls will create a self-reinforcing mechanism. For political candidates and politicians it can become a nightmare, as they struggle to get traction in the mire of the media's obsession with polls.

In 1988, the campaign of Democratic presidential candidate Michael Dukakis felt overwhelmed by reporters' constant references to polls. "We were constantly being asked about the polls," said Kirk O'Donnell, a Dukakis aide. "Tracking polls took over. 'What were your overnight numbers?' was always the first question I'd get on the plane every morning."[11] Dukakis began to attack the journalistic obsession with polling by firing back: "Pollsters don't vote, people do."

Republican candidate Bob Dole faced a similar problem in 1996. "The tracking polls by CNN were the most memorable and regrettable aspect of the campaign," said Christina Martin, deputy director of communications for the Dole campaign. "We felt they were becoming a self-fulfilling prophecy." Dole pollster Tony Fabrizio attributed Dole's continuing poor performance to an error in CNN's methodology. Fabrizio even took the step of writing to CNN to ask for a change in the network's use of registered voters without reference to refusal rates or their likelihood of voting.[12]

The perception of momentum and viability is just one of the by-products of a poll-obsessed political process. In the universe of impression democracy, polls have propaganda value that can yield real results. Polls can translate into the critical resources needed to propel a campaign. Certainly no pollster can argue with the fact that polls are the gateway to fund-raising and financial resources. One reason this is the case, many political scientists and media critics posit, is that media coverage mirrors poll results. As a candidate shows strength in the polls, journalists and pundits become more likely to cover the campaign. This increases the candidate's "free media" exposure. Being perceived as a potential winner increases the success of fund-raising, which leads to more "paid media" influence as the candidate finances radio and television ads.

Could impressionable voters' preferences be driven by the perceptions of victory created by salvo after salvo of polls raining down on them during election time? People like the idea of supporting a winner. When Americans are asked who they voted for in past elections, the winning candidates always get *more* support than they actually received at the polls. Could polls have the same effect? Could they actually reinforce, not just passively record, the opinions of voters? It would seem, at the very least, that we ought to consider the proliferation of polls as an unknown variable in a volatile formula whose final result may not be the stable sample of public opinion once thought. Pollsters agree that tragedies, news events, and media coverage can affect polling results. If they are right, it would seem to follow logically that the aggregate effect of media polls and their coverage could affect the methodology of individual polls. In other words, the pollster might be able to speak with authority on the science of a single poll, but the concatenation of these polls appearing week after week might have an unexplored impact on individual surveys.

Such a theory isn't impossible or even unknown to the realms of psychology or sociology. The Rand Technique takes advantage of the psychological need for individuals to be part of the group and uses the expression of aggregate opinion in surveys to build consensus and pressure for the majority opinion. Individuals may be polled about an issue and then given the results of that poll. The feedback from the first canvass of the group's members often drives a change of opinion in dissident individuals. This feedback loop may be continued over and over again to reinforce the majority opinion.

There are other reasons to suspect that the one-sided coverage of the polls could distort an election. Experts, media observers, and journalists generally agree that negative campaign ads turn off voters and decrease voter turnout. Does it not follow that the consistent and negative message of a candidate's defeat could similarly depress supporters and prospective voters? The question here isn't meant to suggest exact parallels or solid evidence of a bandwagon effect. The continuing thesis of this book is that polling now plays a powerful role in American democracy, and, as such, the art of polling deserves the same scrutiny and balanced judgment that is applied to other institutions that influence political debate and deliberation. As with the Heisenberg uncertainty principle in science, the pollster's act of observation can influence the process being observed.

Even setting aside the idea that the voter can be affected by the polls, the existence of a bandwagon effect is quite conceivable because polls drive so much of what journalists perceive and report in the political horse race. Even though we can't prove that some voters respond to a bandwagon effect, what should worry us is that we know the media do. Media reportage follows perceived winners, and polls help shape that coverage. But if the media's perception of strength is based on

> If the media's perception of strength is based on a methodological artifact, then shouldn't we be concerned about their loss of objectivity?

a methodological artifact, then shouldn't we be concerned about their loss of objectivity?

When Voters Refuse . . .

In 1992, Britain's Conservatives stunned pollsters when they won re-election despite weeks of polling that showed the Labor Party ahead in the polls. Pollsters were flummoxed, if not actually embarrassed. Their explanations, not just their inaccuracies, deserve special consideration as we discuss methodology. Pollsters did not fault their methods of polling. Rather they were faced with another problem rarely discussed—a deceptive sample. Academics declared that the Conservatives' surprise victory was the result of a "spiral of silence." In other words, respondents lied to interviewers.

Because of media coverage and social pressure, the pollsters posited, many voters were reluctant to admit that they were going to vote Conservative. Thus many supporters of John Major simply claimed to be undecided or else refused to answer polling questions. A similar phenomenon occurred in 1980 when pollsters underestimated Ronald Reagan's victory margin. Experts suspect that Reagan Democrats weren't ready to admit during surveys that they were going to vote for the conservative Republican. And like the "stealth" Major supporters, these voters concealed their views until Election Day when they stood in the privacy of the voting booth.

The lesson is that even when pollsters have immaculate methods for finding a random sample, there may still be other obstacles to getting an accurate measure of public sentiment. In the cases of Reagan and Major, voters weren't forthcoming, and that translated into potent victories for the conservative politicians. Such difficulties aren't isolated. The problem of getting people to answer pollsters' questions is exacerbated by rising refusal rates. This problem has been dubbed polling's "dirty little secret." It's becoming more and more difficult for pollsters to get a random and representative sample.

To be statistically sound, as we have seen, an entire sample must be equally available for random selection. Rising refusal rates are hazardous to pollsters' methodology. John Zogby reports that refusal rates have risen substantially in the past decade. How much? There are no official industry estimates, and many of the same pollsters who champion the public's right to be part of the political process flatly decline to divulge their refusal rates.[13] According to Zogby, however, in the 1980s about 35 percent of those called refused to answer pollsters' questions; by 1999, that number was as high as 65 percent.

The proliferation of polls has come during a period when voters are tuning out those same polls, presenting us with a paradox. Even though voters have gained a greater role in the selection of candidates in primaries and can be heard through talk radio, the Internet, and the constant use of polling, the "little guy" is getting harder to find. Polling has done nothing to increase citizens' sense of involvement with and importance to the political process. Could it be that the incessant use of polling actually makes Election Day and one person's vote appear irrelevant? Pollsters haven't grappled with this question, but the effect of constant polling may actually be to mute the message of voters by making the results appear a *fait accompli*.

"There are so many polls and they are reported on so much of the time, people are just beginning to shrug their shoulders," says Larry Sabato, professor of political science at the University of Virginia.[14] People aren't just shrugging their shoulders; they are hanging up the phone. And this has broad consequences for the sound methodology of polls. With an increase in two-income households, fewer voters are happy to answer at dinnertime some stranger's questions about whether they think the president is doing a good job in Kosovo. Whether it's a telemarketer or a polling interviewer, tired American moms and dads and busy young adults don't want to surrender their precious time.

Sampling error is also increased because some Americans are more likely to tune out than others. Thus getting a fair sample endangers pollsters' *political* accuracy. "My review of polling over the year strongly suggests to me that demographically speaking, Democrats have a greater tendency to respond than more conservative Republicans," observes pollster John Zogby.

Not everyone agrees, however. Paul Lavrakas, political science professor at The Ohio State University, suggests that too much may be made of the refusal rate question: "New studies indicate that we may not lose accuracy with refusal rates, provided the sample is still scientific."[15] Lavrakas points to a study by the Pew Research Center for the People and the Press conducted in 1999. The organization used two separate surveys to probe the same questions. The first was conducted over a five-day period and contacted one thousand adults. Sixty-five percent responded. The Pew Research Center then put together a second survey over an eight-week period and sent out advance letters informing participants that a pollster would be calling them. As an added benefit, the group also offered a small monetary gift to those who agreed to be interviewed. Nearly eight in ten (79 percent) responded—a response rate just 14 percent higher than that for the five-day poll. Despite the differences in technique, the polling results were virtually the same.

The problem is that a five-day survey is vastly superior to most media surveys—especially the overnight surveys or rushed polls that media organizations push after tragedies or in the midst of red-hot political controversies. Overnight polling is forced by the tyranny of the twenty-four-hour news cycle. In the rush to get data, interviewers have to move on to those who can or will respond to the phone questions. The Pew Research Center's findings, then, indicate that diligence is rewarded. But chances are, if media organizations spent even five days on a poll, we would get different results than with the two- or three-day quickie polls that are the norm.

Once again it is useful to consider how slight changes in methodology can affect the results. Refusal rates and problems of sampling are more likely to plague weekend polls—not just the overnight poll that oversamples liberal Democrats. In January 1996, seven polls emerged about the likely race between Bill Clinton and Bob Dole. Although all the polls showed Bill Clinton ahead, their results were wildly different for methodological reasons.

- A CBS News poll taken January 2–3 of 1,000 adults put Clinton up by 6 points (48 percent to 42 percent).

- An ABC News/*Washington Post* poll taken on January 6–7 surveyed 852 adults and found that Clinton led Dole by 16 points (53 percent to 37 percent).

- A CNN/*USA Today*/Gallup poll taken January 5–7 surveyed 1,000 adults and found Clinton leading by only 1 point (47 percent to 46 percent).

- A Yankelovich Partners poll taken January 10–11 surveyed 1,000 adults and put Clinton's lead at 6 points (47 percent to 41 percent).

- Another CNN/*USA Today*/Gallup poll on January 12–15 found Dole down by 1 point (49 percent to 48 percent) among 1,000 registered voters.

Changing the sample can make all the difference in the world, especially when surveys are conducted so long before Election Day. Only the most politically attuned are awake that early. A sample of all adults is automatically unstable. For instance, when Gallup "screened down" in the January 5–7 poll for those respondents who said they were actually registered to vote, Dole moved into a 3-point *lead.*

But there could be other factors explaining why these polls varied from a 1-point to a 16-point lead for Clinton. Polling on weekends can increase refusal rates or lead to inaccuracies. As Charles Cook, editor of the *Cook Political Report,* notes, "[M]any pollsters over the years have found it very difficult to find representative cross-sections of the public at home and willing to sit through a lengthy telephone interview."[16] Cook points out that the two polls finding a 6-point lead for Clinton were taken on weeknights, not weekends. He hypothesizes that weekday polls may reach a more conservative and active sample. Just as a poll's methodology may be distorted by the propensity of more conservative, Republican-leaning voters to hang up the phone on weeknights, so too may the results be affected when polls are taken on weekends, when active members of the population are less likely to be at home at all.

WEIGHTING THE SAMPLE

Once a sample has been taken, the next step for pollsters is to rebalance the makeup of participants so it conforms to the proportions in the U.S. Census. Not every poll will have an exactly representative sample. Therefore pollsters will rejigger the numbers in favor of those underrepresented or overrepresented in the sample—usually men, young people, the less educated, and racial minorities. This recalculation, or weighting, is necessary because some groups are less likely to take part in the survey.

When it comes to the actual events on Election Day, likely voters are, by definition, the ones pulling the levers of power. In covering elections, the media must understand that American liberty and equality under the law are dependent on a vigilant citizenry. The sample most representative of those who choose to do their duty is the likely voters. Any focus on samples that are merely registered but possibly disconnected voters biases what happens on Election Day by placing polls ahead of democratic representation. It elevates a very narrow notion of public opinion above the dynamic public debate about ideas and representation that was intended by the founders to find the best candidates for leadership.

> In covering elections, the media must understand that American liberty and equality under the law are dependent on a vigilant citizenry.

Who Paid for It?

Despite their growth and increased use, polls are still an expensive proposition for any party, candidate, or media organization. Polling requires sophisticated computer technology, phone banks, pollsters to write questions, and interviewers to ask respondents their opinions. These results have to be gathered, tallied, and analyzed. And none of these steps is easy or inexpensive.

That's why media outlets began forming strategic partnerships. During the 1976 presidential election cycle, the *New York Times* joined forces with CBS News to conduct polls on the campaign. The other networks soon followed. ABC News teamed up with the *Washington Post,* and NBC News shared costs with the *Wall Street Journal.* CNN works with *USA Today,* and Gallup and Fox News use Massachusetts-based pollster Opinion Dynamics. Reuters, the British-owned news syndicate, uses New York's Zogby International.

Knowing something about the internal dynamics and institutional interests of the people commissioning a poll adds insight to one's interpretation of a poll's results. At the very least, who pays will affect the way that questions are designed, which plays a critical role in what kind of answers a pollster will get. Most people are familiar with surveys sponsored by a large media organization, such as CBS or the *New York Times*. A large news organization will commission dozens of surveys a year, with some, such as CNN, using tracking polls like a campaign. Advocacy groups and think tanks also commission surveys. Usually these organizations have a political agenda or way of looking at the world that they wish to push. Polls—not just the wording of questions—become a way of framing policy issues. Such polls deserve to be examined with the strictest methodological and rhetorical scrutiny. Finally, of course, political candidates and politicians commission polls all the time. The results of their polls tend to be held securely within the walls of the campaign, but occasionally information will be leaked to the media or used to inform donors and supporters.

MEDIA POLLS: THE WORST OF THE LOT

The sponsors of a poll usually provide more than just the financial resources. They also help guide pollsters toward their ends. Just because a poll is sponsored by a public media organization does not mean that it is unbiased or more accurate than one paid for by an interest group. Indeed, in some ways, the opposite is true. Private polls can be far more accurate than "public" polls conducted by the media because private business and candidates have an incentive to be as precise as possible. The more accurate the information, the better they can develop their product or campaign. Private polls may ask the same question worded in different ways, contradictory questions, and hypothetical questions that help illustrate opinion to get as complete a view as possible. On the other hand, "[i]n public polling, all the subtlety disappears," says Scott Rasmussen, president of Rasmussen Research.[17] What Rasmussen means is that the public polls conducted by the media are not guaranteed to be more accurate than private polls.

Public opinion polls in the media work on an imperative different from private polls. The media must concentrate on speed, and they are often restrained by their polling budgets, which must be spread over many polls. Media polls are also shaped by how they'll be used for stories, which means that question wording isn't examined with the same attention that a private pollster might use. As Rasmussen explains: "Sometimes [public] polling is made to sound too scientific. If you are writing something, you can find a poll to support any position." Rasmussen isn't the only person expressing such a view. Skepticism and animosity toward polling have grown over the past decade to include a vocal group of critics who charge that polls are protean vehicles that may be shaped into any expression of public opinion.

A media organization's political beliefs or journalistic interests determine when a poll is taken, how the questions are asked, and what findings will be emphasized when a story is reported. Take, for instance, two questions posed in similar polls taken in 1996. The *New York Times* asked 1,111 adults the following:

> Medicare recipients pay a fee of $46.10 a month for their coverage of doctors' bills. Would it be acceptable or not to you if Congress raised that fee each year so that it reached $90 a month by the year 2002?

Only 31 percent said that such a policy change would be "acceptable." Sixty-three percent thought the change was "not acceptable." Another 7 percent didn't know. Around the same time, GrassRoots Research, a private polling firm, asked 1,000 voters this question:

Under current law most retirees will pay a monthly Medicare premium of $70. Under the budget plan just passed by Congress, this monthly premium would increase to $88. Over seven years, this change will save the government $47 billion in Medicare costs. Would you favor or oppose the increase?

The difference in results was stark. Nearly six of ten registered voters who responded (59 percent) favored the idea of Medicare reform when it was explained this way. Another 39 percent opposed it. Only 2 percent were uncertain.

Both questions probed the same public policy issue: How did the public feel about Congress's reform plan for Medicare? Yet the final results aren't just different, they call for a radically different news article, policy debate, and even legislation in Congress. The fact is that although the media and political elite accord polls a great deal of influence, tiny changes in methodology and wording can have extensive effects on the final numbers in polls. Could the organizational imperatives of the media affect the time, wording, or framing of questions?

Clearly the GrassRoots question was more thorough and technical, contextualizing the Republican plan based on the numbers and intentions being used by Congress to deal with the budgetary pressures on Medicare. Was the *New York Times* poll biased? Both polls were methodologically sound, but as anyone who has followed the *Times'* coverage of budget issues could attest, its poll mirrored the political vocabulary of the editorial page, headline writers, and news directors at the Gray Lady. The *Times'* editorial writers, long-time Republican critics and supporters of a progressive and assertive government, were fond of calling GOP Medicare policy changes "cuts," with frequent recourse to dire terms such as "slashing" and "draconian reform."

The polls that are most likely to shape debate, mold opinion, and have the most comprehensive consequences are those conducted by the nation's biggest media organizations. The media have tried to maintain their independence and objectivity by developing their own polling arms, but there is plenty of evidence to suggest that Americans should be just as leery of media pollsters' claims of objectivity. Journalists are notoriously resistant to any charges of bias. The common rejoinder from the media professional is that "bias is in the eye of the beholder." Perhaps. But unless journalists, producers, and editors are made of different stuff from the rest of the nation they cover with a skeptical eye, the vigilant citizen should be prepared to scrutinize even the most respected media organization's polls.

> Unless journalists, producers, and editors are made of different stuff from the rest of the nation they cover with a skeptical eye, the vigilant citizen should be prepared to scrutinize even the most respected media organization's polls.

THE ACCURACY OF CAMPAIGN POLLS

"The information from a poll is only as good as the information you put into it," says Sarah Simmons, former political consultant with Public Opinion Strategies. POS did polling for Florida Governor Jeb Bush, presidential contender Senator John McCain, and more than three dozen House candidates in 1998. "In private polling, you learn to ask the bad questions about yourself. It is the likely direction of a campaign, so you want to know what voters will think."[18]

Private pollsters working for candidates and politicians are more likely to ask questions that emphasize nuance, conflict, misgivings, and gray areas rather than ideology. Because candidates and campaigns have to maneuver in the gray areas of public opinion, their polling questions tend to avoid the black-and-white, winner-loser, conservative-versus-liberal questions. To discover voter subtleties, private pollsters will ask multiple questions about the same issues using different words or will present questions that test voter intensity by demanding trade-offs. For instance, a skilled politician such as Bill Clinton in 1995 might detect from his polling that there was a politically rewarding position beyond the usual spending-and-taxing of Democrats versus the social indifference of Republicans. Clinton realized that a balanced budget was a concern for most Americans. But instead of taking a traditional liberal position, he sought to protect left-wing programs *and* balance the budget. Using nuanced polling and Clintonian opportunism, he advocated at various points a five-, seven-, and ten-year balanced budget.

While a media poll usually looks for a quick answer to a series of questions, private pollsters tend to ask overlapping questions so they can paint a picture of how voters are approaching an issue. This isn't to say that media polls don't sometimes demand trade-offs and tough choices from voters. But private polling, unless it is a purely political push by an advocacy group, usually asks tougher and more balanced questions. When a candidate's internal pollster sits down to write a poll, there is every incentive to be truthful. The success of the candidate depends on getting detailed and nuanced results.

ADVOCACY POLLS

Now contrast private polls with the realm of the advocacy poll. For think tanks, consumer groups, unions, and all other special interest groups, polls are bludgeoning devices, offering leverage in the public policy process. For example, in 2000, Lockheed Martin commissioned a poll from Democratic pollster Mark Mellman showing that a majority of Americans thought drug use was rising. (In reality, it was falling.) The poll also showed that the public was more likely to blame Democrats than Republicans for this state of affairs. The Lockheed Martin poll results introduced a second public opinion curiosity that soon drew Democratic support in the anti-drug-funding debate: 56 percent of the public supported using U.S.-built and U.S.-financed aircraft for drug interdiction in drug-producing countries. It shouldn't surprise readers that Lockheed Martin just happens to build such aircraft. The result was bipartisan support for a $1.7 billion bill for drug interdiction and aircraft.

> The media have accelerated polling and, in many cases, have become less conscious of polling's limitations than private pollsters are.

The methodology of media polls is subjected to a different kind of pressure than that of polls by ideological think tanks and advocacy groups. The shortening of the news cycle has given polling a new urgency. Combined with the competition from the Internet, talk radio, and twenty-four-hour news operations, the media have accelerated polling and, in many cases, have become less conscious of polling's limitations than private pollsters are.

The Meaningless Primary Polls

While the methodology of conducting a poll has improved immensely in the past sixty years, the field is still far from being an exact science. For the reader unfamiliar with the process of polling, the prior discussion may seem abstract. But all the small obstacles and challenges in the way of getting a good sample add up, and nowhere is this more apparent than in the Holy Grail of polling: the quest for solid, reliable primary polling.

Primary polling suffers from nearly all of the aforementioned methodological challenges. In addition, voters are often uninformed about and uninterested in the seemingly unimportant task of primary voting. Just as crippling to the task, journalists make unreflective use of polls in an attempt to get a sounding of voter sentiment, even when that sentiment is unstable.

Finding likely voters in the environment of the primary often looks more like snipe hunting than a scientific search for sound public opinion. Warren Mitofsky, president of Mitofsky International, warned fellow pollsters and journalists that he wouldn't pay attention to polls from any primary or caucus state, except for New Hampshire. Turnout is so low in primaries that it is difficult to get an accurate sample of prospective voters. "Find the likely voters, I dare you," he told an audience of fellow pollsters and journalists in 2000.[19]

Most news organizations use polls to inform and educate voters during the election season. The problem is that polls have come to dominate the primary season as candidates vie for funds, media attention, and support. From the viewpoint of sound methodology, primary polling is most inaccurate during this period. Voters aren't just ignorant of most of the candidates, they typically don't tune in until the last few weeks of the campaign. Nevertheless the media polling machine rolls into action, measuring support for candidates. Primary polling runs into several obstacles, including the difficulty of finding "likely voters." The first obstacle occurs in those states that hold open primaries. The second is finding out who *exactly* is going to vote.

These two problems are interrelated. In 2000, pollsters did poorly in the early primaries. In New Hampshire, voters surprised the media by handing Senator John McCain, Republican of Arizona, a 19-point victory over Texas governor George Bush (49 percent to 30 percent). The final CNN/*USA Today*/Gallup poll conducted on the Saturday, Sunday, and Monday before the election showed McCain ahead 44 percent to Bush's 32 percent. CBS News, on the other hand, found McCain up by only 4 percentage points. This wasn't the first time polls had horribly miscalculated. In 1988, Gallup's final poll in New Hampshire's GOP primary was off by more than 17 points. Gallup had Senate Minority Leader Bob Dole leading Vice President George Bush by 8 points. Bush ended up *winning* by 9 points. [20]

Pollsters weren't any more accurate when it came to the Democratic contest in 2000. The CNN/*USA Today*/Gallup poll showed Vice President Al Gore up by 54 percent over New Jersey senator Bill Bradley's 42 percent. Once again CBS News was off by more, reporting in its poll that Gore led Bradley by 16 points. The final results at the ballot box were very tight: Gore beat Bradley by only 4 percentage points (50 percent to 46 percent).

"Polls definitely had trouble in New Hampshire," says Murray Edelman, editorial director of Voter News Service. "The polls underestimated the independents who would show up. It's very difficult to find out who will vote in primaries."[21] There is evidence that McCain might have pulled independents from Bradley during the primaries, making the results less stable. Still, pollsters and journalists should know, after three decades of symbiosis between polling and the media, that the closing days of an election can see some curveballs, especially as the parties have grown weaker and more Americans now call themselves independents.

The polling results of 2000 didn't bother Kathleen Frankovic, director of surveys at CBS News. "Polls fundamentally got the right share of the vote for the national front-runners," she told the *New York Times*. "But the polls were too low on the two challengers because of late-deciding voters and the influence of independents."[22] When polls are off by 6 or 7 percentage points, however, and media pollsters still consider them relatively accurate, we have to ask ourselves a question: What justifies reporting small 4- to 5-point movements as an important shift in voter sentiment?

Imagine if such strange logic were applied to stock car racing. In the trial heats, drivers would vie for poll position. Fans, crews, and announcers would rave over the split-second differences in the time trials that would determine just where rivals would start. Race officials and pre-game shows would use these tiny differences to handicap the race. Yet when the race day arrived, all the rules would be suspended. We'd be told that that it doesn't matter where a driver finishes as long as it is within six or seven cars of his time-trial rival.

> The sad truth is, the polling industry doesn't know how to evaluate the accuracy of its results.

The sad truth is, the polling industry doesn't know how to evaluate the accuracy of its results. Despite the power of polls in democratic debate, there is no agreed-upon methodology for determining when or how accurate final pre-election polls are when compared with Election Day. The Social Science Research Council looked at the different ways to judge the accuracy of polls after the debacle of 1948, but the group failed to establish an industry-wide standard.

As pollster Warren J. Mitofsky argues, "[I]t is clearly an undesirable state of affairs for scholars who wish to study the question of poll accuracy with fairness and precision."[23] Accuracy is all the more critical in the Age of Polls, when the presence and influence of polls have made them an institution in the democratic debate. Yet without a means for journalists and other pollsters to evaluate a poll, the institution of polling is unaccountable to the citizen—for whom these tools of democracy ostensibly speak.

Of course, pollsters are quick to remind the lay reader and television viewer that polls don't predict the future. Pollsters stress that these polls give us "a snapshot in time." With this disclaimer, polls can't be blamed for the wild gyrations and shifts in sentiment that occur in the final days of an election. Nor are polls to blame when independent voters can't commit or late-deciding voters change their minds at the last minute. Yet it is just such volatility that demands that polling be held *more* accountable, and all the more reason for journalists and pollsters to scrutinize the methodologies used during campaigns.

The "snapshot" defense doesn't prevent the media from hypothesizing about races and strategies based on poll results. The minute poll numbers are in hand, journalists race out and pundits ponder what could happen weeks later on Election Day. Such a game of handicapping and blitzkrieg journalism rarely notes the methodological dangers. Campaign stories saunter on, with no warning labels to caution voters, supporters, or even candidates that media polling is notoriously volatile during primaries and the early part of general elections.

Indeed we come to another paradox of polling: As a race gets tighter and media interest grows, the more powerful the influence of polls is likely to be. Yet it is during those times that polls are more likely to affect and be affected by media coverage. Journalists will jump on new results, pundits will watch trends, and campaign managers will try to spin the findings to show newfound strength. From a methodological point of view, we have encountered a problem similar to the one that plagues lawyers facing a big murder case. Even though prospective jurors are selected at random, this does not mean they won't be influenced by media coverage.

Random sampling is the foundation of polling. But while methodologically valid in the cool and isolated air of academia, random sampling does little to tell us about what truly energizes voters. Most media polling gives only a crude sense of voter support or opposition to specific policies. The people who move politics and drive debate are far more driven than is the disconnected voter who is chosen by Lady Luck to answer the questions of a survey.

In *Federalists* Nos. 10 and 51, James Madison writes about the dangers of factions and the containment in an "extended republic." Most journalists are familiar with the lesson of this work: that political parties and organizations preserve freedom by policing, competing, and even opposing other political parties and organizations. Polling may call the citizen to be judge, jury, and executioner on these public policy struggles, but "random sampling" of the populace does nothing to tell us why "factions" are moved to enter the arena of debate. Whatever our political differences with our fellow citizens, passion is part of patriotism. Why the disconnected, apathetic, willfully ignorant voter is thought to be a more authentic voice of democracy than the concerned and hopeful citizen who gets personally involved in debate and organizations is a mystery of the polling culture.

Indeed the next great debate in American democracy concerns who we should sample and why. The debate about "likely voters" is really a debate about who participates in the political *act* of expressing public opinions through political associations, talk radio, letters to the editor, local parties, and fund-raising. Many pollsters and media players argue that polls are a democratizing device. Using this logic, polling *should* cast the widest net possible. But if you agree with Madison that our interests are represented by our elected leaders and the private associations we support to communicate our beliefs, then random sampling becomes a methodologically sound way to tap into the opinions of people who don't care. As we shall see in later chapters, most Americans aren't just disconnected from the political system, they are grossly ignorant and even apathetic about their responsibility to vote. By including such individuals in polls and then using the results as a bludgeoning device to browbeat politicians on policy questions, we distort the process. Every Election Day will be a surprise unless we attempt as much as possible to plumb the opinions of those citizens who conscientiously go to the polls, research the issues, and then vote for their representatives.

Why reward with a say in government the apathetic citizen who does not take the time to vote? If the methodological basis of polling depends on polls and reportage that observe rather than drive opinion, then perhaps the first step is to ensure that we do our best to tap the best informed and most involved. Everett Carll Ladd, director of Roper, charged that the proliferation of polling hammered away at the chances of Bob Dole to be considered a real contender for office. But when Election Day came, Bill Clinton failed to win a majority and Dole did well in the electoral college. If Ladd is right, then polls may feed a herd mentality among journalists and a bandwagon effect flowing from the soft support of impressionable voters.

In 1932, the magazine *Literary Digest* predicted that Al Smith would handily defeat Franklin Delano Roosevelt. Pollsters point to this poll as an example of poor methodology. The *Literary Digest* results depended on affluent subscribers who were more likely to back Smith. But the problem of rising refusal rates has led at least one election observer to advocate mail-in questionnaires. "One of the toughest parts of election polling is figuring out who, of all those voting-age citizens out there, [is] actually going to vote. Their proportion keeps getting smaller, and that makes identifying them harder," writes Philip Meyer, holder of the Knight Chair in Journalism at the University of North Carolina, Chapel Hill.[24] "The low response in mail surveys might not be a flaw at all if the people who respond to the surveys are the same interested, socially concerned citizens who are going to vote in those particular elections."

Meyer studied the results of pre-election surveys sponsored by the *Columbus Dispatch*. The paper polled voters by mail, and the self-selected responses consistently mirrored the final results of elections, despite the fact that this method violated the rules of conventional polling. Such polling veers widely from a random sample because the more animated and more energetic voter is more likely to respond. Pollsters can't rely on such numbers, even though their accuracy challenges the methodological accuracy of current practices.

"One of the toughest parts of election polling is figuring out who, of all those voting-age citizens out there, [is] actually going to vote."

Random selection is a basic rule of sampling theory. By following these rules, pollsters can measure the results with confidence within a margin of error. But in the day-to-day of flesh-and-blood politics, this may be subtly misleading. Meyer ponders whether conventional theory "may have made us obsess over sampling and pay insufficient attention to other sources of error"—such as who actually gets to the polls.

The methodology of polling has improved immensely in the past fifty years. It has allowed voters a new channel for their voices to be heard. But as carefully as we ought to police the methodology of polling, it is all the more critical to realize that polling is not perfectly fitted to American representative democracy, in part because the United States is not third-century Athens. We do not select our rulers by lot. Our federal system, the free associations and special interests that vie to change policy and safeguard liberty, and our many representative officials are no less the voice of the people than a randomly selected group of voters.

As ensconced and insulated as political players in Washington may be, responsibility for the final decisions on policy is still given to representatives of the people who are selected on Election Day by private citizens who choose to vote. Is this a less representative process than methodology that taps average citizens? That's debatable. Consider: Even when pollsters are deployed to find out what Americans think, they are still forced into using a *representative* sample. They can't possibly capture and synthesize every opinion of the little guy. Even so, the soundness, attentiveness, and knowledge of that random sample are yet more reasons to question the power of polls in shaping our political future. Ignorance and apathy are real problems. Therefore we should debate about what makes a media poll and selected questioning of randomly chosen Americans more accurate than the system set up by the founders for deliberation and selection of the best the Republic has to offer. Beyond the problems of polling methodology are deeper and more pressing issues of self-rule: problems that are worthy of a debate that extends beyond a few column inches, that deserve more attention than a few minutes of telephone questioning, and that have consequences that can't be measured by a statistical margin of error.

CHAPTER FOUR

The Definition of "Is"

The Complex Nature of Wording

*Polling is often as much a measure of the evolution of
words as it is a measure of change of opinion.*

■ ■ ■

POLITICS IS A WAR OF WORDS, and nowhere is this more
apparent than in opinion polls. A poll's methodology is often
the least understood part of a poll and, for the media, too
often the untold story. How a question is worded can greatly
change the response. A poll may be methodologically sound,
yet with the addition of only a few words, a single lead-in
question, or even just politically charged "code words," the
results may be skewed and citizens' responses drastically
changed.

The subject of wording is so complex and powerful that it
is almost impossible to overstress its importance to polling.
This chapter focuses on how question wording can change or
even distort polling results. It also considers the implications

of those "response effects" generated by wording—namely, does the very significance of question framing and wording have deeper implications for how we should think about polls and public opinion?

It's easy to overlook how polling questions are worded. The constant temptation when reading any story about poll numbers is to make the data the story. Poll numbers are often employed like statistics spouted by an avid baseball fan—a recourse used enthusiastically to definitively end debate. In the illusive world of politics, with all its spin, deception, and hidden intent, poll numbers give the appearance of fact. They are often the only anchors in a swirling sea of partisan storms. But the importance of wording should always receive close attention from the media and the alert citizen.

> How a pollster frames, words, and asks political questions should be examined with the greatest skepticism and care.

How a pollster frames, words, and asks political questions should be examined with the greatest skepticism and care. As when an independent counsel questions the president, every word matters, because at any moment the respondent's answer may hinge on the slightest shade of meaning or interpretation of the question. In this game, we must all scrutinize what the definition of "is" is.

In looking at any polling question, certain rules can help us hack through the thick bramble patch of political language to reach an understanding of what exactly is going on in public opinion. Any conscientious citizen should ask the following questions, no matter who conducted the poll or how seemingly sound the pollster's methodology:

- What was the sequence of the questions? Were there lead-in questions?

- Were words used that could bias or influence responses?

- Were there words, terms, or even ideas that would be affected by recent news?

- Do questions explain or define terms in ways that could affect the outcome?

This important task is, unfortunately, made difficult if not impossible because the news media rarely, if ever, give readers or viewers enough information to explore all the questions and their actual wording. Bear in mind that the polling questions that follow aren't tilted, biased, or deliberately manipulative in the way that a false dilemma is presented. They aren't questions such as "Have you stopped beating your wife?" The examples that follow are a reminder that, for many Americans, how a question is framed and presented can be as important as what a person says he or she believes.

Lead-In Question

In 1996, the California media jumped on the results of a Mervin Field poll that showed that support for the California Civil Rights Initiative had plummeted to only 56 percent. Later known as Proposition 209, the initiative was designed to prohibit state and local agencies from using race, sex, color, ethnicity, or national origin as a basis for preferential treatment policies.

The low level of support was indeed surprising. For more than a year, the *Los Angeles Times* had been polling on the issue and finding that roughly two-thirds of registered voters backed the measure. Thus the Field poll results appeared to show that something cataclysmic had happened. The new and inexplicable drop in support provided fodder for the media and for foes of the initiative. But if we look closer, the drop looks less like a new trend and more like a problem in how the poll was constructed. In their main question, both the

Los Angeles Times polls and the Field poll used language similar to that on the ballot, but the Field poll asked the following lead-in question:

> Have you seen, read, or heard about a ballot initiative that would abolish state and local laws relating to affirmative action, referred to as the California Civil Rights Initiative, that will appear on the November 1996 ballot?

Without knowing the lead-in question, it is tempting to draw the wrong conclusions. But a deeper consideration of the Field question shows why the setup was important in explaining the smaller amount of positive responses received by the follow-up question. Two problems appear immediately. The first is the word "abolish." As California pollster Arnold Steinberg remarked at the time, "The word 'abolish' is too unsettling to the status quo."[1] Words that demand radical change, revolutionary reforms, or bold new institutional prerogatives are likely to lower support for ideas or to bias answers. Americans are reasonable compromisers, not partisan extremists.

The second problem with the Field question is that it subtly prods voters to claim they know something about the initiative, when they might not. The clause "Have you seen, read, or heard about" puts pressure on the respondent to look closely at the reform that threatens to "abolish" the current way of life. It is a sad fact, but voters are often ignorant of public affairs, even during the hottest of political controversies. In 1990 and 1992, only three out of ten voters in California could connect the gubernatorial and senatorial candidates with their positions on abortion and the death penalty—hot topics in these state races. So when the Field poll asked for a self-evaluation of civic knowledge, no doubt many respondents felt pressure to claim that they knew more about the California Civil Rights Initiative than they did.

With so much going on in this lead-in question, it's not surprising that the results were used in the political debate. Opponents of Proposition 209 could claim that CCRI wasn't just losing support, it was losing support from "people who have seen, read, or heard" about it. In other words, more civic-minded voters were split on the issue, especially as they learned more about it. The subtle implication: The ignorant voter supported CCRI, and support would fall as the word got out.

What makes the lead-in question dangerous is that the media and the pollster do not report it. With the limited space and time constraints of the twenty-four-hour news cycle, most media organs do not present all the questions or their order in the survey. Instead they may present the results of a single question to the reader *without reference to the lead-in.* A second question might be relatively innocuous and, on close inspection, might actually seem fairly balanced, but tipped by a lead-in, the results can be very misleading.

> Words that demand radical change, revolutionary reforms, or bold new institutional prerogatives are likely to lower support for ideas or to bias answers.

This isn't the only example of how a lead-in question can throw results. Ask Americans about their support for military intervention, and certain lead-in questions can almost always boost support. For instance, a polling question that probes support for a public policy initiative gains advocates if the lead-in states that the president of the United States favors the move. As pollsters Michael W. Traugott and Paul J. Lavrakas note, "When questions are asked this way, especially in a period of an international crisis or conflict, experiments show respondents are more likely to express support for that policy than if the question did not include that phrase."[2] Simply put, Americans like to support their president, and that can boost approval for foreign policy ventures.

Question Wording—First Frame the Issue, Then Get the Power

The power of lead-in questions is just one form of question "framing." How questions are worded, what "salient" ideas they raise in voters' minds, and the way they make a person think about a public policy question show the power of the pollster's words to influence the responses from those interviewed. To demonstrate the power of words, let's examine two issues that the public is divided about: education reform and taxes. Word choice is particularly important when addressing these continuing controversies in public policy.

SCHOOL CHOICE— WON'T SOMEONE THINK OF THE CHILDREN?

Polls generally show that support is growing for letting parents use vouchers to send their children to schools of their choice, whether public or private. But how that question is asked directly affects whether there is majority support for vouchers. Consider the following three polls taken at about the same time in 1997:

> The left-of-center Joint Center for Political and Economic Studies asked: "Would you support a voucher system where parents would get money from the government to send their children to the public, private or parochial school of their choice?"
> *Some 48.1 percent of the general public said yes; 46.1 percent said no. Among African Americans especially, support for school choice is high. Some 57.3 percent of blacks said yes; 37.9 percent said no.*

> The pro–school choice Center for Education Reform, a Washington-based think tank, asked almost two thousand

> people: "How much in favor are you of allowing poor parents to be given the tax dollars allotted for their child's education and permitting them to use those dollars in the form of a scholarship to attend a private, public or parochial school of their choosing?"
>
> *About 73 percent responded that they "strongly favor" or "somewhat favor" the idea. Only 23 percent were against it.*

> The professional education fraternity Phi Delta Kappa conducts its own regular poll of the public's views on education. It asked: "Do you favor or oppose allowing students and parents to choose a private school to attend at public expense?"
>
> *About 44 percent favored that plan.*

What explains the wide variation? In part, it's due to the intense, often bitter, debate to define the real nature of school choice. For teachers unions, the education establishment, many liberal politicians, and some section of the electorate, such a simple reform could have devastating and immoral consequences. It would mark the end of America's long tradition of public schooling.

Janet Bass, spokeswoman for the American Federation of Teachers, the nation's second-largest union, warns that this would be a "siphoning of public dollars" signaling the "end of public education." The National Education Association, the nation's largest teachers union, agrees, charging that "tuition vouchers are a means of channeling public dollars to private schools and thus undermining American public education."[3]

Vouchers (usually "taxpayer-funded vouchers"), critics charge, take money from the public schools and "cream" the top students from the schools, leaving private schools with more money and the best students. Even if public education weren't destroyed, say these critics, the inevitable result would be a two-tier system.

On the other side of the equation are reform groups who
see public schools as hopelessly gridlocked and incapable of
change because of a lack of accountability. Bureaucratic rules,
burdensome litigation, political power blocs, and selfish special interests have undermined serious reform for the past
thirty years. School choice is seen as a way to shake up the
system, provide a little bit of *perestroika* for the state-run mo-
nopoly of education, and open a way out for low-income kids
trapped in awful schools. It does so by empowering parents
by letting them choose what's best for their kids. By creating
financial incentives for schools to listen and serve taxpayers,
parents would be back in charge.

So those are the battle lines—drawn clearly and defined
unequivocally with words. How do you find neutral questions to get the public's "real" opinion? You don't. Only by
looking at the question from different angles with different
wordings is it possible to get a sense, and then only a rough
sense, of what Americans really want, other than better
schools.

Regardless of the questions, support for school choice has
grown. Even the education establishment's PDK polls have
shown growing support for school choice over the years. In
1993, slightly less than 25 percent of those polled backed the
idea. Even with adverse wording, that number nearly doubled. Is all this just hot air and spin from pollsters?

All of these polling questions were conducted in a
methodologically sound manner, although the Center for Education Reform leads respondents a bit with its "how much in
favor are you" wording; the question should allow for dis-
agreement. Even so, why is wording so important? If Americans felt strongly about education issues, did their homework,
and followed public policy, then they ought to have well-
developed opinions on the direction of reform. If Americans
were strong-minded on political issues, they would see
through such wording variations. Yet clearly they don't.

For those in the political arena, the importance of wording is well known. The American Federation of Teachers tried to prevent the misuse of polling data by issuing a press release that urged editors and education writers to reexamine the way they approach the voucher/choice issue. "What's the difference between vouchers, choice, and opportunity scholarships?" the AFT asked. "Nothing, except that the last two *sound* better. A voucher by any other name is still a voucher—public dollars leaving public schools for private schools."

Jeanne Allen, president of the Center for Education Reform, has her reasons for using the word "scholarship" in the CER poll. She says that too often, polls use the term "voucher" to load the dice. "Vouchers are negative and do poll negatively," Allen said. "But it's a vapid concept. Most people don't understand the term and view it as a policy-wonk term. So why do a poll on terms people don't understand? We use the word 'scholarship' because everyone knows what that means."

GOP pollster Frank Luntz stresses how important wording can be for school choice. In a guide distributed to Congress, *The Language of the 21st Century*, Luntz states in no uncertain terms: "Don't use the word 'voucher.'" He explains: "If you want to support greater choice in education, there is even a right and wrong way to describe the issue." He adds, "It's parental choice, not school choice . . . they're opportunity scholarships, not vouchers."

There is no perfectly neutral or wholly objective way to ask questions without disturbing the pool of public opinion.

The AFT called Luntz's writing on the subject "Orwellian." Yet both sides agree that language is the decisive factor in assessing public opinion on this issue, although very few media stories emphasize this fact. The terms "voucher," "tuition voucher," "taxpayer-funded voucher," "school choice," "scholarships," and even "opportunity scholarships" have all been used in polling questions. Which one is correct?

Some of these terms, such as "taxpayer-funded voucher" and "opportunity scholarship," are specially modified to tilt opinion to one side of the debate or the other. But for our purposes here, it is important to note that they have all been used in methodologically sound surveys. There is no perfectly neutral or wholly objective way to ask these questions without disturbing the pool of public opinion. In the Age of Impression Democracy, what once might have been debated in public speeches and rostrum address as part of normal political discourse is now dependent upon the assumptions and choices made in developing the polls.

TAXING QUESTIONS—
IS IT SPENDING OR WASTE?

When Governor George W. Bush declared victory on Super Tuesday 2000, he presented his policy ideas, outlining several of his top priorities. Bush said he wanted to reform Social Security, rebuild the military, and cut taxes. On this last point, Bush charged, "After eight years of Clinton-Gore, we have the highest tax burden since World War II. And yet we are told that taxes are not an issue. . . . The polls say cutting taxes is not popular. I'm not proposing tax relief because it's the popular thing to do; I'm proposing it because it's the right thing to do."

To reporters, this apologetic appeal made perfect sense. Many, after all, had reported on polls showing little public support for tax cuts. The surplus, the public seemed to be saying, should be spent on new government programs. And many reporters pinned Bush's loss in New Hampshire to his decision to push a sizable tax cut as the centerpiece of his campaign—at the cost, of course, of the journalistically popular issue of campaign finance regulation.

But the truth of the oft-repeated claim that the public doesn't want a tax cut isn't at all clear; it's even dubious. Compare the wording and results for two questions asked by Pew Research Center for the People and the Press following President Bill Clinton's 2000 State of the Union address. The pollsters set up the question in the news context:

> President Clinton has proposed setting aside approximately two-thirds of an expected budget surplus to fix the Social Security system. What do you think the leaders in Washington should do with the remainder of the surplus?

Under the first variation, Pew asked:

> Should the money be used for a tax cut, or should it be used to fund new government programs?

Phrased this way, three out of five (60 percent) of those polled supported a tax cut. Only 25 percent backed spending on new programs. Another 11 percent wanted the money spent on "other purposes," and 4 percent didn't know.

What seems like an overwhelming majority disappears, however, when the wording reorients the average American's mind to think of specific and well-intentioned spending. In the second variation, the Pew Research Center asked the same setup question but then provided the following options for spending:

> Should the money be used for a tax cut, or should it be spent on programs for education, the environment, health care, crime-fighting, and military defense?

Under this format, only 22 percent of citizens favored a tax cut. Nearly seven in ten (69 percent) liked the wish list of spending presented by the pollster. Finally, 6 percent wanted the money used for "other purposes," and 3 percent didn't know. Writing in 1991, pollster Daniel Yankelovich stated, "People automatically oppose government spending in the abstract but simultaneously endorse programs that involve government spending for causes they support, such as the war on drugs."[4]

Now take a look at a poll of 880 likely voters by Zogby International. It asked the tax question in a significantly different way:

> The U.S. government will take in $3 trillion over the next 15 years that it currently has no plans to spend. Do you want to keep some of the money in the form of a tax cut or have the government make plans to spend it on federal programs?

Zogby found much more support for tax cuts when the debate was framed in this way. A strong majority of those polled, 56.3 percent, said they preferred a tax cut; just 31 percent wanted more government spending. Overall support was higher, but among Democrats support also went up, with 41.6 percent saying they'd prefer tax cuts in this scenario. Even more surprising, less than a majority (44.7 percent) said they preferred more government spending.

Key Democratic constituencies also favored tax cuts when the question was asked this way. More than half of union members (50.4 percent) said they preferred a tax cut, and 40.8 percent said they preferred government spending. In the suburbs, where the parties battle each other for the vote, 54.5 percent said they preferred a tax cut, and a relatively scant 30.4 percent said they preferred government spending. Adds Richard Noyes of the Media Research Center, "If every pollster asked the question using Zogby's words, the wave of polls showing support for tax cuts would lead to a very different conventional wisdom than we have now, it would seem."[5]

Such results aren't unknown to pollsters; they just go unreported by media anxious to use polls for their stories and prejudices. Wording has become especially important *because* the media fail to report on issues. Voters aren't just uninterested in politics; chances are that when they tune in, they aren't going to see reports balanced with facts or issue discussions to help them. They might know what former Vice President Al Gore thinks of plans to cut taxes—it's a "risky scheme"—but not why it might endanger the economy.

Polling on taxes or any other policy question is also limited in value because the media often frame the issue with a liberal bias.

> Polling on taxes or any other policy question is limited in value partly because the media often frame the issue with a liberal bias.

Noyes found in one of his media studies that journalists rarely note the arguments *for* tax cuts.[6] His work shows that the media are less likely to use statistics that show the burden of taxation than they are to emphasize the "risky" nature of tax cuts. The media often ask the GOP how to "pay for" tax cuts, with subtle hints that pit tax reform against the future of Social Security or Medicare or "the environment." Thus voters are left without a balanced base of knowledge when they hear about tax cuts. Do such numbers make a difference when the pollsters are deployed to ask about public views? Absolutely.

The wording and background reportage of polling questions aren't the only factors that have an effect on perceived support for tax cuts. Polls are an extremely limited forum for explaining the complex and nuanced public debate about taxes, or any other issue for that matter. The wording of polling questions doesn't just "frame" the voter's mind; it is often the only source for the meager facts a voter will use to determine his or her opinion.

In 2000, while many journalists enjoyed reporting a diminution in support for tax cuts based on polls in the Republican primary, none based their explanations on polling questions that specifically tested whether tax cuts "don't resonate with the public." Rarely do journalists ask questions that could disprove their own theories or that contradict their preferred wording. Low poll numbers for tax cuts in Bush's case were used to explain his foundering in the Granite State—and to explain away support for any cuts at all, implicitly backing the economic status quo.

But at least one candidate, who spoke for tax cuts repeatedly and who actually interacted with citizens from around the nation, offers another explanation of the apparently low numbers. Steve Forbes, publisher and former GOP presidential candidate, sums it up this way: "People tend to regard the tax issue the way they do the weather, because they've been burned so often."[7] They support the idea, but they find it hard to rally because of the politicians' fickleness.

> Rarely do journalists ask questions that could disprove their own theories or that contradict their preferred wording.

The wording of polling questions must be examined carefully. Pollsters, pundits, and journalists should discuss the results using only the actual wording, and even then, there can be reason to doubt the results. The explanations and nuances of politics are many—a fact too often ignored when wording issues are left unexplored.

Range of Answers— Choosing Between "A" and "A"

Even if a question passes muster and isn't biased (a dubious proposition in itself), it's still possible that the results can be biased by the *choice of answers*. Polling isn't a substitute for

dialogue, debate, or the rhetorical exchange that should characterize a healthy representative democracy. Politics isn't always painted in the stark black-and-white ideological hues of
the political junkie. For the average voter, the world is made
up of gradations, subtleties, even inconsistencies in personal
belief. Thus Ohio University political science professor Herbert Asher warns:

> Individuals and groups with an ax to grind can easily construct
> questions that will generate desired responses. The response
> alternatives they provide to the interviewees can also help
> them achieve the intended result. . . . If a middle alternative is
> not listed as one of the choices, then fewer citizens will opt for
> that choice, and this can alter the interpretation of a poll.[8]

Nowhere does the choice of answers play a more important role than with the issue of abortion. Pundits and journalists wrestle over the pro-choice/pro-life makeup of the nation.
They like to discuss how the issue plays out over time and
during elections.

But measuring views on abortion is difficult and highly
dependent not just on how a question is worded but also on
the kind of responses that are offered. Most journalists report
that a majority of Americans are pro-choice. For instance, in
January 1998, a CBS/*New York Times* survey asked about
abortion this way:

> If a woman wants to have an abortion, and her doctor agrees
> to it, should she be allowed to have an abortion?

The results flowing from this question seem to lend unequivocal support to the perception that Americans are in favor of a
woman's right to choose: Nearly six in ten (59 percent) said a
woman "should" be allowed to get an abortion under such
circumstances. Only 24 percent said she "should not" have

such a right. These were the only two answers allowed by the questioner. Survey respondents could answer "it depends" only if they volunteered the answer. In other words, a middle-ground position was effectively excluded in a Procrustean effort to fit Americans into an ideological position worthy of media coverage. Yet most Americans, on either side of the issue, don't hold such a stark position. Thus when media, political parties, or advocacy groups try to force Americans into expressing polarized views, the inevitable result is distortion of public debate and deliberation. In fact the evidence seems to indicate that the "it depends" category is the position of choice for most Americans. If you provide voters with a wider range of answers, the results seem to indicate a vastly different point of view on abortion.

> "Individuals and groups with an ax to grind can easily construct questions that will generate desired responses."

Pollsters Everett Carll Ladd and Karlyn Bowman collected the polling data concerning the public's views on laws limiting abortions.[9] Americans were asked: Do you favor or oppose each of the following proposals?

A law requiring women seeking abortions to wait twenty-four hours before having the procedure done.
More than seven in ten (73 percent) "favor" such a law. Oppose: 23 percent.

A law requiring doctors to inform patients about alternatives to abortion before performing the procedure.
Favor: 86 percent. Oppose: 11 percent.

A law requiring women under 18 to get parental consent for any abortion.
Favor: 78 percent. Oppose: 17 percent.

> A law requiring that the husband of a married woman be notified if she decides to have an abortion.
> *Favor: 70 percent. Oppose: 26 percent.*

These seem like powerful endorsements of more restrictions on abortions. But what *do* Americans actually believe? Is the support for such limits on abortion an indication of a pro-life disposition that merely lacks its eloquent Lincoln? Or should we take as the objective truth on the matter the results of the CBS/*New York Times* survey, which seems to show strong support for the woman's right to choose abortion in the safety, cleanliness, and private supervision of her doctor's office? One way or another, the wording of the question and the answers that purport to speak for all Americans will be important, if not decisive.

This issue also comes up in priority polls, which purport to discover what issues voters think are most important. But these polls are general and communicate little more than a wish list. Voter priority polls are problematic, in part because they are so dependent on how the wish list is constructed, what makes the list, and how the questions are asked.

For instance, during the 2000 campaign, a Portrait of America poll found that the second most important issue to voters after the economy was "government waste." Seventy-three percent of likely voters considered it "very important." Polls from other organizations had shown high rankings for education, the economy, and Social Security as top issues. Not one other campaign poll of voter priorities from the media giants had come up with a similar result. Then again, it could be because the Portrait of America poll was the only one to include government waste as a possible answer.

It is the critical job of the pollster and the media to make sense of polling results and to orient public discourse. Because the framing of the question and the answers disposes voters to respond in a certain way, knowing about this volatility places a special burden on pollsters and the political class that uses polls.

"I want you to know as consumers and watchers of the polls," said Kellyanne Fitzpatrick, president of The Polling Company. "My job is not to be a political pollster, as much as to be a cultural anthropologist and really pay attention to the way people are making their choices and living their lives."[10]

Clarity of the Wording— Confusion Is for the Tax Code

Even if the intent is pure and the choices are representative of the complex beliefs of the populace, the actual wording of questions must be *grammatical.* In 1993, the Roper Organization conducted an infamous poll on American views about the Holocaust. Roper's data suggested at first that almost one-quarter of Americans doubted that the Holocaust—the Nazis' systematic effort to kill Jews, Gypsies, and other unwanted groups—ever occurred. Media groups leapt on and widely spread the numbers. And Jewish groups, understandably, expressed alarm. After all, the denial of the Holocaust has become a hallmark of anti-Semitic propaganda. In short, many Americans were shocked by the data.

Examination of the Roper question, however, suggested another explanation. Roper asked: "Does it seem possible or does it seem impossible to you that the Nazi extermination of the Jews never happened?" The question's double negative undoubtedly confused those polled. (It was a poor translation of a similar question asked by French pollsters.) Once the question was rendered into grammatical English, the number of Holocaust skeptics fell below 5 percent.

This isn't just a lesson about the importance of clear wording. It is also a warning about how the media cover polls. In this case, the media covered a poll that was clearly newsworthy—based on its results. But because the stories made no reference to the actual wording of the poll's question, readers reached an entirely incorrect conclusion about American society. For the unreflective or sloppy journalist, question wording can be all too irrelevant to the imperatives of reportage. If the media don't understand the power of wording, it can be much too easy to treat a poll as merely a vehicle for reporting on "hot-button" issues being debated daily in newspapers and on television. The Roper poll seemed to provide valuable information about what goes on in the hearts and minds of citizens: Is America racist? Is anti-Semitism strong in the United States? Do Americans disguise their real beliefs about others? Tempted by the results, the reporter might leap into action with a front-page story about the dark side of America. Only through a careful analysis of the wording could the truth emerge. Such careful analysis is rare, however, given the twenty-four-hour news cycle and the proliferation of polls pushed into headlines because of cost and institutional incentives.

> For the unreflective or sloppy journalist, question wording can be all too irrelevant to the imperatives of reportage.

Even small changes in wording can distort the clarity and intent of a question in subtle ways. In 1999, the *National Law Journal* conducted a survey that found that three out of four potential jurors were willing to ignore a judge's instructions if they didn't agree with those instructions. Such a finding would seem to point to a certain ignorance of the rule of law, a lack of faith in the legal system, and a profound trust in jury nullification. But the lack of clarity of the question casts doubt on the radical implications of the *NLJ* results.

The *NLJ* asked whether potential jurors agreed with the following statement: "Whatever a judge says the law is, jurors should do what they think is the right thing." At first glance, the wording seems relatively innocuous. For the politically savvy reader, it seems like a simplified poll on the doctrine of jury nullification. But is that how the average potential juror sees it? The flaw in the question is very subtle. "When asked to agree or disagree with complex statements, respondents tend to focus on the last clause of the statement," write Greg Schneiders and Jo Ellen Livingston of the Washington-based consulting firm Frederick Schneiders Research.[11]

When the subject of a polling question is not one of burning importance to respondents, they will tend to answer "yes" to any relatively reasonable statement or idea. This is one reason that almost every modest government spending program polls well. The wording of the question is really drawing a "why not?" from the good-hearted citizen who wants a better world. This is not, however, the same as an enthusiastic "yes."

So subtle is the problem of wording in this question that we must explore one more issue: the use of the word "whatever." We've already recognized that the statement in this *NLJ* poll is not well balanced. We should hope that citizens agree with the general statement that they "should do what they believe is the right thing." To disagree is an invitation to moral anarchy. But in this case, "whatever" reinforces the focus on the last part of the question by telling the respondent to ignore the words contained in the subordinate clause. "Whatever" is a term of disregard. Thus the pollster's wording was an invitation to focus on the main clause with particular attention. When a question is rigged in such a way, the wording occludes the question's intent, which prevents respondents from hearing a clear set of choices that they can weigh carefully.

Worried by these results, Schneiders and Livingston asked their own question about the disposition of voters toward jury nullification. They asked whether citizens agreed with the following statement:

Regardless of how they personally view the case they are hearing, jurors should always follow the instructions of the judge concerning the law in the case.

Nearly three out of four (74 percent) agreed with the statement—a result in direct contradiction with the *National Law Journal* survey. Both polls were methodologically sound and scientifically executed, yet their results could not be more at odds. Of course, Schneiders and Livingston admit that their version "pushed" respondents as well: The word "regardless" in their question functions much like the word "whatever" in the *NLJ* question. It is a tip-off to the respondent indicating the stronger alternative—just what the pollster is looking for. When the respondent gets such a signal, all he or she usually does is see the main statement as one that a

> Polling questions should avoid "pushing" respondents toward a particular answer, and should instead offer clear and balanced alternatives for consideration.

sane and reasonable person could agree to. Polling questions should avoid "pushing" respondents toward a particular answer, and should instead offer clear and balanced alternatives for consideration.

Code Words—
Putting Bombs in Sentences

Over time, certain words used in politics begin to take on new meanings. As with the entire English language, the passage of time causes political terms to evolve, shift, change, and adapt for new circumstances and different perceptions of reality. In many cases, terms that were once popular develop a negative connotation. Polling can be a measure of this evolution of words as much as of actual changes of opinion. At first this may seem a counterintuitive statement. But in polling, wording plays such a critical role in eliciting public opinion that we cannot ignore the fact that certain words have the power to shift opinion just by their mere presence.

As we have seen, Americans' beliefs aren't as fixed as media reports suggest. Change the code words, and the results can change markedly. The words "welfare" and "social spending" both drive down support, for instance. But if you replace "welfare" with "spending for the needy," polling numbers will rise. Political scientists Howard Schuman and Stanley Presser found that Americans don't like to "forbid" behavior. But ask them if certain behavior should "not be allowed" and support will rise. Similarly ask voters if abortion should be made "illegal" and support drops. Ask if abortion should "not be permitted" and support can rise 5 to 10 percentage points.

Earlier in this chapter we noted that both sides in the debate over school choice believe that the word "voucher" drives down support. Because this is a relatively new policy debate, polling questions on the topic yield unique insights into how a word can become a code word. Not surprisingly, the pejorative nature of "voucher" grew out of an extended political battle finally decided in the election booth. In 1993, California voters considered Proposition 174, a voucher initiative that would have given parents $2,600 per child to send their children to the school of their choice. Voucher opponents spent $25 million to defeat the initiative, and much of that money was spent on focus groups and survey research to find a pejorative label for the policy.

" 'Voucher' isn't the best descriptive term and that's exactly why it's used," said Arnold Steinberg, a pollster for Proposition 174. " 'Voucher' has the sound of bookkeeping or accounting. It's far different from the actual idea of school choice, which is a glamorous and vibrant concept." Steinberg added that the word also has overtones of "entitlement," which is the kiss of death to many middle-class voters.

Code words are also problematic because they are often used unconsciously by the media and then absorbed into the polling culture. Phrases such as "right to privacy" or "right to choose" can be used in polls on issues ranging from gun ownership and control to medical reform and abortion. Other code words include terms such as "liberal"—sullied after Vice President George Bush's attacks on Michael Dukakis in 1988. "Big government" carries a negative connotation all its own. "Reform," as in campaign finance reform or welfare reform, can garner support just as a patients' "bill of rights" biases support toward a nice-sounding, vaguely understood idea. Budget "cuts" and "slashes" are particularly powerful code words used both in media stories and in polling questions, often without the conscious knowledge that they are the spark destined to set off some explosive emotions.

The results invariably activate certain antennae in the body politic for those abstract ideas Americans value or distrust. Americans do not follow politics closely, they are uninterested in debate, and very few have the philosopher's disposition toward self-reflection and internal consistency. Most of us rarely test and carefully apply our beliefs. Instead we are (according to the evidence of polls) a basket of contradictions. The power of polling—and especially of code words—is derived in part from the phenomenon Daniel Yankelovich calls "compartmentalized thinking": "Frequently, compartmentalized thinking is linked to certain words or phrases that have become politically tainted—code words to which the public responds in ways that do not reflect their true feelings."[12]

We might argue with this idea of "true feelings" as being excessively simplistic. A person may be pro-choice on abortion but may be against the right of parents to choose which schools their children attend. A voter may favor smaller government but support huge increases in defense spending. These are examples of issue compartments in conflict. But the wide differences in polling results, such as those examples discussed here, seem to indicate that it isn't just that people's compartments of thinking are in conflict with one another. The real issue seems to be deeper, with far more problematic implications for the entire enterprise of polling and the media's unreflective reportage on public opinion.

The Scary Implications of Wording Effects

Response effects resulting from question order, wording, or politically charged code words reveal that Americans do not have strong, unequivocal beliefs about the burning issues of the day; rather, they may give different responses to different polling questions on the same issue. The real danger of polling, therefore, is that it gives us a false sense that people's views are settled and well established. For many elites—especially journalists and advocates who don't give the issue much thought—polling ostensibly provides an insight into what Americans think about controversial political questions. They see in polls vindication for their reportage as well as numerical measurement of the public's beliefs. Wording, as well as question order and the content of lead-in questions, doesn't get much scrutiny because the political and chattering classes are spellbound by the aura of numerical exactitude. Question wording, unless grossly biased, is an afterthought because political issues are already well defined in the mind of the politico-media establishment. The elites are simply looking to public opinion to deliver them from gridlock into action and power.

Most journalists understand that a poll can yield distorted results, but few report on its decisiveness or level of dependability. The wording of a question about tax cuts, education, abortion, or any other policy controversy is more likely to generate media interest based on themes already familiar to the political cognoscenti. Thus wording rarely receives close inspection in the media. Polling questions are regarded as merely a vehicle for carrying the media's hot issues to the public.

But the power of wording, as evidenced by polls on the same subject that differ radically in their results, indicates that there is conflict, contradiction, inconsistency, and just plain ignorance in the policy beliefs of most Americans. Code words and response effects in general trigger certain spheres of thought on public policy issues that can be openly inconsistent when compared with one another. Thus pollsters wield tremendous power because their choice of words determines which ideas will be made "salient" to the respondent. The skilled pollster is both aware of this danger and probably gifted in its manipulation.

> Americans do not follow politics closely, they are uninterested in debate, and very few have the philosopher's disposition toward self-reflection and internal consistency.

What do all these questions about wording really mean? Should we abandon polling? Is there no neutral ground on which to ask people their opinions? Why do lead-in questions matter? Why does "framing" have such a decisive effect on the responses given by citizens? All these questions are the pollster's curse: If the American voter is really attuned to public events, then shouldn't he or she have firm, well-thought-out views on the political issues of the day? In a democracy, public opinion matters. But these nagging questions cast doubts about whether polling is indeed the perfect outgrowth of democratic ideals and a guaranteed way of improving public deliberation.

Within the academic community, unlike among journalists and pundits, polling results aren't seen as a hard-and-fast measure of public opinion. UCLA political science professor John R. Zaller denies that there is "any true position" held by individuals or the public as a whole. "If different frames or different question orders produce different results, it is not because one or the other has distorted the public's true feelings," he continues. "It is, rather, because the public, having no fixed true opinion, implicitly relies on the particular question it has been asked to determine what exactly the issue is and what considerations are relevant to settling it."[13]

The lesson of how wording affects polls, for those who choose to look closely enough, is that polling is a *part* of the political process. It is not above debate. It is not a serene castle in the air that sits above the tumult of politics. It is not a neutral ground in political debate. In the quest to use numbers to explain everything, citizens should realize that polls are subject to human bias.

Polling is not a serene castle in the air that sits above the tumult of politics. It is not a neutral ground in political debate.

We might attempt to find what pollster Daniel Yankelovich calls the "mushiness" of public opinion by deliberately asking the same question in different ways. If the responses are consistent, then polling may indeed be a straightforward and accurate way to measure public opinion. But if the answers vary with the phrasing of the question, then we would do well not to draw any grandiloquent conclusions from particular polls. Yet in this era of ubiquitous polling, the media rarely let concerns about conflicting poll results humble their reportage. Instead there is a drive, even a journalistic imperative, to present public opinion as hard news.

How we talk about politics in a republic is nearly as important as what we decide. Political judgment, negotiation,

THE DEFINITION OF "IS" • 173
mislabeled

and even involvement are dependent on words. Such conclusions aren't new, of course. Throughout history, many civilizations and thinkers have looked at words as the coin of the realm in the marketplace of ideas. Debasing that currency may lead to strife, faction, intolerance, and social discord.

The pollster's desire to be a neutral part of the process is admirable. But like the media ideal of objectivity, perfect neutrality isn't possible. As social scientists Donald R. Kinder and Lynn M. Sanders write:

> Those of us who design surveys find ourselves in roughly the same position as do those who hold and wield real power: public officials, editors and journalists, newsmakers of all sorts. Both choose how public issues are to be framed, and, in both instances, the choices seem to be consequential.[14]

But why does wording play such a decisive role in the results? It stands to reason that if Americans had strong beliefs on political questions, their responses to different polls would not be affected by the wording of the questions. Zaller concludes, "[I]ndividuals do not typically possess 'true attitudes' on issues, as conventional theorizing assumes, but a series of partially independent and often inconsistent ones. Which of a person's attitudes is expressed at different times depends on which has been made most immediately salient by chance and the details of questionnaire construction, especially the order and framing of questions."[15]

As we look more closely at the use and effect of words, we must conclude that polling is more art than science. Polling results can be affected by so many factors that the list seems almost endless: the conception of the questions, the timing of the survey, the ongoing debates, the charged code words, and, not least, the psychology and honesty of those polled. We can declare polling to be a science only in methodological terms.

The techniques of polling have been accepted and established as a valid statistical tool. But the sound methodology of polling shouldn't be considered *the* truth. The wording of a soundly conducted poll can be enough to bias or slant results. It may be tempting in this age of technological wonder to equate scientific method with unequivocal truth. But the almost infinite number of contradictions on education, budget, Medicare, and tax issues casts serious doubt on the exactitude of polling.

> For too many people—especially those in the media—polls have the appearance of the one true reality in the ephemera and illusion of politics.

Yet it is precisely this temptation to call polling a science that gives it such power in American democracy. For too many people—especially those in the media—polls have the appearance of the one true reality in the ephemera and illusion of politics. Thus polling becomes the independent force amid the spin and worldly bluster of political rhetoric and manipulation.

Polls Can't Replace Elected Leaders

The problem that words pose to the process of deliberation in democracy wasn't unknown to the founders. Indeed the struggle over ratification was a struggle over words, with both the Federalists and the anti-Federalists striving to control the way the questions were being framed. James Madison cautioned readers in *Federalist* No. 37:

> Besides the obscurity arising from the complexity of objects, and the imperfection of the human faculties, the medium through which the conceptions of men are conveyed to each other, adds a fresh embarrassment. The use of

words is to express ideas. But no language is so copious as to supply words and phrases for every complex idea, or so correct as not to include many, equivocally denoting different ideas. Hence it must happen, that however accurately objects may be discriminated in themselves, and however accurately the discrimination may be conceived, the definition of them may be rendered inaccurate, by the inaccuracy of the terms in which it is delivered. And this unavoidable inaccuracy must be greater or less, according to the complexity and novelty of the objects defined. When the Almighty himself condescends to address mankind in their own language, his meaning, luminous as it must be, is rendered dim and doubtful, by the cloudy medium through which it is communicated.[16]

The complexity of political issues is given short shrift by polling and media coverage. The ideas of compromise and the ability of the people's representatives to discuss and meet are poorly served by the overly simplified language of polls. The wording of polls does not only influence individual responses, it also influences the entire political process by seeking answers, solutions, and feedback in the course of a few fifty-word questions. How do we spend $1.88 trillion? How should we manage the agencies and departments of government? How should we handle Kosovar Albanians who attack U.S. troops following a war with Serbia? Media reportage presents the responses elicited in polls on such complex issues as *vox populi, vox dei.* With nary a word about the power of words, politicians and the public itself are badgered into positions whose popularity has been measured by a group of people who thought up their answers on the spot, after little research and little thought.

The pollster's problem is really the age-old philosopher's problem of how words express reality. Philosopher George Santayana called language "the great engine of fanaticism." He even wished for a way out of the problem that words can create in political discussions. He wrote in *Dominions and Powers: Reflections on Liberty, Society, and Government:*

> A critic of politics finds himself driven to deprecate the power of words, whilst using them copiously in warning us against their influence. It is indeed in politics that their influence is most dangerous; so that one is almost tempted to wish that they did not exist and that society might be managed silently, by instinct, habit and ocular perception, without this supervening Babel of reports, invectives, laws, arguments and slogans.[17]

Words have long been thought to be the decisive force in politics. But we must remember that polling does not extricate us from the chief blessing and curse of politics; polling only obscures politics under the pastiche of numbers and pseudoscientific credibility.

Couple this polling obsession with the practical necessity to cut down what even the most comprehensive survey shows to fit a 1,200-word article, and you get democratic debate that is shallower and weaker. Deliberation and compromise are part of the process of sounding out and clarifying public opinion. When we forget the importance of words, openly and eloquently expressed, the consequences are frustration, alienation, and disconnect in the body politic.

Amid the maelstrom of polling, public deliberation becomes a narrow battle over the terms of polling questions, waged by the hired-gun pollsters who represent the special interests and parties in politics who pay their way. The debate about words has always been the chief challenge to actors in the political drama. Politics in a representative democracy is a lawful contest over how to frame issues to voters. But now, because of the proliferation of polling, the battle goes to the political forces that can push the polls that support their beliefs. The media no longer judge political figures on the basis of their eloquence in representing issues and explicating ideas, but rather on their fealty to their polling numbers. For many officeholders, this has undercut discussion and deliberation about the great ideas and challenges of the day and has created a niche for the worst sort of politician—one who panders to the latest expression of what the public "believes."

Polling does not extricate us from the chief blessing and curse of politics; it only obscures politics under the pastiche of numbers and pseudoscientific credibility.

We should be concerned about this state of affairs because, as citizens, instead of enjoying a vigorous and enriched public policy debate conducted by the nation's brightest and best, we now get flashy, slick leaders who race to abandon principle for the popular and fleeting causes that appear in whatever polls catch the media's attention or pummel the Capitol into submission.

CHAPTER FIVE

Democratizing Ignorance

The dirtiest secret of all: Polling is an industry built to exploit ignorance—and there is plenty of it.

■ ■ ■

FOR NEARLY FORTY YEARS, lawmakers, reformers, and educators have fought over a simple idea that would undeniably change the state of public education: school choice. In various shapes and guises, the debate over school choice has come to symbolize all the frustration with and hopes for public education. The pro-voucher camp argues that choice is a way to bring accountability and competitive pressure to a failing school system. Under the simplest plan, parents would be given back a portion of the taxes they already pay in the form of a voucher that would cover the cost of educating their child. In the most far-reaching plans, they could send their kids to any school—public, private, or religious. Voucher foes warn that the idea, if put into practice, would mean nothing less than the end of public education, and would quite possibly breach the First Amendment's prohibition on the establishment of religion.

As with every great public policy fight of the past half-century, the struggle to influence public opinion is at the heart of the school choice controversy. Both sides have deployed an army of pollsters to measure public support for their positions. But even when opposing parties survey public opinion at roughly the same time, using statistically valid methods, the results may differ widely. There seems to be a hidden problem.

According to an annual survey by the professional educators group Phi Delta Kappa, support for vouchers rose from 24 percent in 1993 to 41 percent in 1999. But separate polls by the nation's two largest teachers unions, the National Education Association and the American Federation of Teachers—the most implacable opponents of vouchers—showed the public dead set against the idea. Meanwhile, polling by reform-minded groups also found a majority in support of their position in 1999 and even revealed a public ready for some sort of change that would empower parents, if it meant ending the stagnant results and shattered dreams of failing schools.

How do we explain these disparate results? Chapters 2 and 4 illustrated the critical role played by the wording of polling questions. When the issue is presented as a question of freedom and parental choice, support for vouchers and opportunity scholarships rises. But when it is described as a scheme that would starve public schools in order to finance the private education of rich kids, support for school choice plummets. Academics call such changes "response effects," or changes in public attitude based on the framing of the question, as opposed to actual public opinion shifts. And as we've seen, such effects show that the public isn't ideological or even strongly opinionated.

But there is more to this disparity than a mere difference in wording. As both sides brandished their polls as conclusive "proof" that their position had the backing of the people, another poll at the end of 1999 called the veracity of all sides' polls into question by asking some fairly obvious and basic questions. Public Agenda, a nonprofit group based in New York, provided an important object lesson in the limitations of polls and their unreflective use. In December 1999, the group released the results of a poll that asked whether the average American even knows what a school voucher is. As Public Agenda's results show, there is a tremendous divide between the elite arguments and the public knowledge about this reform. And as we shall see, this problem extends to almost all aspects of political debate.

It would appear that most Americans have no clue what vouchers are. Only 17 percent of the 1,200 members of the public (including 394 parents of school-age children) could give a basic definition of school vouchers. And, at best, only another 11 percent showed they had a general, but foggy, notion. More than six in ten (63 percent) of those polled admitted they knew little or nothing at all about vouchers.[1] And 80 percent said they "need to learn more about vouchers before they can form an opinion." Even more amazing was that more than half of community leaders (53 percent), such as local politicians, CEOs, presidents of colleges, and editorial writers, admitted they didn't know enough about vouchers to have an opinion.

> There is a tremendous divide between the elite arguments and the public knowledge.

To most Americans, even to most politicians, these results are amazing. Why, in the course of a decade of polling and media stories, had this fundamental fact gone unnoticed? What Public Agenda found, and what the media overlook, is that public ignorance has a larger role here than any party to the voucher debate may have realized. Although some may find consolation in the four-fifths of respondents who admitted that they needed to learn more, the bigger picture is a bleak one.

A Representative Democracy Requires Reflection and Choice

If ignorance is rife in a republic, what do polls and the constant media attention to them do to deliberative democracy? As Hamilton put it, American government is based on "reflection and choice." Modern-day radical egalitarians—journalists and pollsters who believe that polls are the definitive voice of the people—may applaud the ability of the most uninformed citizen to be heard, but few if any of these champions of polling ever write about or discuss the implications of ignorance to a representative democracy. This is the dirtiest secret of polling.

Political decisions flow from a voter's sense of the world. King Solomon wrote that "[a]s a man thinketh, so is he." It follows that as men and women think, so is a democracy. In a democratic nation, right makes might, by virtue of the thinking and deliberation of the citizenry. Thus the perceptions of the citizenry, whether factual or imaginary, have a direct bearing on how citizens vote.

For instance, many of the laws regulating business and child labor came after Americans were exposed to the horrors of nineteenth-century factory conditions. Many citizens began to support civil rights laws in the 1960s once they saw discrimination with their own eyes. Images of water cannons loosed on peaceful black citizens and of black schoolgirls facing white policemen and guard dogs changed the base of knowledge and opened the eyes of many Americans about the horrors of state-imposed discrimination and segregation. It is the ability of democratic societies to change that gives them cohesion and moral force in times of crisis. But only democratic debate and new information can bring such change.

Absent from most polling stories is the honest disclosure that American ignorance is driving public affairs. Basic ignorance of civic questions gives us reason to doubt the veracity of most polls. Yet the incessant media focus on polls serves to inject that ignorance into the political process. We already know that polls may be skewed by outside factors, such as wording, question order, sample size, and recent news and media coverage.

> Absent from most polling stories is the honest disclosure that American ignorance is driving public affairs.

These response effects cast doubt on the pollsters' claim that public opinion surveys are actually measuring concrete public attitudes about policy issues. The framing problem, in which polling results differ depending on how public policy questions are presented, points to a populace with unreflective, even contradictory thoughts about political issues. Were Americans armed with strongly held opinions and well-grounded knowledge of civic matters, they would not be open to manipulation by the wording of polls. This is one of the strongest reasons to question the effect of polls on representative government.

Politicizing Polling

Polls tell us what Americans are *feeling* about a news event or a policy issue. The Founding Fathers feared direct democracy precisely because public opinion could be unstable and even self-destructive when citizens made decisions based on emotions or on "temporary or partial considerations."[2]

Polling can be the starting point and endpoint for what most politicians will consider in terms of legislation. In the hands of an aroused media, polls can build upon news coverage and propel legislative change, or even save a president from ouster. But because of the public's ignorance of the issues, polling can only tell us about people's likes and dislikes, about their sentiments and tastes. For companies, market research, with its elaborate polling and use of focus groups, really is useful. When a corporation spends tens of millions of dollars to learn whether the public is likely to buy its new kind of soap rather than Brand X, it usually gets its money's worth. There is a substantial difference, however, between which brand of soap three out of four people prefer and what those same people think of how the president of the United States is handling the Irish situation.

"Polls have become 'players' in the political process," says CBS News polling director Kathleen A. Frankovic. To say the least: We need look no further than the debate over President Clinton's impeachment. One week before the House of Representatives voted on articles of impeachment, a CBS News/ *New York Times* poll asked half of a sample: "If the President is impeached, would it be better for the country if he resigns?" Fifty-seven percent of respondents said "yes." But when the other half of the sample was asked: "If the House voted to send articles of impeachment to the Senate for a trial, would it be better for the country if the President resigns?" only 40 percent said "yes."

> Polls, and the media that report them, tend to take the "informed voter" for granted.

Frankovic said the difference was that the second poll explained the "two-step" nature of the process. "One reason for the difference is that, up until the time of the House's vote, nearly one-third of the public was under the mistaken impression that impeachment was the same thing as removal from office, in which case it was logical to them that Bill Clinton should just leave quietly, instead of being dragged kicking and screaming from the White House."[3]

In this era of polls, basic ignorance carries costs. It is the challenge of every politician in every age to bring his or her message to the people. No matter what their education or knowledge, in a democracy, the people have the final say. Should that ignorance extend to specific issues, polls may or may not show the immediate effect. Polls, and the media that report them, tend to take the "informed voter" for granted. But to get a usable response, polls pander to the lowest common denominator.

What Americans Know

Almost any look at what the average citizen knows about politics is bound to be discouraging. Political scientists are nearly unanimous on the subject of voter ignorance. The average American citizen not only lacks basic knowledge but also holds beliefs that are contradictory and inconsistent. Here is a small sample of what Americans know:

- Nearly one-third of Americans (29 percent) think the Constitution guarantees a job. Forty-two percent think it guarantees health care. And 75 percent think it guarantees a high school education.[4]

- Forty-five percent of Americans think the communist tenet "from each according to his abilities, to each according to his needs" is in the Constitution.[5]

- More Americans recognize the Nike advertising slogan "Just Do It" than know where the right to "life, liberty, and the pursuit of happiness" is set forth (79 percent versus 47 percent).[6]

- 90 percent of Americans know that Bill Gates is the founder of the company that created the Windows operating system. Just over half (53 percent) correctly identified Alexander Hamilton as a Founding Father.[7]

- Fewer than half of adults (47 percent) can name their own congressperson.[8]

- Fewer than half of voters could identify whether their congressperson voted for the use of force in the Persian Gulf War.[9]

- Just 30 percent of adults could name Newt Gingrich as the congressperson who led Republican congressional candidates in signing the Contract with America. Six months after the GOP took Congress, 64 percent of Americans admitted they did not know.[10]

- A 1998 poll by the Pew Research Center for the People and the Press showed that 56 percent of Americans could not name a single Democratic candidate for president; 63 percent knew the name "Bush," but it wasn't clear that voters connected the name to George W. Bush.[11]

- According to a January 2000 Gallup poll, 66 percent of Americans could correctly name Regis Philbin when asked who hosts *Who Wants to Be a Millionaire,* but only 6 percent could correctly name Dennis Hastert when asked to name the Speaker of the House of Representatives in Washington.

Political scientists Michael X. Delli Carpini and Scott Keeter studied 3,700 questions surveying the public's political knowledge, beginning with polls conducted in the 1930s. Delli Carpini and Keeter concluded that people tend to remember or identify trivial details about political leaders, focusing on personalities or simply latching onto the policies that the press plays up. For example, the most commonly known fact about George Bush while he was president was that he hated broccoli. During the 1992 presidential campaign, 89 percent of the public knew that Vice President Quayle was feuding with the television character Murphy Brown, but only 19 percent could characterize Bill Clinton's record on the environment.

Delli Carpini and Keeter then show the full absurdity of public knowledge: More people could identify Judge Wapner (the longtime host of the television series *The People's Court*) than could identify Chief Justices Warren Burger or William Rehnquist. More people had heard of John Lennon than of Karl Marx. More Americans could identify comedian-actor Bill Cosby than could name either of their U.S. senators. More people knew who said, "What's up, Doc," "Hi ho, Silver," or "Come up and see me sometime" than "Give me liberty or give me death," "The only thing we have to fear is fear itself," or "Speak softly and carry a big stick." More people knew that Pete Rose was accused of gambling than could name any of the five U.S. senators accused in the late 1980s of unethical conduct in the savings and loan scandal.[12]

> Fewer than half of adults (47 percent) can name their own congressperson.

In 1986, the National Election Survey found that almost 24 percent of the general public did not know who George Bush was or that he was in his second term as vice president of the United States. "People at this level of inattentiveness can have only the haziest idea of the policy alternatives about which pollsters regularly ask, and such ideas as they do have must often be relatively innocent of the effects of exposure to elite discourse," writes UCLA political science professor John R. Zaller.[13]

All of this would appear to be part of a broader trend of public ignorance that extends far beyond politics. Lack of knowledge on simple matters can reach staggering levels. In a 1996 study by the National Science Foundation, fewer than half of American adults polled (47 percent) knew that the earth takes one year to orbit the sun. Only about 9 percent could describe in their own words what a molecule is, and only 21 percent knew what DNA is.

Esoteric information? That's hard to say. One simple science-related question that has grown to have major political importance is whether police ought to genetically tag convicted criminals in the hopes of linking them to unsolved crimes. In other words, should police track the DNA of a convicted burglar to see if he is guilty of other crimes? Obviously issues of privacy and government power are relevant here. Yet how can a poll about this issue make sense if the citizenry doesn't understand the scientific terms of debate? Asking an evaluative question seems pointless.

WHAT ABOUT THE NEXT GENERATION?

The next generation of voters—those who will undoubtedly be asked to answer even tougher questions about politics and science—are hardly doing any better on the basics. A 2000 study by the American Council of Trustees and Alumni found that 81 percent of seniors at the nation's fifty-five top colleges scored a D or F on *high school*-level history exams. It turns out that most college seniors do not know the men or ideas that have shaped American freedom. Here are just a few examples from *Losing America's Memory: Historical Illiteracy in the 21st Century,* focusing on people's lack of knowledge about our First Citizen—the man whose respect for the laws of the infant republic set the standard for virtue and restraint in office:

- Barely one in three students knew that George Washington was the American general at the battle of Yorktown—the battle that won the war for independence.

- Only 42 percent could identify Washington with the line "First in war, first in peace, first in the hearts of his countrymen."

- Only a little more than half knew that Washington's farewell address warned against permanent alliances with foreign governments.

And when it comes to actually explaining the ideas that preserve freedom and restrain government, the college seniors performed just as miserably:

- More than one in three were clueless about the division of power set forth in the U.S. Constitution.

- Only 22 percent of these seniors, from such elite universities as Harvard, Stanford, and the University of California, could identify the source of the phrase "government of the people, by the people, and for the people" (from Lincoln's Gettysburg Address).

- Yet 99 percent of college seniors knew the crude cartoon characters Beavis and Butthead, and 98 percent could identify gangsta rapper Snoop Doggy Dogg.

Failing Civics

Apparent ignorance of basic civics can be especially dangerous. Americans often "project" power onto institutions with little understanding of the Constitution or the law. Almost six in ten Americans (59 percent) think the president, not Congress, has the power to declare war. Thirty-five percent of

Americans believe the president has the power to adjourn Congress at his will. Almost half (49 percent) think he has the power to suspend the Constitution (49 percent). And six in ten think the chief executive appoints judges to the federal courts without the approval of the Senate.[14]

Some political scientists charge that American ignorance tends to help institutions and parties in power. That is hardly the active vigilance by the citizenry that the founders advocated. Political scientists continue to debate the role of ignorance and the future of democracy when voters are so woefully ignorant. As journalist Christopher Shea writes, "Clearly, voter ignorance poses problems for democratic theory: Politicians, the representatives of the people, are being elected by people who do not know their names or their platforms. Elites are committing the nation to major treaties and sweeping policies that most voters don't even know exist."[15]

> Most college seniors do not know the men or ideas that have shaped American freedom.

Of course, all these references to polls that show the extent of voter ignorance might seem to compromise the very thesis of this book. Is there an inherent contradiction in my argument because these polls are being used to show what the public does not know? No. Polls of public knowledge differ substantially from the media-generated polls on public attitudes about policy issues because they are *content-oriented*. Polls of public knowledge plumb the depth of knowledge (however shallow the pool) in a populace that is continually asked to comment on and judge political matters. The criticism in this book focuses on the media's use and misuse of polls. Polling can provide positive benefits, but it is not a surrogate for deliberative democracy. Indeed, how can a populace deliberate without a proper knowledge of simple, uncontestable facts?

For instance, Delli Carpini and Keeter conclude that most Americans make fundamental errors on some of the most contested and heavily covered political questions. "Americans grossly overestimate the average profit made by American corporations, the percentage of the U.S. population that is poor or homeless, and the percentage of the world population that is malnourished," they write. "And, despite twelve years of antiabortion administrations, Americans substantially underestimate the number of abortions performed ever year."[16]

> Most voters in the election booth can't identify a single position of the incumbent, but if they've seen the candidate's name before, that can be enough to secure their vote.

With most voters unable to even name their congressperson or senators during an election year, the clear winner is the establishment candidate. Studies by Larry Bartels at Princeton University show that mere name recognition is enough to give incumbents a 5-percentage-point advantage over challengers: Most voters in the election booth can't identify a single position of the incumbent, but if they've seen the candidate's name before, that can be enough to secure their vote. (In many cases, voters can't even recognize the names of incumbents.)

Media polls are typically searching in vain for hard-nosed public opinion that simply isn't there. Polls force people to say they are leaning toward a particular candidate, but when voters are asked the more open-ended question "Whom do you favor for the presidency?" the number of undecided voters rises. The mere practice, in polling, of naming the candidates yields results that convey a false sense of what voters know. When the Vanishing Voter Project asked voters their presidential preferences without giving the names of candidates, they routinely found that the number of undecided voters was much higher than in media polls. Just three weeks before the 2000 election, 14 percent of voters still hadn't made up their minds.

The Vanishing Voter

The Vanishing Voter Project is a program of the Joan Shorenstein Center on the Press, Politics, and Public Policy at Harvard University. Starting in April 2000, the project randomly sampled registered voters on twelve content-based questions every week. Six questions focused on the Republican nominee's policy positions, and six focused on the Democratic nominee's views.

Unlike most horse-race polls, the Vanishing Voter survey asked voters where Bush stood on gun registration, defense spending, campaign finance restrictions, abortion, and tax credits for health insurance for the poor. The results:

Do you happen to know whether Bush favors or opposes requiring people to register all guns they own?
Favors: 20 percent. Opposes: 34 percent (correct). Haven't heard/Don't know: 46 percent.

Do you happen to know whether Bush favors or opposes a substantial cut in defense spending?
Favors: 9 percent. Opposes: 45 percent (correct). Haven't heard/Don't know: 46 percent.

Do you happen to know whether Bush favors or opposes a ban on very large contributions to political candidates?
Favors: 22 percent. Opposes: 14 percent (correct). Haven't heard/Don't know: 63 percent.

Do you happen to know whether Bush favors or opposes placing new restrictions on abortions?

> *Favors: 33 percent (correct). Opposes: 16 percent. Haven't heard/Don't know: 51 percent.*

> Do you happen to know whether Bush favors or opposes giving low-income people a tax credit that they can use to buy private health insurance?
> *Favors: 31 percent (correct). Opposes: 11 percent. Haven't heard/Don't know: 58 percent.*

Note that a simple majority of Americans could *not* answer any of these questions correctly. On every question, between 9 and 20 percent of voters actually got it *wrong*. Those who said they didn't know or hadn't heard ranged from 46 percent to a staggering 63 percent—three weeks before Election Day.

Not even on income taxes—the linchpin of all three televised presidential debates—could most Americans say whether Bush favored a large tax cut. Just 43 percent said Bush favored a substantial tax cut. Forty-eight percent said they didn't know or hadn't heard. And a 10 percent swath of semiconscious citizens said Bush opposed tax cuts.

Gore fared no better. His six questions probed voters' knowledge of his positions on school choice, Medicare, the environment, Social Security, affirmative action, and foreign policy.

> Do you happen to know whether Gore favors or opposes allowing parents to use tax dollars to send their children to a private or parochial school?
> *Favors: 24 percent. Opposes: 25 percent (correct). Haven't heard/Don't know: 52 percent.*

Education, the issue that the polls claimed to be the number one issue for the electorate, was completely beyond these voters' ken. Gore, the sworn enemy of school vouchers, was mislabeled a *supporter* of school choice by 24 percent of voters polled. Another 52 percent said they hadn't heard about or didn't know his position. Only 25 percent got it right.

Voters' knowledge of Gore's other positions was similarly spotty. His position on prescription drugs for the elderly was the only one that a majority of voters polled managed to get right.

> Do you happen to know whether Gore favors or opposes expanding Medicare for retirees to cover the cost of prescription drugs?
> *Favors: 59 percent (correct). Opposes: 3 percent. Haven't heard/Don't know: 39 percent.*

Even then, only 59 percent were on target. Not coincidentally, this was also the most popular campaign issue with the media the month before—lending credence to the idea that polls function more as measuring devices for media saturation than as measures of well-grounded opinion.

Even Gore's decade-old, loudly trumpeted environmentalism was a mystery to voters:

> Do you happen to know whether Gore favors or opposes a ban on offshore oil drilling in federal waters as a way of protecting the environment?
> *Favors: 30 percent (correct). Opposes: 14 percent. Haven't heard/Don't know: 56 percent.*

> Do you happen to know whether Gore favors or opposes allowing workers to invest a portion of their payroll taxes in private retirement accounts rather than having all of it go toward Social Security?
> *Favors: 17 percent. Opposes: 28 percent (correct). Haven't heard/Don't know: 55 percent.*

> Do you happen to know whether Gore favors or opposes affirmative action policies that would allow the use of race

as a consideration in college admissions and government contracts?
Favors: 25 percent (correct). Opposes: 11 percent. Haven't heard/Don't know: 64 percent.

Do you happen to know whether Gore favors or opposes placing substantial restrictions on trade with China because of its human rights record?
Favors: 14 percent. Opposes: 18 percent (correct). Haven't heard/Don't know: 69 percent.

The results of this poll, taken just three weeks before a presidential election, were staggering. After three debates, one very substantive vice presidential debate, two political conventions, and more than $20 million in campaign ads, just one-third to barely one-half of all voters could correctly match one of the candidates to his campaign ideas, and only after being given twelve chances to do so. Only once did a majority of voters pass. Yet long before the conventions or the debates, media pollsters insisted on probing and journalists insisted on covering this so-called public opinion.

But as discouraging as the October 15, 2000, poll was, it was nothing compared with the previous months' surveys. Voter ignorance was so widespread that anywhere from 60 to 70 percent of voters admitted they didn't know or hadn't heard where the candidates stood on the issues.

Magical Polling: The Illusion of a Knowledgeable Public

Even when polling covers subjects on which a person should have direct knowledge, it can yield misleading results because of basic ignorance. The nonpartisan Center for Studying

Health System Change (HSC) found that how people rate their health care is attributable to the type of plan they *think* they are in more than their actual health insurance. The center asked twenty thousand privately insured people what they thought of their coverage, their doctor, and their treatment. But instead of just taking their opinions and impressions, the center also looked at what coverage each respondent actually had.[17]

Nearly a quarter of Americans misidentified the coverage they had. Eleven percent didn't know they were in an HMO. And another 13 percent thought they were in an HMO but were *not*. Yet when people believed they were in a much-maligned HMO (even when they actually had another kind of insurance), their perceived satisfaction with their health care was lower than that of people who believed they had non-HMO coverage (even when they were in an HMO). Similarly, on nearly all ten measures studied by the center, those HMO enrollees who thought they had a different kind of insurance gave satisfaction ratings similar to those who actually had those other kinds of insurance.

Once center researchers adjusted for incorrect self-identification, the differences between HMO and non-HMO enrollees nearly vanished. Could it be that HMOs are victims of negative publicity and media-driven sensationalism? Certainly some of the frustration is well deserved. But what is critical here is that even on something as personal as health care, citizens display a striking and debilitating ignorance that quietly undermines many polling results.

> Even on something as personal as health care, citizens display a striking and debilitating ignorance that quietly undermines many polling results.

After looking at the carnage of polls that test voter knowledge rather than impressions, James L. Payne concluded in his 1991 book *The Culture of Spending:*

[S]urveys have repeatedly found that voters are remarkably ignorant about even simple, dramatic features of the political landscape. The vast majority of voters cannot recall the names of congressional candidates in the most recent election; they cannot use the labels "liberal" and "conservative" meaningfully; they do not know which party controls Congress; they are wildly wrong about elementary facts about the federal budget; and they do not know how their congressmen vote on even quite salient policy questions. In other words, they are generally incapable of rewarding or punishing their congressman for his action on spending bills.[18]

Ignorance of basic facts such as a candidate's name or position isn't the only reason to question the efficacy of polling in such a dispiriting universe. Because polls have become "players in the political process," their influence is felt in the policy realm, undercutting efforts to educate because they assume respondents' knowledge and focus on the horse race. Is it correct to say that Americans oppose or support various policies when they don't even have a grasp of basic facts relating to those policies? For instance, in 1995, GrassRoots Research found that 83 percent of those polled underestimated the average family's tax burden. Taxes for a four-person family earning $35,000 are 54 percent higher than most people think. Naturally when practical-minded Americans look at political issues, their perceptions of reality influence which solutions they find acceptable. If they perceive that there are fewer abortions or lower taxes than there really are, these misperceptions may affect the kinds of policy prescriptions they endorse. They might change their views if introduced to the facts. In this sense, the unreflective reporting on public opinion about these policy issues is deceptive.

The *Wall Street Journal* editorial page provides another example of how ignorance affects public debate. Media reports during the 1995 struggle between the Republicans in Congress and the Clinton White House continually asserted that the public strongly opposed the GOP's efforts to slow the growth of Medicare spending. A poll by Public Opinion Strategies asked one thousand Americans not what they felt but what they actually *knew* about the GOP plan. Twenty-seven percent said they thought the GOP would cut Medicare spending by $4,000 per recipient. Almost one in four (24 percent) said it would keep spending the same. Another 25 percent didn't know. Only 22 percent knew the correct answer: The plan would increase spending to $6,700 per recipient.

Public Opinion's pollsters then told respondents that true result of the GOP plan and explained: "[U]nder the plan that recently passed by Congress, spending on Medicare will increase 45 percent over the next seven years, which is twice the projected rate of inflation." How did such hard facts change public opinion about Medicare solutions? Six of ten Americans said that the GOP's proposed Medicare spending was too *high*. Another 29 percent said it was about right. Only 2 percent said it was too *low*.

Indeed polling and the media may gain their ability to influence results from voter ignorance. When a polling question introduces new facts (or any facts at all), voters are presented with a reframed political issue and thus may have a new opinion. Voters are continually asked about higher spending, new programs, and the best way to solve social ills with government spending. But how does the knowledge base (or lack of knowledge) affect the results of a polling question? That is simply unknown. When asked in a June 2000 *Washington Post* poll how much money the federal government gives to the nation's public schools, only 31 percent chose the correct answer ("less than a quarter"). Although

> Polling and the media may gain their ability to influence results from voter ignorance.

only 10 percent admitted to not knowing the correct answer, fully 60 percent of registered voters claimed they knew but were wrong. Is there any doubt that voters' knowledge, or lack thereof, affects the debate about whether to raise school spending to ever higher levels?

Reporters often claim that the public supports various policies, and they use such sentiment as an indicator of the electoral prospects of favored candidates. But this, too, can be misleading. Take, for instance, the results of a survey taken by The Polling Company for the Center for Security Policy about the Strategic Defense Initiative. Some 54 percent of respondents thought that the U.S. military had the capability to destroy a ballistic missile before it could hit an American city and do damage. Another 20 percent didn't know or refused to answer. Only 27 percent correctly said that the U.S. military could not destroy a missile.

What's interesting is that although 70 percent of those polled said they were concerned about the possibility of ballistic missile attack, the actual level of ignorance was very high. The Polling Company went on to tell those polled that "government documents indicate that the U.S. military cannot destroy even a single incoming missile." The responses were interesting. Nearly one in five said they were "shocked and angry" by the revelation. Another 28 percent said they were "very surprised," and 17 percent were "somewhat surprised." Only 22 percent said they were "not surprised at all." Finally 14 percent were "skeptical because [they] believe that the documents are inaccurate."

Beyond simply skewing poll results, ignorance is actually amplified by polling. Perhaps the most amazing example of the extent of ignorance can be found in Larry Sabato's 1981 book *The Rise of Political Consultants*. Citizens were asked: "Some people say the 1975 Public Affairs Act should be repealed. Do you agree or disagree that it should be repealed?" Nearly one in four (24 percent) said they wanted it repealed.

Another 19 percent wanted it to remain in effect. Fifty-seven percent didn't know what should be done. What's interesting is that there was no such thing as the 1975 Public Affairs Act. But for 43 percent of those polled, simply asking that question was enough to create public opinion.

Ignorance can threaten even the most democratic institutions and safeguards. In September 1997, the Center for Media and Public Affairs conducted one of the largest surveys ever on American views of the Fourth Estate. Fully 84 percent of Americans are willing to "turn to the government to require that the news media give equal coverage to all sides of controversial issues." Seven in ten back court-imposed fines for inaccurate or biased reporting. And just over half (53 percent) think that journalists should be licensed. Based on sheer numbers—in the absence of the rule of law and dedication to the Bill of Rights—there is enough support to put curbs on the free speech that most journalists (rightly) consider one of the most important bulwarks of liberty.

Ignorance of the Process of Polling

Ignorance extends to the polls themselves. Most Americans don't understand the workings of polls, particularly sampling. In 1998, University of Michigan researchers interviewed 1,001 adults about the credibility of poll findings. Only 15 percent thought that a sample of 1,500 or 2,000 people "can accurately reflect the views of the population." Almost half (45 percent) of those polled said they thought "public opinion polls are [typically] right in reporting how people feel about issues." But 37 percent agreed with the statement that "polls do more harm than good in our society," with 29 percent saying that polls do not have a very good record of predicting election outcomes.

Then again it depends on how you ask the question. Two other polls came up with quite different results. What's truly bizarre is that a 1999 Center on Public Attitudes study found that many of those same Americans who think Congress should more closely follow the polls do not actually trust those polls:

> When you read about a poll, how much confidence do you have that you can judge whether it was done in a fair and scientific manner—a great deal, a fair amount, not very much, or none at all?
> *A bare majority (50.4 percent) said they had a "fair amount" of certainty, with another 5.8 percent saying they had a "great deal." But 29.8 percent said they had "not very much" confidence, and 12.7 percent said "none at all." That's 42.5 percent in the camp of the skeptics.*

A Gallup poll conducted just six weeks later yielded somewhat similar findings on public skepticism about polls, even though Gallup found the public distrustful of politicians who consult polls. Gallup asked:

> Generally speaking, how much do you trust what you see or hear in the public opinion polls—a great deal, a fair amount, not very much, or none at all?
> *When asked this way, 4 percent believed a "great deal" in the polls and 34 percent a "fair amount." Fully 45 percent did not trust the polls very much, and another 16 percent said they had no trust at all. That's 61 percent of Americans in the camp of skeptics or outright disbelievers.*

Taken at their word, these people think they know what they are talking about:

> Just from your own standpoint, how much do you know about how the polls work—a great deal, a fair amount, not very much, or nothing at all?

> One out of ten respondents said that they knew a "great deal" about polls. Another 44 percent judged themselves as knowing a "fair amount." Some 38 percent said they knew "not very much," and 7 percent admitted they knew "nothing at all."

Where do these experts of "great" and "fair" knowledge really score? Gallup asked an open-ended, content-oriented question:

> By any chance, do you happen to know roughly how many people are interviewed in a typical national opinion poll?
> Nearly half (49 percent) said they had no opinion. Twelve percent said the typical survey sample is fewer than 500 people. Three percent said 500, just 2 percent said 501 to 999, and 12 percent said 1,000. Another 2 percent said the typical survey interviews 1,001 to 1,999 respondents. Finally a stalwart band comprising 20 percent of American adults believed, both optimistically and wrongly, that the typical poll uses more than 2,000 respondents.

Despite this ignorance about a device that has had a profound effect on American democracy, polling still plays an important, if not hypnotic, role. How do voters evaluate polls, then? According to a study by the University of Maryland's Stanley Presser, the public attraction to what other people are thinking is policy voyeurism. Presser writes, "[J]udgments about polls are significantly affected by whether the poll results coincide with an individual's own preferences," and that "limits the extent to which

"Judgments about polls are significantly affected by whether the poll results coincide with an individual's own preferences."

poll reports, despite their ubiquity, can shape people's assessments of what the public believes." Thus polls are given credence not through reflection or deliberation but simply through egoism. The result is a kind of unrepentant ignorance that furthers mob thinking by strengthening the majority and disheartening the minority.

The Power of the Pollster: A Little Knowledge Works Wonders

In an era when Americans have neither the time nor the interest to track politics closely, the power of the pollster to shape public opinion is almost unparalleled when united with the media agenda. As media critic S. Robert Lichter notes, "Polls are both information and ammunition for politicians and the media. People who want the world to look a certain way can create that world to some extent by using polling. When you take a poll, you are creating a temporary opinion and you don't know how it is going to affect ideas already out there."[19]

For elected leaders, voter ignorance is something they have to confront when they attempt to make a case for new policies or reforms. But for the media, ignorance isn't an obstacle. It's an opportunity for those asking the questions—whether pollster or media polling director—to drive debate. As more time is devoted to media pundits, journalists, and pollsters, and less to candidates and leaders, the effect is a negative one: Public opinion becomes more important as arbiter for the chattering classes. But in a knowledge vacuum, public opinion also becomes more plastic and more subject to manipulation, however well intentioned.

Pollsters often try to bridge the gap in public knowledge by providing basic definitions of terms as part of their questions. But this presents a new problem: By writing the questions, pollsters are put in a position of power, particularly when those questions will be used in a media story. The story—if the poll is the story—is limited by the questions asked, the definitions supplied, and the answers that respondents are given to choose from.

The elevation of opinion without context or reference to knowledge exacerbates a problem of modern democracies. The dismissal of truth as the coin of the realm in public deliberation puts government affairs in the hands of those with the biggest media megaphone. Self-expression may work in NEA-funded art, but it robs the political process of the communication and discussion that marries compromise with principle. Clearly "opinion" isn't the appropriate word for the melange of impressions and sentiment that are presented as the public's beliefs in countless newspaper and television stories. If poll respondents lack a solid grasp of the facts, surveys give us little more than narcissistic opinion.

> As history has so painfully shown, when truth is sacrificed for political expediency, civilizations can be put in peril.

As history has so painfully shown, when truth is sacrificed for political expediency, civilizations can be put in peril. As intelligent and precise thinking declines, all that remains is a chaos of ideologies in which the lowest human appetites rule. In her essay "Truth and Politics," historian Hannah Arendt writes: "Facts inform opinions, and opinions, inspired by different interests and passions, can differ widely and still be legitimate as long as they respect factual truth. Freedom of opinion is a farce unless factual information is guaranteed and facts themselves are not in dispute."

One of the dangers of polling is that it assumes and often controls the presentation of the relevant facts. As a blunt instrument, the pollster's questions fail to explore what the contrary data may be. This is one reason that public opinion can differ so widely from one poll to another. When the citizens of a republic lack basic knowledge of political facts and cannot process ideas critically, uninformed opinion becomes even more potent in driving people. Worse, when the media fail to think critically about the lines of dispute on political questions, polls that are supposed to explore opinion will simplify and even mislead political leaders as well as the electorate.

Let us return to a primary thesis of this book: The modern proponents of polls consider polls to be valuable because they yield insights into what voters think. But this claim ignores the dynamic process by which a representative democracy discusses and weighs decisions. When the media drive opinion by constant polling, the assumption of an educated public undermines the process of public deliberation that actually educates voters. Ideas are no longer honed, language isn't refined, and debate is truncated. The common ground needed for compromise and peaceful action is eroded because the discussion about facts and the parameters of the question are lost. In the frenzy to judge who wins and who loses, the media erode what it is to be a democracy. Moments of change become opportunities for spin, not for new, bold responses to the exigencies of history.

If this line of logic is correct, then not only are polls influenced, shaped, and even dominated by voter ignorance, but so is political debate. The evidence shows that ignorance is being projected into public debate because of the pervasiveness of polls. Polls are leading to the democratization of ignorance in the public square by ratifying ill-formed opinions, with the march of the mob instigated by an impatient and unreflective media. Polls—especially in an

> Polls are leading to the democratization of ignorance in the public square by ratifying ill-formed opinions, with the march of the mob instigated by an impatient and unreflective media.

age marked by their proliferation—are serving as broadcasting towers of ignorance.

Political science professor Rogan Kersh notes, "Public ignorance and apathy toward most policy matters have been constant (or have grown worse) for over three decades. Yet the same period has seen increasing reliance on finely tuned instruments for measuring popular opinion, and more vigorous applications of the results in policy making."[20] And here is the paradox in the Age of Polls: Pollsters and political scientists are still unclear about the full consequences of running a republic on the basis of polls—polls that can be manipulated by framing their questions. The cost of voter ignorance is high, especially in a nation with a vast and sprawling government that, even for the most plugged-in elites, is too complicated to understand. Media polling that does not properly inform viewers and readers of its limitations serves only to give the facade of a healthy democracy, while consultants, wordsmiths, and polling units gently massage questions, set the news agenda, and then selectively report results. Even for the most strident supporter of polling as the best tool of democracy, this state of affairs is manifestly undemocratic. It is like the marionette player who claims (however invisible the strings) that the puppet moves on his own.

CHAPTER SIX

The Dangers of Ignorance
Be Afraid, Very Afraid

*Polls measure opinion, belief, and impression—
but only occassionally admit the depth or costs of
ignorance.*

■ ■ ■

THERE'S AN OLD JOKE about the basketball team owner
who takes aside a troubled player who once had brilliant
prospects. "I can't figure out what your problem is," he
says. "Are you ignorant or just apathetic?" The player lack-
adaisically responds, "I don't know, and I don't care."
When it comes to politics, the average American is just like
that athlete. It's hard to find out where ignorance ends and
apathy begins.

For the most part, journalists, academics, and especially
media polling ignore the implications of disconnected,

apathetic, and uninformed voters. As political science profes-sor Rogan Kersh of Syracuse University writes, "[S]ocial sci-entists seem inclined to overlook or explain away the dangers accompanying an uninformed populace."[1] Even when the civic ignorance is reported, it's easy to miss the overall influ-ence of voter ignorance on the flux of conflicting and soft atti-tudes called public opinion. John R. Zaller writes in *The Nature and Origins of Mass Opinion:*

> [N]o one knows quite what to make of the multiple va-garies of mass opinion. Most analysts truly believe that public opinion is a more substantial entity than is indi-cated by the evidence. . . . [A]nd yet gloomy indications are all too real. Being unable to square all the facts with what one believes is true, one simply puts aside the trou-bling evidence for the time being, leaving it to survey methodologies to work out, and writes about those as-pects of public opinion one does understand. An obvious problem with this approach is that it conceals informa-tion from the reader. Another is that it relinquishes the opportunity of making realistic statements about how mass opinion, in all of its elusiveness, forms and changes.[2]

The consequences of ignorance and apathy are, first and foremost, to create an obstacle for pollsters trying to express meaningful, well-grounded public opinion. For the media, it may not matter that public opinion can be distorted by lack of information or substantive knowledge, but for the conscien-tious pollster, ignorance and apathy are a serious problem in any poll. Numbers do not public opinion make. To portray the public as more informed and opinionated than they are is to hide the sandy foundations of public opinion for profit and media opportunism.

Searching for Quality Needles in Ignorant Haystacks

In *Coming to Public Judgment,* professional pollster Daniel Yankelovich studies the relationship between public ignorance and public opinion with great care. The issue of voter intelligence and awareness concerns "nothing less than the ability of Americans to govern themselves in keeping with the principles of democracy."[3] Yankelovich admits that voters lack specific knowledge about politics, but does not regard the ignorance of the average voter as reason enough to dismiss the value of public opinion polling. "I have come to the conclusion that equating quality opinion with being well informed is a serious mistake. . . . To assume that public opinion is invariably improved by inundating people with information grossly distorts the role of information. A society operating on this assumption misconstrues the nature and purpose of public opinion in a democracy."[4]

> The issue of voter intelligence and awareness concerns "nothing less than the ability of Americans to govern themselves in keeping with the principles of democracy."

Unfortunately, few media pollsters are so frank. The issue before us, however, isn't whether the media and politicians should deluge voters with useless political factoids. If anything, the kind of horse-race coverage that characterizes modern journalism probably aggravates the problem of uninformed voters. Under the modern imperatives of reportage, journalists bombard voters with useless information, insider accounts, and Monday-morning quarterbacking. Entire debates about Medicare funding, spending battles, and foreign policy can take place with very little reference to specific details or critical facts. Yet the media will still poll voters on these matters.

Disconnected information or unnecessary details aren't the best way to return mental vitality to a body politic plagued by ignorance. The problem is deeper than that. It isn't just a populace disconnected from government, it is a journalistic corps disconnected from those they purportedly serve. The first steps to understanding the problem require a little humility and a little realism. Voters are asked to give their opinions on political matters because they are members of a democratic community. Their opinion matters because their vote matters. But we should remember that their sacred expression of opinion might be based on little more than impressions, gut feelings, fragments of knowledge, or simple prejudice. In fact, their knowledge may be limited to just the information provided in the questions in the poll. As a pollster chooses and presents a few critical facts, the result is public opinion shaped, not always reported.

Yankelovich, however, wants to find that elusive and true public opinion. He recognizes ignorance as a serious challenge to the pollster. He attempts to define the nature of the problem of voter ignorance by asking what is meant by quality public opinion. According to polling pioneer George Gallup, quality public opinion was the Holy Grail of polling. He wrote in 1947 that he wanted a "method in opinion research to distinguish between people's 'snap judgments' and opinions that have been carefully thought through—an unmistakable dimension of quality."[5] Yankelovich's solution is for pollsters to distinguish between "mass opinion" and "public judgments" by defining *mass opinion* as "the defects of inconsistency, volatility, and nonresponsibility."[6]

Nonresponsibility refers to the citizen's "failure to take the consequences of their views into account." This means that in cases where they are asked a question, they do not see the consequences or unintended side effects of a particular course of action. For example, if respondents are asked their opinions on a spending initiative, they are nonresponsible if their answers change depending on whether they understand that a specific spending initiative might require cuts in another program or unleash higher taxes. Respondents are responsible when they say "yes" to a policy question with direct knowledge of what is being sacrificed or demanded to put that policy into action. Yankelovich labels these responsible responses "public judgment" for good-quality public opinion that is "stable, consistent, and responsible."[7]

Yankelovich believes that "By focusing on public judgment we can crawl out from under the quality-as-information trap. We can begin to shape a concept of public opinion in which quality is defined by evidence that the public has faced up to the consequences of its convictions."[8]

There is much to praise in Yankelovich's more nuanced view of what exactly makes quality public opinion, especially in light of the ample evidence of public ignorance on basic policy matters. But what Yankelovich recommends is a kind of public opinion survey vastly different from those used by the media today. Overnight polls and shallow questions may get instant results and mesmerizing numbers, and give the Sunday morning talk shows plenty of drama to discuss, but the results don't often stand up when the wording is altered or issues are framed in another way.

For this reason, Yankelovich considers media polls incomplete and sloppy, and reports about public knowledge greatly misleading. He suggests three tests for determining whether a poll is just a report of mass opinion or a credible insight into public judgment:

> One test is to ask questions in opinion polls in several slightly different ways that do not change the essential meaning of the question. If people change their answers in response to slight shifts in question wording[,] this is a sure

sign that their opinions are volatile. A second test is to plant questions that probe for inconsistencies and contradictions—another sign of mass opinion. My third test is to confront respondents with difficult trade-offs that directly challenge wishful thinking. This approach presents people with the consequences of their views and then measures their reactions.[9]

The tests put forward by Yankelovich take public ignorance and apathy as serious obstacles for every poll to overcome. In his quest to challenge and test public opinion, Yankelovich searches for a deeper pulse of belief than that which courses on the surface of most polling stories. He isn't looking for quickie ratifications of one policy idea or another. Nor does he seek summary judgments on personalities or scandals as so many journalistic polls do. Ignorance and apathy undermine polls because they are the often the reasons why opinions are incoherent and soft. Yankelovich sees the challenge for the pollster and the journalist as finding ways to work around and through such volatility, impression, and prejudice and then digging for the real beliefs of voters. Unfortunately, for most media polls, such caution in the face of public ignorance is simply dismissed as irrelevant. Most media organizations find it more convenient and more profitable to synchronize the Greek chorus of headlines and journalistic outrage with the supposed support of readers and viewers. In such cases, the malleability of the public using cleverly designed questions is just too tempting.

Are Citizens Smarter for Tuning Out?

But we must ask, if quality public opinion is elusive because of ignorant and apathetic voters, then why are voters ignorant and apathetic? Lack of basic knowledge extends to the most fundamental political facts, ideological definitions, even to the most common civic terms used in polling questions. Media polls often assume political knowledge that doesn't exist in the body politic (or manipulate that lack of knowledge through selective information). As was noted in chapter 5, only 17 percent of adults polled could even give a basic definition of a school voucher, despite a decade of debate and polling about the subject. Yet at the same time, media stories cite polls that the public believes that improving education should be a number one or number two political priority.

> The political system offers little reward for the individual who devotes time and resources to becoming well versed in government affairs.

How can this be? If voters really cared about an issue, wouldn't they take the time to become educated about it? And if polls are the voice of democracy, shouldn't journalists learn from such polls and then report more stories about the nuts and bolts of politics?

In 1957, political science professor Anthony Downs introduced the idea of "rational ignorance" to put the disinterest of voters into the context of his economic theory of democracy. His theory attempted to explain voting decisions and electoral choices in the same language and with the same benefit-maximizing mind-set that drive economic decision-making. He posited that voters eventually realize that their vote isn't likely to be decisive in electoral contests. Because there are so many other voters, the chances of actually having a say are very small. The political system, from a cost-benefit analysis point of view, offers little reward for the individual voter who devotes the time and resources to becoming well versed in government affairs.

Consider for a moment the daunting task of sifting through and judging the relevant bits of information required to make a decision about what direction government policy ought to take. As journalist James Bovard writes, "Citizens' ignorance may be increasing as fast as politicians' spending."[10] The problem isn't just that ignorance and spending are running next to each other. Ignorance and the resulting disconnect may be driving spending, or at least allowing its unchecked growth.

Since the New Deal and especially the Great Society, the incentive to follow politics has slowly withered as the size of government has grown and its ability to respond to the citizen has disintegrated. Media polling offers the illusion of control over this behemoth, feeding the growth of government as polls and stories urge the public to support more regulations and more laws and more bureaucracy to fix the lack of accountability and market distortions of the welfare state. Rarely do polls or articles create pressure to reduce the size of government or cut programs. Just as the size, complexity, and sheer scope of federal, state, and local government has made the task of the conscientious voter more difficult, journalists have become unconscious to the waste, unresponsiveness, and unwieldy nature of modern bureaucracy. Instead, journalists scour for new outrages that will demand new programs, which are then tested in new polls.

Then polls ask us for our preferences about what an individual politician should do or what dream policy should be enacted, but this is a fantasyland when compared to the gritty reality. Indeed, the hypnotic attraction of polling may come from the seeming ability for the angry or disconnected voter to demand immediate change despite political reality or practical problems such as the separation of powers, parliamentary procedure, even the Bill of Rights. Polls are often used to judge politicians or parties, especially in those cases where a politician is standing in the way of legislation or ideas favored by journalists and those writing the polls. But trying to ascribe blame in the complicated minuet of the two parties can be difficult and, when in the hands of pollsters, highly misleading.

For instance, on the issue of gun control, media stories typically focus on irresponsible acts and bloody crimes with guns and rarely note the defensive or heroic use of firearms. Likewise, polling questions typically focus on the merits of gun control as opposed to the protection of the Second Amendment. In this familiar schema, Americans are often asked to pass judgment on the National Rifle Association, a group that ranks second only to tobacco companies in the spread of evil, according to liberal theology and the average journalist's universe. Polls are often used to show how politicians are out of step with the American public when they side with NRA positions, particularly after a shooting tragedy.

On the surface this seems like a perfect opportunity for polling to push politicians to "do something about guns in the schools." But often the war in the headlines and then in the polls has little in common with the reality of legislative debate and deliberation. For years, the NRA was assailed for opposing then–President Clinton's anti-gun legislation, because the group wouldn't back a five-day waiting period. In actuality, the NRA wanted an instant background check instead. But only the most astute political observers could track such developments and even then, only with well-developed political beliefs, would they be able to hold accountable the party that was stalling gun control or stopping new anti-crime efforts. Often political debate goes nowhere for a reason. Stalemate is valuable as a fundraising tool, with parties taking antipodal positions to further their other efforts. One of the consequences of an ignorant electorate is that they cannot ascribe blame, punish, or reward politicians because they don't have the knowledge to do so. Yankelovich's suggestion for more in-depth and carefully constructed polls is an excellent starting point and an indictment of most media polls. But it only takes us so far. The need for an informed populace reminds us of the critical role of representatives in the process. Even if voters learn about issues through well-crafted poll questions that challenge their priorities and beliefs, this is hardly a replacement for democratic discussion and debate. Every day, politicians are forced to reckon with ignorance and must carefully explain their ideas, fundamental terms, and answer basic questions as a way to communicate with voters. But a sample of 900 adults randomly selected by pollsters who assume broad knowledge and strong opinions is not more representative than the hundreds of elected officials, thousands of free associations and interest groups, and the hundreds of thousands of activists who take the time to be informed and get involved. It is seriously misleading.

Public ignorance and alienation are something of a paradox. The same telecommunications advances that have made polling more extensive, faster, and cheaper have brought more news and information to the average citizen. In addition, with the smoke-filled rooms and power politics of the two major parties weakened, voters have more say in which candidates are selected. With more Web sites, cable news channels, and radio talk shows than ever before, the voluntary retreat from being informed seems counterintuitive. Many scholars see the attrition of political parties and the dissatisfaction with candidates as the cause of disconnection and voluntary ignorance. Others finger media cynicism and invasive political coverage as the cause of disillusion. Whatever the driving force, voters aren't just ignorant, they are voting less and tuning out more. Even in an era in which government is larger than it has ever been and federal power is more extensive, voters show little interest in mastering the details or learning the basics of the bureaucratic creature than now inhabits every aspect of their lives. While polling and government programs have grown, voter discontent and alienation have, too. In 1960, voter turnout reached an all-time high of 65 percent. In 1996, voter turnout was a record-low 51 percent for a presidential contest. In the early 1960s, three-quarters of Americans said that the government could usually or almost always "be trusted to do the right thing." Less than a quarter of Americans now think the government can be trusted to do the right thing.

Arming the Electorate: Education

Although the theory of "rational ignorance" helps explain alienation and intellectual disinterest, the aggregate effect of rationally ignorant citizens is a populace asleep and vulnerable. Public ignorance doesn't just undermine the credibility of many public opinion polls, it makes voters more defenseless against media manipulation and political spin in the framing of issues.

The many dangers stemming from an intellectually dormant electorate isn't a new idea, it is just forgotten.

The framers of the U.S. Constitution believed that citizen ignorance was a threat to the long-term health of the Republic, and they took precautions to ensure that the people were informed about what their officials were doing in office. We've already explored how the framers constructed a system of laws, institutions, and legal machinery to check the growth of government and limit the ability of any single group or person from monopolizing political power. But checks and balances weren't enough. The dark and designing nature of human ambition made it impossible for a perfect political system to rule over corrupt men.

Whether Federalist or Anti-Federalist, Hamiltonian or Jeffersonian, that first generation of the United States of America was united by a common desire to build a better and more learned citizenry. The Constitution sought to rebuild the balancing act of the British constitution in which the aristocracy, monarchy, and commons checked each other. But because the new nation was a republic, the framers also sought to promote deliberation and learned debate. The framers wanted elected officials to have a sufficient time in office and in the various institutions to acquire information about the needs of the nation. In addition, the framers wanted frequent elections, public debate, and a free press to disperse knowledge, to hold officials accountable, and to educate the citizenry.

In 1789 in the *First Inaugural Address,* George Washington stated: "The preservation of the sacred fire of liberty and the destiny of the republican model of government are justly considered as deeply, perhaps as finally, staked on the experiment entrusted to the hands of the American people."

Thomas Jefferson echoed this sentiment, saying, "I know no safe depositary of the ultimate powers of the society but the people themselves; and if we think them not enlightened enough to exercise their control with a wholesome discretion, the remedy is not to take it from them, but to inform their discretion by education. This is the true corrective of abuses of constitutional power."[11]

Even though many of the founders leaned toward a less democratic, more constitutional system, their faith in the possibilities of American republicanism did not waver. Even Alexander Hamilton, who advocated a constitutional monarchy at the Federal Convention, turned ink into eloquence, warning the American people of the challenge before them:

> It has been frequently remarked, that, it seems to have been reserved to the people of this country, to decide by their conduct and example, the important question, whether societies of men are really capable or not, of establishing good government from reflection and choice, or whether they are forever destined to depend, for their political constitutions, on accident and force.[12]

But as wary as the founders were of pure democracy, they were positive about the role of education and virtue. They wanted a nation based on the rule of law presided over by deliberative statesmen who were policed by an educated citizenry. This is what Hamilton meant by "good government" established on the basis of "reflection and choice." Hamilton, icon of Federalism, saw education and a vigilant populace as the decisive bulwark to freedom in a republic. And he was by no means the only one. Almost to the man, the founders spoke and wrote with a desire to educate and even persuade their fellow patriots to the cause of republicanism and liberty. But the virtue of education, in their minds, went beyond our practical notions of education.

Most Americans don't think of education in terms of republicanism and liberty. Instead, we value education as a subdivision of the economy. Better education means a more competitive worker, more efficient economy, and a more prosperous nation. But the founders believed that an ignorant electorate would be defenseless against the silver tongue of demagogues (today's poll-obsessed politicians) who promise everything, in the face of law, reason, or good sense.

Thomas Jefferson gives perhaps the most frank and well known of the Founding Fathers' thoughts on education—a position that contrasts greatly with the theories that attempt to rationalize or explain away voter ignorance as harmless. "If a nation expects to be ignorant and free, in a state of civilization, it expects what never was and never will be," he wrote in 1816.[13]

An anonymous Federalist writing as "The Worcester Speculator" in 1787 echoed this sentiment. The author saw a

> The founders believed that an ignorant electorate would be defenseless against the silver tongue of demagogues who promise everything, in the face of law, reason, or good sense.

direct relationship between education and liberty. "If America would flourish as a republic, she need only attend to the education of her youth. Learning is the *palladium* of her rights—as this flourishes her greatness will increase."[14] The author describes the role of every citizen as a guardian of the public trust, carefully watching the actions of public officials. "The members of a republic are mutual guards upon each other's conduct: Should a few, from ambitious motives, endeavor to subvert the constitution or aggrandize themselves at the public expense, the community at large would take the alarm, and with united efforts frustrate their designs."[15]

On this founding view, every citizen must be educated and aware, he continues: "But every one, whether in office or not, ought to become acquainted with the principles of civil liberty, the constitution of his country, and the rights of mankind in general. Where learning prevails in a community, liberality of sentiment, and zeal for the public good, are the grand characteristics of the people."[16] Should the citizenry become ignorant, they will be "prey to internal usurpers."[17]

The Constitution is supposed to channel the disagreements and factional sentiments of the public square into reasoned and respectful resolution. And ideally, education and virtue should play a role in tempering vice and ambition in the citizenry. Together the virtues of the public and private realms of human conduct strengthen each other and limit the exercise of lawless power, the temporary delusions of the masses, or the ambition of the designing.

While the founders might have been critical of democracy and its abysmal track record through the annals of history, at bottom, they used it as a spur to cultivate a better-informed citizenry. No one better exemplifies this gritty realism than John Adams, the resident philosopher of Quincy, Massachusetts, who believed that liberty was impossible when the people descended into ignorance and intellectual indolence.

"Education," he wrote, "is more indispensable, and must be more general, under a free government than any other."

Part of that civic education required citizens to gain a consciousness about the rule of law. Adams was the first man to use *republic* as a term of approbation, rather than as a synonym for anarchic democracy. Before him, most used the term in a derogatory sense. But for Adams a republic was "government of laws, not men." Furthermore, he stressed, "All other government than that of permanent known laws, is the government of mere will and pleasure, whether it be exercised by one, a few, or many."

When education and knowledge among the people disintegrate, the inevitable result is tyranny. In *A Dissertation on the Canon and Feudal Law,* Adams makes clear that the Dark Ages arose primarily from the ignorance of the people. Here we must understand the Dark Ages not just as a period of history but as a state of enslavement to a capricious and unchecked elite. "But the fact is certain; and wherever a general knowledge and sensibility have prevailed among the people, arbitrary government and every kind of oppression have lessened and disappeared in proportion," Adams wrote.[18]

Tyranny reigned in the Dark Ages, Adams thought, because of the unholy marriage of the religious powers and the state. All knowledge and law were in the hands of an elite with an incentive to keep the people ignorant and oppressed (ignorance being a form of oppression). The noble orders and the church worked hand in hand: "All these opinions they were enabled to spread and rivet among the people by reducing their minds into a state of sordid ignorance and staring timidity, and by infusing into them a religious horror of letters and knowledge."[19]

Adams saw education as an ally to the continued defense of liberty. The two leaned on each other because education spurred men to watch the public affairs of those in power. "Be it remembered, however, that liberty must at all hazards be supported," he wrote. "And liberty cannot be preserved without a general knowledge among the people, who have a right, from the frame of their nature, to knowledge, as their great Creator, who has given them understandings, and a desire to know; but besides this, they have a right, an indisputable, unalienable, *indefeasible*, divine right to that most dread and envied kind of knowledge, I mean of the characters and conduct of their rulers."[20]

This belief in education as a means for enlightening the citizenry to good government and watchful vigilance was common among the founders. It was one of the reasons the founding generation supported public education—a revolutionary concept at the time—so vigorously. Political scientist and historian Richard D. Brown writes that eighteenth-century America's views of an informed populace was a turning point in history:

> What was crucial in this viewpoint was not the belief that elite education supplied benefits to the whole society, a view that had been a commonplace since the Renaissance. What was new, and potentially radical, was the idea that the very same values, ideas, and information might penetrate and permeate the entire social order, if only in attenuated form, and that the minds as well as the manners of the lower ranks matter.[21]

During the Revolution, John Adams's cousin Samuel defended the idea of an informed, aroused, and educated citizenry. In November 1775, Samuel Adams attacked the policy of those towns that had dismissed schoolmasters because of the costs of defending themselves against Great Britain. This was, in its own way he said, self-defeating: "The leading Gentlemen [the schoolmasters] do eminent service to the public, by impressing upon the minds of the people, the necessity and

Importance of encouraging that system of education, which ... is so well calculated to diffuse among the individuals of the community, the principles of morality, so essentially necessary for the preservation of public liberty." Why? As he said, "[N]o people will tamely surrender their liberties, nor can they easily be subdued, when knowledge is diffused and virtue preserved."

How the founders viewed the place of education is best illustrated by their support for its public funding. Despite a strong and resolute commitment to liberty and limited government, the founders passionately supported public education. George Washington in his farewell address pressed for the establishment of a national university, saying that education is the foundation of a free state. "Knowledge is, in every country, the surest basis for public happiness." Washington believed that education played an especially vital role in the United States because "the measures of Government receive their impression so immediately from the sense of the Community."

> "Knowledge is, in every country, the surest basis for public happiness."

The first president saw a direct relationship among education, public opinion, and deliberation in a representative democracy. An informed and knowledgeable populace, Washington believed, contributed to the health of the republic in a variety of ways. The first is by "convincing those who are entrusted with the public administration, that every valuable end of Government is best answered by the enlightened confidence of the people." Second, education is a defensive measure against manipulation and oppression. It teaches the people "to know and to value their own rights; to discern and provide against invasions of them; to distinguish between oppression and the necessary exercise of lawful authority; between burdens proceeding from a disregard to their convenience and those resulting from inevitable exigencies of society." Finally education gives voters the moral instruction "to discriminate the spirit of liberty from that of licentiousness—cherishing the first, avoiding the last; and uniting a speedy, but temperate vigilance against encroachments, with an inviolable respect to the laws."

An informed populace can police government, keep it efficient, and most of all protect the citizen from government oppression, thereby ensuring that government is the servant of the people. Thomas Jefferson believed so heartily in this defensive role of education that he wanted to broaden the base of the educated populace by establishing a system of education that extended to every citizen. The most powerful presentation of his ideas on education came in his "Bill for the More General Diffusion of Knowledge," which he introduced in 1779. Jefferson wanted a school in every village of the state to ensure that "all the free children, male and female, resident within the respective hundred, shall be entitled to receive tuition gratis, for the term of three years, and as much longer, at their private expense, as their parents, guardians, or friends shall think proper."

An educated citizenry was part of the elaborate defenses needed to keep a people free and government in check. Jefferson took these ideas so far that he wrote that residents of America should *not* be given automatic citizenship for fear that this tradition of educated resistance would be endangered. He endorsed a Spanish statute that required that citizens be able to read and write in order to vote.

Today such ideas strike our ears as strange, perhaps even disturbing. But Jefferson didn't share the modern idea that education was simply a conveyor belt for a factory state. Nor did he view the power to vote, assemble, and speak out as a frivolous right of self-expression. Such citizen action carried with it a burden of responsibility, vigilance, and eloquent persuasion. He would likely dismiss the idea of asking uninformed voters their views of questions of political import.

Jefferson's friend James Madison held similar views on the importance of education to the cause of protecting fragile liberty. In a letter to William T. Barry on August 4, 1822, Madison extolled Kentucky's plan for universal education: "A popular Government, without popular information, or the means of acquiring it, is but a Prologue to a Farce or a Tragedy; or perhaps, both. Knowledge will forever govern ignorance: And a people who mean to be their own Governors, must arm themselves with the power which knowledge gives." Madison singled out Kentucky's effort to expand education to the poorest citizens as a policy worthy of praise. "Learned Institutions ought to be favorite objects with every free people. They throw that light over the public mind which is the best security against crafty & dangerous encroachments on the public liberty."[22]

What the founders had in mind was not a warm-and-fuzzy notion of education. The lessons of history and the science of politics warned the enlightened citizen that freedom had to be protected and government watched closely. As John Adams wrote, "Liberty under every conceivable form of government is always in danger. Ambition is one of the more ungovernable passions of the human heart. The love of power is insatiable and uncontrollable; there is danger from all men. The only maxim of a free government ought to be to trust no man living with power to endanger the public liberty. Be upon your guard then, my countrymen."

Fisher Ames, another High Federalist, thought it laughable that citizens could guide a nation based solely on democratic self-expression absent of education and reflection. "It may be of some use in this argument [against pure democracy], however, to consider that it would be very burdensome, subject to faction and violence; decisions would often be made by surprise, in the precipitancy of passion, by men who either understand nothing, or care nothing about the subject; or by interested men, or those who vote for their own indemnity. It would be a government, not by laws, but by men," he wrote.[23]

Rediscovering Ancient Trepidations

The founders were right: There are dire consequences when the citizenry fails to be informed and vigilant.

Citizen ignorance may be rational at the individual level, but in the context of society, the multiplier effect is costly. As Bovard notes, "The only way to presume that citizen's ignorance of government is irrelevant to democracy is to presume that government is inherently benevolent and that people do not even need to know what it is doing. People can ignore the details of government policies—since they are essentially making a choice between two competing political caregivers— in the same way that an infirm person might choose between two nurses competing for hire, with no understanding of the drugs the nurses planned to inject him with."[24]

Political scientists Michael X. Delli Carpini and Scott Keeter show similar concern about the costs of ignorance in *What Americans Know About Politics and Why It Matters.* They agree with the founders that a republic is a perilous high-wire act—spectacular when it works, but dangerous when the participants don't know what they are doing: "The American political system was designed to balance a belief in the public's civic authority with doubts about the public's civic competence."[25] Echoing the sentiments of the founders' warning, they state, "To the extent that citizens are uninformed, the system is less democratic."[26]

There is also a second consequence of voter ignorance: For pollsters and political consultants, it becomes easier to manipulate the citizenry when political knowledge is low and convictions weak. The media's ability to set the agenda of political debate through pollsters' wording of questions increases as the public lowers its intellectual defenses—something the Washington pollster understands all too well.

"The one thing about polling that's a little cynical is that we understand that most people in this country don't have a lot of time to read politics or watch C-SPAN or watch PBS," says Democratic pollster Fred Yang. "They really get their politics in short sound-bites. And what our job as consultants is to do is to pick those four or five relevant themes or messages that convey something about the candidate, test those in polling, and find out how popular they are, and then use those for the campaign's message."[27]

> For pollsters and political consultants, it becomes easier to manipulate the citizenry when political knowledge is low and convictions weak.

Political science professor Margaret Stimman Branson, a specialist in civic education, agrees that civic ignorance carries civic costs. "The real obstacle to effective interchange of ideas between the electorate and officeholders, however, is citizens who do not know how to exercise their rights and responsibilities and/or who do not believe in themselves and their power to influence public policies," she told the International Conference on Education for Democracy. "Officials are quite aware of how little citizens appreciate their own importance."[28]

Even some government officials view ignorance as dangerous to the long-term prosperity and health of the nation. The Federal Reserve Bank of Minneapolis devoted a special issue of *The Region,* a quarterly magazine, to the subject of the economic ignorance of the American public. Todd G. Buchholz, president of Victoria Capital, warned, "An economically illiterate public can be bullied or inveigled into thinking that the victims of good economics exactly offset the beneficiaries."[29] Economic ignorance, much like polling questions that fail to disclose the cost of a new program, brings errors into public policy.

With voter knowledge so low on economic matters (or those few policy matters that aren't tied to economic questions), voters tend to go along with the subtle push provided in the wording of the poll questions. The average citizen doesn't think in terms of the costs of one government policy versus another unless expressly demanded to do so. This most fundamental law of economics—that there is scarcity—is too often forgotten by journalists and advocates anxious to prove support for one policy or another. But such questions about nice-sounding programs and more government spending prey on voter ignorance. In such cases, respondents might express support for price controls, government intervention, or intrusive regulatorions unaware of the true costs to economy and personal liberty.

There is yet another ramification of public ignorance: It undermines debate and discussion of ideas. As economics professor William R. Walstad writes, "This knowledge deficiency affects people's ability to evaluate economic matters and produces uninformed opinions. Among the informed, of course, there will still be differences about what should be done on an issue, but it provides a solid basis for a reasonable discussion of economic alternatives."[30]

The most ardent advocates of polling insist that polling contributes to the democratic process of spreading information. By publishing what the public thinks, the media believe they serve the public good in finding the appropriate policies for elected officials to debate and pursue. Yet in the absence of key knowledge about terms and policies, it is impossible to have the kind of debate that is most likely to further the good of the nation. Working with Gallup, Walstad found that "less than 4 in 10 high school seniors or adults could answer basic questions about economic terms and concepts that are essential for understanding economic events and issues reported in the news media."[31]

Even the most basic knowledge about economics can affect the outcome of economic survey questions. For instance, Walstad's survey asked the following question:

> To the best of your knowledge, the prices of most products in a <u>competitive</u> market, like the United States, are determined by: (a) supply and demand for products; (b) the consumer price index; (c) local, state, or Federal government; (d) the monetary policy of the Federal Reserve.

Only 5 in 10 knew the correct answer was "a"—prices are determined by supply and demand for products.

Walstad then asked these young adults to apply their knowledge to the following situation:

> A bicycle manufacturer raises the prices of bikes because the demand increased even though the cost of producing bikes has not increased. Do you think the manufacturer should be allowed to raise prices?

Two out of three students opposed the company's response to inexorable market forces. But the results become even more interesting as Walstad cross-tabulated the responses to the knowledge of basic economic principles. For those who knew that supply and demand determine prices in a free market, 6 out of 10 would allow the price increase. But among those ignorant of the basic laws of economics, just 41 percent thought the company was acting within the parameters of competition and economic reality.

Such a discussion goes a long way to explaining how government intervention can gain such political momentum in policy debates. The bike-manufacturing example mirrors many debates about health care price controls, prescription drugs, the cost of energy, and a host of other issues. When polls claim to show support for state interventionism when it is based on such fundamental ignorance, a true reckoning of public opinion should note what people *know*, not just what they *believe*. Newspaper articles should print more than the margin of error and the size of the sample.

They should show what knowledge or lack of knowledge may be influencing the results.

Negative Campaigning: Catering to Ignorance

Voter apathy, combined with the shallow horse-race obsessions of the media, exacerbates the low levels of knowledge in the citizenry. It assumes knowledge and strong opinions where they don't exist.

The grim reality is that as citizens become less interested and more ignorant about what's going on in politics, the incentive for politicians and consultants to aim for the lowest common denominator increases. Like a radio shock jock, politicians' on-air tactics and language must stay ahead of the devolution of the audience.

John Adams once warned that democracy was always threatened because the people applaud "artifices and tricks . . . hypocrisy and superstition . . . flattery, bribes, [and] largesses." Once a virtuous and alert citizenry descends into the amoral indifference and selfishness of a mob, its manipulation by the politically cunning is assured. Rome disintegrated as the emperors used *panem et circenses,* bread and circuses, to satisfy the lowest appetites of the crowd. Gross accusation, smeared reputations, and the use of public welfare to bribe the populace became so common that Roman historians rarely affected surprise at the vicious circle of greater handouts and more bloody gains by the ambitious. The operative emotion in the political sphere, like ours today, was usually disgust and cynicism.

When the public becomes indifferent to the process of politics, democratic institutions become the pawns of the politically cunning. The media's focus on the horse race and reliance on the polls has sapped political discourse of content. And with the need for politicians to poll-test every idea to break through the veil of the uninformed, the chances of hearing substantive speeches from elected leaders have declined. The vacuum of public ignorance and apathy has enabled the rise of a new political weapon suited for the sound-bite environment: the negative ad.

As citizens become less interested and more ignorant about what's going on in politics, the incentive for politicians and consultants to aim for the lowest common denominator increases.

Ironically, the negative ad has become one of the only places left for substantive knowledge about candidates to appear. As Stephen Ansolabehere and Shanto Iyengar write in *Going Negative: How Negative Advertisements Shrink & Polarize the Electorate,* "The relatively low levels of concrete information that voters bring to political campaigns represents an enormous opportunity for candidates to educate the public."[32]

The television ads that bombard voters in the last days of a campaign are one of the only resources for a voter to be able to consider the record of a candidate. With its sinister black-and-white pictures, unflattering still shots, and harsh newspaper headlines floating across the screen, the negative ad has become the popular punching bag of pundits, media scholars, and even self-righteous politicians. It is also the cynical monument to an ignorant public and a self-absorbed media, whose "Gotcha!" partisanship has trivialized the role of the free press and made the public sick of politics.

Ignorance Empowers Focus-Group Clichés

Negative ads work not only because voters are ignorant, but also because they often pick up where journalists fail, bringing up issues that distinguish one candidate from another. But the truly effective ad isn't a long policy discourse or learned debate. It has 30 seconds to strike a chord in the viewer. And this means that the negative ad has to have emotional resonance.

With public discourse so dependent on emotional appeal, political candidates turn to focus groups whose goal is to "gain access to private, non-communicable, unconscious feelings and emotions."[33] The pollsters, consultants, and candidates get to see beyond the quantitative numbers of a poll. More important, they can find out what words and phrases will help shape the impressions they present. In modern politics the focus group and the poll work hand in hand.

A poll may tell a politician what the people believe when a question is framed a certain way, but a focus group can give insights into how voters feel. The rise of focus groups in itself indicates both the limitations of polls in reading voters' minds and the suggestibility of those minds.

GOP pollster Frank Luntz believes in the power of focus groups precisely because voters are largely ignorant in a time of dynamic political change. "With the rise of talk radio and 24-hour television news channels, not to mention C-Span and public access cable, there is a rapidly increasing number of semi-informed voters out there with only half-formed political views. The elements that make up public opinion have changed; so must its measurement."[34]

Bill Clinton was an expert at using focus groups to deal with especially prickly problems during his presidency. For example, throughout 1995 and 1996, consultant Dick Morris tested Republican and Democratic Medicare ads on focus groups to get a sense of how the commercials might change the way voters viewed the debate. In addition, Clinton's tactics for handling the various scandals that plagued his administration—from Gennifer Flowers, to allegations of draft dodging, to his health care program, and even to impeachment—were driven by careful exploration of wording and presentation, both of which were then tested in focus groups. When voters swooned to his promise of "ending welfare as we know it," they were hearing the echoes of their own political unconscious, derived from their fellow citizens in focus groups.

What makes the focus group so effective in the hands of a skillful politician is the ability to tap the unspoken inclinations and intentions of millions of voters, many of whom are more responsive to *how* something is said than to *what* is said. Public ignorance opens the door to negative advertising with its disconcerting, ominous delivery as well as the factory-tested, focus-group-approved political vocabulary. As long as media reports trade issue-oriented substance for insider baseball and cynical put-downs, voters will tune out. And as long as voters tune out, the public square will continue to resort to what James Madison called the "vicious arts" of politics—the kind of well-tested chicanery that gets attention and hits voters at the level of emotion rather than reason.

The founders of the nation saw political debate as a way to ennoble and educate voters, as well as hold accountable the dangerous impulses of elected officials. The Senate, the presidency, and the judiciary were checks on popular rampages of ignorant or enraged voters. The House with its frequent elections was meant to give air to popular ideas. The system was meant to mediate the whims of a populace that would want everything from government at the cost of liberty. Frequent elections were meant to give voters the final say about their representatives. Today, elections are an afterthought in the long train of polls, focus groups, pundit debates, and journalistic advice.

Ignorance Casts Doubt on Journalistic Explanations

During the 2000 presidential election, the Gore-Lieberman campaign considered a unique way to battle the ignorance that causes voters to judge candidates based on personality and likeability. Convinced by journalists and talking heads that he had won the third presidential debate, then–Vice President Al Gore said he was going to buy 90-minute blocks of time on cable stations in swing states. Gore believed that rebroadcasting his debate with George W. Bush would help clarify their political differences and help him win the election.

But there was serious reason to believe this misguided effort would not only fail to attract votes, it could also help Bush bury Gore once and for all. The reason is that voter ignorance causes the average citizen to watch a debate in a very different way from the average Beltway commentator or political junkie.

Thomas Patterson, political scientist at Harvard University, has studied how voters watch debates. What voters were looking for in the 2000 debates may explain why Bush, not Gore, saw his fortunes surge in the polls in the wake of the televised exchanges. Unlike the journalistic establishment, voters don't keep score based on who can cram the most data and policy wonkery into debate answers. Simply put, because of ignorance voters don't have the political knowledge to keep score. "Viewers do respond favorably to a poised and artful candidate, but they are looking for something deeper—an indication that a candidate is 'big enough' for the presidency," states Patterson.[35] In fact, voters have no problem declaring one man more knowledgeable (Mondale and Gore), but then deciding the rival would make a better president (Reagan and Bush).

The big variable in 2000 was the relative health of the economy in a time when voters didn't have a clear choice.

Both sides had successfully blurred the ideological lines for the electorate. Throughout the election, most Americans did not know which candidate stood for what ideas. Just three weeks before the election—after three debates, one very substantive vice-presidential debate, two political conventions, and more than $20 million in campaign ads—a simple majority of voters could match only one of the candidates correctly with *one* of his political beliefs: 59 percent of voters knew Gore was in favor of prescription drug benefits becoming part of Medicare. Less than 50 percent of registered voters knew where Bush stood on gun registration, defense spending, campaign finance restrictions, abortion, tax cuts, and tax credits for health insurance for the poor. And voters did no better identifying Gore's policies on school choice, the environment, Social Security, affirmative action, and sanctions against China. In short, voters are stunningly uninformed and tragically ignorant. So what are voters looking for? According to Patterson, "Second-by-second analyses indicated that the audience responds most favorably to the candidates when they are talking about an issue that people care deeply about and are able to frame the position in a way that shows they understand why people are concerned about the issue."

> Voter ignorance causes the average citizen to watch a debate in a very different way from the average Beltway commentator or political junkie.

Note that viewers don't keep a tally of verbal hits. They aren't even looking specifically for numbers, data, or loads of detail from information dump trucks. What voters want is softer and far less tangible. They are looking for assurance that the candidate has empathy and decorum. This may have been the source of the problem for Gore, who aggressively and relentlessly defended his positions with excruciating wonk-numbing detail. Journalists were clearly concentrating on this aspect of the debate, so they declared Gore the winner. But voters may have gotten hung up on Gore's smallness and meanness. If Patterson is right, Gore's huffing and puffing, lunging and sighing, quibbling and last-minute harangues were as important to voters as any Rube Goldberg recitation of his tax "cut" plan.

In fact Patterson studied how voters watched a dozen debates from the past 20 years. Among them, he found that no one ranked lower in his debate performance than Gore when he savaged Bill Bradley in New York City in the fall of 1999. Replaying his debates with Bush may have seemed to be a smart plan to Al Gore. It may have been good for the nation to have the differences between the candidates clarified. But it may also have invited more voters to judge a man on his professionalism and conduct, not just his policy proposals—a move that could have proven costly. Voter ignorance and the average citizen's interests are so different from elite opinion that they cast doubt on the ability of any journalist to divine what is motivating voters to change their allegiance from candidate to candidate or issue to issue.

Journalists repeatedly said that the people sided with then–Vice President Al Gore "on the issues," despite George W. Bush's lead in the polls. To anyone who has truly studied polling, such claims ring hollow because issue polls or voter priority polls depend almost entirely on how questions are framed to voters. As polls of voter knowledge show, however, even if (and that is a big "if" dependent on the wording of the poll questions) voters did side with Gore, they could not reward him with their political support because they didn't know where *he* stood. In fact, in most cases, voters rarely know specifically where any politician stands.

Pushed by media coverage, prodded by previous polls, voters give vague impressions and are forced into ill-considered, partisan positions in polling. Perhaps voters are ignorant because they tune out the very media that are supposed to educate them; that media being too busy telling them what they think and who's up or who's down rather than covering issues. Whatever the reason, voters are often so uninformed that it is impossible to say exactly what motivates them or how they reason. In this hostile climate of ignorance, there's only one question left for pollsters and journalists to ask: Which is greater—the ignorance of the voters or the arrogance of the journalists who say they can read minds?

Recognizing the Problem

The founders of this nation knew all too well the dangers of ignorance and the consequences of a sleeping citizenry. Aware that those in power are always seeking more control, the founders sought to build a system that encouraged political deliberation and education of the electorate, and restrained the ambitious demagogue.

To frustrate the human tendency toward lawlessness and vice, the founders sought to build a government that prevented any single man, faction, or party from gathering all the elements of power—the legislative, executive, and judicial functions—into their hands. Tyranny was defined as the ability to wield the authority of all three branches with impunity.[36]

We forget in this Age of Polling, with all its impatience and demand of action, that the system the founders established refracted power to prevent its abuse and ensure accountability. With polling, it is easy for the power of media and the patina of popularity to make majority sentiment the *sine qua non.* Too often today, media polls are an enemy of the Constitutional ideas of deliberation, patience, the rule of law, and the rights of the individual.

Such a system of impression democracy—combining media sensationalism, unreflective politicians, and an uninformed electorate—would have alarmed the founders of our nation. Back then, numbers and majorities weren't enough to justify political action. Freedom was too precious to be put in the hands of any one body, whether it was rule by the few, the many, or the one.

John Adams wrote to his friend Thomas Jefferson in 1815, "The fundamental article of my political creed is that despotism or unlimited sovereignty or absolute power is the same in a majority of a popular assembly, an aristocratic council, an oligarchic junto, and a single emperor—equally arbitrary, cruel, bloody, and in every respect diabolical." Jefferson held a similar position in *Notes on the State of Virginia:* "It will be no alleviation that these powers [executive, legislative, and judicial] will be exercised by a plurality of hands, and not by a single one. 173 despots would surely be as oppressive as one." Illuminating the focus of the revolution and the art of constitution making, he added, "An *elective despotism* was not the government we fought for; but one which should not only be founded on free principles, but in which the powers of government should be so divided and balanced among several bodies of magistracy, as that no one could transcend their legal limits, without being effectively checked and restrained by the others."

> Too often today, media polls are an enemy of the Constitutional ideas of deliberation, patience, the rule of law, and the rights of the individual.

All forms of government are susceptible to tyrannous domination by ambitious citizens—especially oppression of those in the minority. The founders considered direct democracy dangerous because, as a result of the demand for immediate reform, immediate action, and the immediate satisfaction of the majority, a new and fearful tyranny could gain ascendance—one that abhors deliberation, law, compromise, and respect for minority rights—all in the name of the people.[37]

INCREASED DELIBERATION

James Madison, in his masterpiece, *Federalist* No. 10, suggested an answer to the problems of faction and party machinations. He argued for what he called an "extended republic," giving special emphasis to the Constitution's ability to control faction and foster deliberation and public education. (Note how his description of the Constitution is yet another reminder of the founders' distrust of unchecked and unreflective democracy.) "The instability, injustice, and confusion, introduced into the public councils, have, in truth, been the mortal diseases under which popular governments have everywhere perished," he wrote.[38] Pure democracies too often allow the "mischiefs of faction" easy access into the public arena. That is why "democracies have ever been the spectacles of turbulence and contention; have ever been found incompatible with personal security; or the rights of property; and have, in general, been as short in their lives, as they have been violent in their deaths."[39]

Madison turned the ancient argument for small republics on its head, defending the ability of a large republic to reduce the influence of the violent passions or momentary whims of the people. The "extended republic" with its representative structure can "refine and enlarge the public views, by passing them through the medium of a chosen body of citizens" and prevent the public interest from being sacrificed to "temporary or partial considerations."[40]

Madison and the other framers of the Constitution wished to avoid direct democracy, instead favoring a republic where the best rose to the top and deliberated on the course for the nation. The conversations would ramify through the nation, informing and fostering a vigilant citizenry empowered to check government and defend its rights.

Madison, like the other founders, saw threats to freedom loom like Scylla and Charybdis: government tyranny on one side, and mob rule on the other. He continues:

[T]here are particular moments in public affairs, when the people, stimulated by some irregular passion, or some illicit advantage, or misled by the artful misrepresentations of interested men, may call for measures which they themselves will afterwards be the most ready to lament and condemn.[41]

The founders' reservations about pure democracy are also evident in their defense of the long terms of office for the Senate and president. They did not want a government whipsawed by the madness of the crowd. Longer terms of office would help bring stability. Hamilton eloquently expressed the fear of unreflective democracy in *Federalist* No. 71, defending the four-year term of the president. The independence and strength of the executive branch were a bulwark for freedom, not a threat, he argued. Longer terms encouraged political officials to act independently of the people when they are deceived or momentarily deluded by their passions. Hamilton wrote that the "republican principle demands, that the deliberate sense of the community should govern the conduct of those to whom they intrust [*sic*] the management of the affairs."[42]

For Hamilton, good government made up of a free citizenry "does not require an unqualified complaisance to every sudden breeze of passion, or to every transient impulse which the people may receive from the arts of men, who flatter their prejudices to betray their interests."[43]

Fisher Ames also cast doubt on the notion that freedom is best secured in a democracy that moves with every whim of the populace. Representatives of the people are elected for a term of office to develop their skills and education. Thus, ridiculously short tenures in office—or, one might speculate, the pressure of never-ending campaigns expressed in polls—could undermine the higher objects of a representative government. "I consider [frequent elections] as one of the first securities for popular liberty, in which its very essence may be supposed to reside. But how shall we make the best use of this pledge and instrument of safety?" Ames asked. "A right principle, carried to an extreme, becomes useless. It is apparent that a declaration for a very short term, *as for a single day, would defeat the design of representation* [emphasis mine]. The election in that case would not seem to the people to be of any importance, and the person elected would think as lightly of his appointment."[44]

Hamilton is often mistakenly accused of having called the collected citizenry "the beast," but his thoughts in *Federalist* No. 71 are far more subtle and sympathetic to the long-term concerns of the people. Hamilton argues for restraints on direct democracy not for fear that the people will act wickedly toward some minority, rather, that out of ignorance or passion they may injure their own interests. "It is a just observation that the people commonly *intend* the PUBLIC GOOD," writes Hamilton. "This often applies to their very errors."

The four-year term of president and other constitutional devices were intended to counter the "wiles of parasites and sycophants." In fact, elected leaders should find the courage to stand firm. Hamilton believes, "When occasions present themselves, in which the interests of the people are at variance with their inclinations, it is the duty of the persons whom they have appointed, to be the guardians of those interests; to withstand the temporary delusion, in order to give them time and opportunity for more cool and sedate reflection."[45]

Hamilton and the other founders did not live to see the rise of polling, so we cannot know how the Federalist luminaries would view the effect of public opinion polls on the process of deliberation. But Hamilton wasn't alone in his desire for constitutional mechanisms that would slow down the translation of public opinion into immediate and thoughtless action. He wanted "cool and sedate reflection," not the impatient, ignorant, and unreflective press to deploy the power of the state to secure desired ends. The atavistic sound of "temporary delusion" and its implication that the people could be subject to error is an indication of how America has changed.

The six-year terms and the structure of the Senate were also designed to moderate the dangers of impression democracy. In *Federalist* No. 63, Madison argues that the Senate will become a haven for the wise and able-bodied to govern the young Republic. Had Athens and the other Greek democracies had such a "safeguard" against "the tyranny of their own passions," he continued, "Popular liberty might then have escaped the indelible reproach of decreeing to the same citizens, the hemlock one day, and statues the next."[46] The Senate was a perfect example of the kind of institution that was needed as an "anchor against popular fluctuations" and would serve to "blend stability with liberty."[47] In short, the Senate was a "defence [*sic*] to the people against their own temporary errors and delusions."[48]

Get Used to Disappointment: The Constitution Strikes Back

As we consider the power of polls to express the changing demands of the people, it becomes clear that the American system of government is not designed for immediate majority action. When media-sponsored polls purport to show support for nationalizing health care, passing a balanced budget amendment, or imposing campaign finance regulations, we must remember that the Constitution slows the process of enactment, which often allows opponents of new ideas to present the other side of the story, the economic costs, and the dangers to liberty. The distribution of power was intended to protect liberty, property, and the rights of the minority. The rule of law embodied in the Constitution is not designed for the daily expressions of opinion by the people prompted by the polls. Even if polls weren't dependent on wording and how the media report them, they are ill suited as a replacement to our representative institutions.

The work of Madison, Hamilton, and the other founders limits the power of government to give in to the immediate demands of the people. As an anonymous apologist for the Constitution, "A Citizen" wrote in the *Carlisle Gazette* on October 24, 1787: "The sole intention of [the new Constitution] is to produce wise and mature deliberation."[49]

Broad representation was meant to further the rule of law and keep government within an energetic, but limited, sphere. At first glance, it might seem that polls are the ultimate instrument

> The American system of government is not designed for immediate majority action.

giving voice to the people for just this purpose. But as we have seen, the real power isn't given to the people. Rather, those who write the polling questions and choose which results to report direct much of the voice of the people. A progressive elite wields public opinion surveys like weapons to push for government action, not for government restraint.

The very structure of our government is meant to do what so many advocates, special interest groups, and unreflective journalists try to accomplish through the blitzkrieg deployment of new polls: that is, to represent the people. The Constitution provides for representation by synthesizing and channeling public opinion. The current use of polls is almost invariably a device for advocacy, one that fits into the prerogatives of a media that sees federal government activism as the solution to the problems highlighted by left-leaning reporters and editors. One need only ask when the last time a poll asked for the repeal of laws. The same people who set the news agenda and then report on the results of the polls are the ones who write the questions. The result is often a measure of how much the public has absorbed the media message, not an objective measure of the deliberation of elected officials interacting with the public.

For those of us living in the Age of Polling, it should be clear that the framers weren't against democracy, but they were, without a doubt, wary of it. The federal Constitution was an experiment. Or as Hamilton pointed out in *Federalist* No.1, it was a test of whether "societies of men are capable or not, of establishing good government from reflection and choice."[50] The reason for trepidation is that experience, for all the founders, indicated that there was reason to be cautious of directly empowering the people, who might oppress minorities out of ignorance or passion. Part of their challenge was devising a government that would, as well as possible, limit the power of government to encroach on the individual and the community's rights and build a citizenry of enough virtue and education to restrain itself and police those in power.

Today we view individual participation in the political process as a kind of political performance art; the symbolic expressiveness of the act, however incoherent or strange, is of value to the public. Despite ignorance or apathy, the pollster tells us that polls are a valuable part of the process. Yet while public opinion is undoubtedly the ultimate basis for any government, it does not mean that the long-term health of the nation is preserved by half-baked opinions based on little more than momentary impressions.

The implications of this line of logic should irritate or at least make us feel uncomfortable. An ignorant and lazy electorate demanding quick and easy answers isn't a cause for celebration, but a reason to ponder the grim consequences looming in the long run. It is hard to imagine the wisdom of the people when so little thinking goes on. We must ask: Does the proliferation of polls contribute to our representative institutions? Or have polls begun to makes us "careless with the Constitution," as Senator Daniel Patrick Moynihan warned? How do the pressures of the polls fit in with the founding principles of this nation? We aren't the first generation to wrestle with these questions. The framers of the Constitution also had good reason to doubt the constant and direct interaction of the people in government.

CHAPTER SEVEN

Politicians and Polls

Everything You Say
Can and Will Be Used Against You

Politicians understand public opinion and the limitations of polls far better than the media.

■ ■ ■

WINSTON CHURCHILL, Britain's greatest leader in the twentieth century, once attacked the idea of the craven politician. In the dark days of 1941, he said to the House of Commons, "I see that a speaker at the week-end said that this was a time when leaders should keep their ears to the ground. All I can say is that the British nation will find it very hard to look up to leaders who are detected in that somewhat ungainly posture." The proliferation of public opinion polls has introduced a new dynamic into public discourse. Although polls are popularly derided as a temporary spine for the spineless, the truth is more complex. Many politicians attempt to influence polls as much as polls influence them. The skill with which Washington's politicians employ polls to push their messages shows that they are far more conscious of the power and limitations of polling than are most journalists. Journalists claim that the polls they write are a mirror of the public's views. For politicians, polls are a valuable tool. Politicians use the bandwagon effects of polling and media coverage to gather support for their ideas, and they exploit the journalistic obsession with polls to garner attention. Politicians realize that polls are more a measure of how an issue is framed than a measure of the fixed, well-informed opinion of an ideologically committed public.

"[T]he polling business gives the patricians an idea of what the mob is thinking, and of how that thinking might be changed or, shall we say, 'shaped,'" suggests left-leaning journalist Christopher Hitchens. "It is the essential weapon in the mastery of populism by the elite. It also allows for 'fine calibration,' and for capsules of 'message' to be prescribed for variant constituencies."[1] Such criticisms aren't new to activists on the left or on the right. Political science professor Daniel Greenberg wrote in 1980:

> Given the devastation that opinion surveys have brought to the American political process, we shouldn't be asking how polls can be sharpened but rather why they are endured and how they can be banished. . . . Polls are the life-support system for the finger-to-the-wind, quick-change politics of our time, and, as such, are the indispensable tools for the ideologically hollow men who work politics like a soap-marketing campaign. . . . The effect of this—on campaigns, as well as on administrations between campaigns—is an obsession with salesmanship rather than governance.[2]

That "salesmanship" gives politicians tremendous wiggle-room for tailoring their ideas to those of the public. Polling isn't the sole cause of issueless "soap-marketing" campaigns, but public polling has mixed with other dominant trends to make it more difficult for political leaders to educate, debate, and persuade the electorate.

"Salesmanship," or the marketing tactics and strategies of political players, has become very important to candidates who must test-market their ideas because they now sell themselves directly to the public. Television and the decline of the influence of political parties have cast politicians adrift to appeal directly to the voter, often without party support. At the same time, politicians must work around a media filter that values conflict and controversy—even before the "new product campaign" begins.

> Public polling has mixed with other dominant trends to make it more difficult for political leaders to educate, debate, and persuade the electorate.

Politicians Know Polls Are Only the Beginning

The ways in which politicians use polls show that they are familiar with the many limitations and gray areas of polling—even if journalists aren't. Political scientists Lawrence R. Jacobs and Robert Y. Shapiro argue that despite popular perception, politicians are not ruled by polls. Jacobs and Shapiro believe that politicians are more apt to use polls to manipulate the public and the media.

In the 1993 health care reform debate, Jacobs and Shapiro found that congressional staffers tended to ignore polling that showed support for health care reform. They identified four reasons that staff members of Congress did not buckle before the polls and pass some version of national health care:

1. The polls from media, party organizations, and lobbyists weren't considered credible. Many in Congress believed that "findings were manufactured through the use of slanted question wording and biased sampling."

2. Staffers discounted public opinion polls because they were too crude to pinpoint public sentiment about complex proposals.

3. The public was too uncertain, with as much as a third of the electorate holding no opinion on major policy issues.

4. Legislators believed public opinion was an "inappropriate" guide for governing.[3]

These four points are perfect examples of the limitations of polls, and they all come down to the same core problem: the American voter. Due to ignorance and apathy, the average voter has withdrawn from the political process and only participates in a minimal way, if at all. Members of the House and Senate understand that the world of politics is far more intricate and complex than the polling conducted by left-leaning media.

During the debate about Medicare reforms, the national media hammered away at Republican proposals as a "gutting of the social safety net," "draconian cuts," and "savage slashes." In the common media schema, Republicans are the reactionaries or obscurantists opposing the will of the people. Similarly it seemed at first that national health care would be just another liberal entitlement to sail through Congress in some form or another.

Initial polling, at least in the eyes of the media, contributed to this notion. But polls often fail to present the trade-offs and opportunity costs for certain courses of action, and even when they do, voter reasoning on complex multibillion dollar ideas can still be quite primitive. So in the beginning, new government programs or rules tend to poll well.

But the political process was designed by the founders to modulate and slow the enactment of legislation so the people and their representatives could look more closely.

The relationship among public opinion, polls, and political leadership is complex. For instance, a politician can't just read the polls and expect to succeed. Even the most plastic politician doesn't solely read the polls because he or she has to choose which polls to read. As Jacobs and Shapiro state, "The efforts of politicians to weigh the costs and benefits of policy and electoral goals are most significantly influenced by their constituents, but constituents do not provide a clear and uniform signal to politicians about which goal to favor."[4]

Politicians See the Reciprocity of Polls and Media

While most pollsters reject the idea that polls produce a bandwagon effect among voters, politicians understand there is such an effect in the media. They understand that polls can drive coverage and therefore attract supporters. In seeking office, donors, or ways to advance their favored issues, politicians know that polls play a critical role in convincing journalists and the public that their ideas are legitimate, popular, and politically feasible.

> Politicians know that polls play a critical role in convincing journalists and the public that their ideas are legitimate, popular, and politically feasible.

Candidates and officeholders recognize the hypnotic power that polls—even unscientific ones—have over journalists. The media obsession with polling makes the preprimary "straw polls" in Iowa, Florida, and Louisiana nearly as important as any other primary poll. Politicians have come to realize that the media have little or no self-control when faced with irresistible measures of the horse race. Even when reporters add a caveat or two about the unscientific nature of the straw poll, the news coverage is nearly the same as any other poll, no matter which channel you watch or which paper you read. That's why politicians will spend hundreds of thousands of dollars to bus in supporters and pay for votes at straw polls. Phil Gramm in 1995 and Steve Forbes and Gary Bauer in 1999 spent huge sums trying to boost their showings in the straw polls.

Polling has a powerful influence on the type of coverage that politicians get, so naturally they try to control or exploit the polls as much as possible. As Tom Rosenstiel said of the Democratic primaries in 1992, even the most issue-oriented politicians are forced to play to the polls.

For example, 1992 Democratic presidential candidate Senator Paul Tsongas had promised voters that he was "no Santa Claus." He sought to tell a more balanced story about Washington's liberal spending and the need for responsible budgeting. According to Rosenstiel,

> In his own way, Tsongas used the press as well. Campaign manager Dennis Kanin found out when major newspapers would be conducting opinion polls, and timed the first Tsongas commercial in December to air just before them to influence the results. The trick pushed him into an early tie for first place.[5]

In 1995, during the Medicare reform debates with Congress, Bill Clinton aired commercials throughout the country. His plan was to drive up public opposition to the GOP legislation, but in such a way that it seemed spontaneous. Clinton knew that the media focus on tactics and strategy, so the White House "air war" was conducted outside the major media cities of New York, Los Angeles, and Washington,

D.C. As the negative campaign progressed, journalists were left with a story that appeared to be built on a spontaneous public surge: Americans opposed the "cuts" and "slashes" in the Republican-proposed reforms.

So it was in the 2000 presidential race. Vice President Al Gore, after months of bad press, came out of the Democratic convention with newfound support and a more united base of core Democratic supporters. As Gore's poll ratings rose, crossover support for Governor George W. Bush naturally faltered. In the zero-sum politics of journalism, reporters and pundits had any number of explanations. Gore's passionate and unexpected kiss of his wife before his acceptance speech received some of the credit, as did Gore's laundry list of favored left-wing ideas. Finally, some of the blame went to Bush's ideas, specifically his tax-cutting plan. Gore had previously attacked the Bush proposal as a risky scheme, and as soon as Bush began to slide, media scrutiny was unloaded on the idea of cutting taxes.

> Politicians understand how the media read and misread polls, and they understand how to manipulate polls and public opinion to drive journalistic coverage.

Unknown to many journalists at the time, the Gore campaign had purchased airtime in markets across the country during the convention, but avoided major media markets that might draw attention to the seemingly renewed interest in Gore. Gore suddenly rose to a 10-point lead in the polls. And Bush retreated from his tax plan, admitting he "needed to do a better job of explaining" the effect of across-the-board cuts. Politicians understand how the media read and misread polls, and they understand how to manipulate polls and public opinion to drive journalistic coverage.

Politicians Tailor Their Message to Ignorant Voters

Politicians, unlike journalists, do not assume a high level of voter knowledge. They understand the limitations of public opinion polling and the consequences of public ignorance. They know that their job is not to produce long lists of public policy plans—the kind of "specifics" that journalists say the public craves. Rather, most candidates—and especially their consultants—realize that Americans view politics through a prism of gut feelings, impressions, and even prejudice. Therefore reaching voters and attracting their support goes beyond a mere recitation of numbers and data. It is a far more complex process that often leads candidates to tailor their messages to affect the public's impressions.

Polling and focus groups play an important role in giving politicians insight into touching heartstrings as well as crafting language for the voter. For journalists, this manipulation is mere showmanship. But politicians have an incentive to find the best way to communicate to voters. Although the task of the politician is split between talking to reporters and talking to voters, the methods of impressing each group differ markedly.

In appealing to the people and in trying to move the polls, politicians are often forced to dumb down their message. As author William A. Henry III wrote, there is a vitiating effect on campaigns when candidates conduct "politics by saxophone"—a phrase Henry coined for campaign stunts that try to make presidential candidates appeal to everyone. In 1988, it was blue-blood Vice President George Bush's revelation that he likes pork rinds and country music. In 1992, it was Clinton's reputed love for junk food and his saxophone-blowing appearance on *The Arsenio Hall Show*.

Henry's ideas about "politics by saxophone" were prescient. In 2000, both presidential candidates fought for the attention of talk-show host Oprah Winfrey. Bush delighted morning talk-show host Regis Philbin by wearing Philbin's trademark monochromatic shirt-and-tie combination. Likewise Al Gore sought to win over Regis's audience by demonstrating how to hypnotize chickens.

"The problem with fostering a personal link with the electorate is that this kind of pseudo-chumminess makes it difficult to lead or inspire. It is not enough to be elected," wrote Henry. "A President must renew his mandate, in a close equivalent to campaigning, virtually every day—the ultimate triumph of populist egalitarianism."[6] This state of affairs creates an interesting dynamic, as opinion elite lament every election year in political cartoon and written complaint: Are these really our choices? Journalists tend to be harsh critics, driving up cynicism with contemptuous coverage of the two choices facing the voters. Usually such critiques come with acid-tongued commentary about how the candidates "avoid specifics," refuse to "talk issues," or fail to put forward any policy "substance."

But polls have led politicians to view the world of public opinion differently. Politicians are challenged with getting their message out to a tuned-out populace, which even in the closest races cannot correctly identify political candidates according to their proposals. In addition, political coverage during elections or public controversy is often biased, cynical, and lacking in substance; voters willfully helicopter their brains out of the wasteland of this coverage. Of course there is little excuse for voter ignorance in the age of the Internet. The average citizen has tremendous resources at his or her fingertips for investigating and researching candidates.

But if average citizens do not take it upon themselves to find this information, chances are they won't get it from the media. This is because, for the most part, television and even newspapers tend to eschew the responsibility of serious, substantive real-issue reportage in favor of gaffes, one-liners, and campaign blunders. This creates an environment that encourages consultants, candidates, and campaigns to find ways to reach voters without resorting to bold and enterprising ideas that could prove costly in the polls. Instead political players orchestrate tightly controlled publicity events and soft, subtle messages that keep opponents and the media from savaging *any* ideas.

Politicians Understand the Challenge Is Framing

Unlike journalists, politicians are deeply conscious of just how conflicted Americans are. Politicians test their ideas in polls and in focus groups. They deliberately tap code words, or create new code words, that will excite or enrage voters. Perhaps one of the most familiar mantras to make its way into American political debate was President Clinton's simultaneous attack on Republicans and defense of "Medicare, Medicaid, education, and the environment." That series of ideas quickly and decisively communicated Clinton's attempt to stand for concerns of the poor, the elderly, parents, and liberal groups, and it subtly indicted his opposition.

Public opinion is far more malleable for politicians than it is for journalists.

Public opinion is far more malleable for politicians than it is for journalists. Whereas reporters use polls to pound and discipline unruly politicians who stand against the public, politicians and partisan pollsters are very capable of exploiting the contradictions in public opinion. This is why, for elites, politics is so maddeningly divided and ideologically inconsistent. Public opinion doesn't bring harmony. Politicians battle over "targeted tax cuts" while advocating tax code simplification. Some advocate balanced budget amendments in the face of billions in extra social spending. School choice supporters fight with those who want greater public school funding and federal control. Neither side can claim victory because it isn't just the electorate that is divided; the individual voter is also most often of two, contradictory mind-sets. As John Zaller notes:

> Political leaders are seldom passive instruments of majority opinion. Nor, it seems to me, do they often attempt openly to challenge public opinion. But they do regularly attempt to play on the contradictory ideas that are always present in people's minds, elevating the salience of some and harnessing them to new initiatives while downplaying or ignoring other ideas—all of which is just another way of talking about issue framing.[7]

What makes a politician's task all the more difficult is the tremendous power of the media, which limits the ability of the politician to make his or her case by setting the news agenda and framing the way new ideas are tested in polls.

CASE STUDY: BILL CLINTON, MASTER OF POLLS

When most political observers think of Bill Clinton, they think of a protean man driven by the polls. They think of him polling in 1996 on where to vacation. They note his shifting support for balanced budgets and welfare reform. And perhaps most conspicuously, Americans think of his 1998 polling on whether he should admit to the American people his adultery and perjury.

Clinton shaped public opinion, just as public opinion shaped his positions. He avidly pursued the best language and issue framing to accomplish his own ends. As far back as 1990, Bill Clinton searched for a way to reach the public. In his famous "Field of Dreams" speech to the Democratic Leadership Council, he talked about the need to change the politics of the Democratic Party and back new, more moderate policy proposals.

Clinton's moderation and involvement with "New Democrats" served as a trial run for his presidential bid. At the time, Clinton couldn't afford to do any polls, but he held town meetings, using them as his "National Focus Group." It was here that Clinton began to tailor his middle-of-the-road message.

Clinton was young and fresh. He differentiated himself from what people didn't like about the Democratic Party. His pollster Stan Greenberg attributes Clinton's later victory in 1992 to these efforts. "Clinton won the ideas primary," Greenberg said. Clinton's ideas, such as community policing, time limits for welfare, and public school choice, had a huge impact. His "surest applause line" was voluntary national service. It was a break with what Clinton called the "politics of something for nothing."[8] Clinton sought lines that could break through the net of media coverage and communicate simple evocative sentiments to the public.

Bill Clinton is in many ways the perfect study of polling in action. But he was not merely a creature of the polls, he was also their master. From the very beginning, Bill Clinton learned to read and even write polls. As Dick Morris states, "In our Arkansas days together, Clinton would spend hours reviewing each detail of a questionnaire before we gave it to the interviewers to field."[9] Indeed, it was this common interest in polls that created their friendship. As Morris's White House rival George Stephanopoulos wrote, "They bonded by poring over polls and bantering about campaign strategy the way baseball fans study box scores and relive their favorite plays."[10] But it was just such a devotion to polling that made Clinton keep Morris hidden from his White House staff to work secretly. Morris, Stephanopoulos charged, was a reminder to Clinton of that part of himself "that confused power and popularity with public service."

Just how did Clinton use polls? Morris puts it this way:

> In a room, [Clinton] will instinctively, as if by a canine sense of smell, find anyone who's reserved toward him, and he will work full time on winning his or her approval and, if possible, affection. . . . America is the ultimate room for Clinton. For him a poll helps him sense who doesn't like him and why they don't. In the reflected numbers, he sees his shortcomings and his potential, his successes and his failures. For Bill Clinton, positive poll results are not just tools—they are vindication, ratification, and approval—whereas negative poll results are a learning process in which the pain of the rebuff to his self-image forces deep introspection. Intellectually, polls offer Clinton an insight into how people think. He uses polls to adjust not just his thinking on one issue but his frame of reference so that it is always as close to congruent with that of the country as possible.[11]

After Democrats were slaughtered in the 1994 mid-term elections, Clinton turned to Morris once again to revive his political prospects, just as he had done when he lost the Arkansas governorship. His old staff members, those who had fought their way from Arkansas to the White House, were left behind as Morris and his tactics took control. Clinton's old pollster, Stanley Greenberg, was left behind as the new Morris strategy was put into effect. But we do well to pause and ask, What was Greenberg's sin? According to Stephanopoulos, Greenberg didn't give Clinton enough recommendations.[12]

Such an assertion lends significant weight to the polling critics' case that polling isn't value neutral. In other words, polling isn't just a matter of politicians asking the public what to do and then doing it. It is far less than an objective, neutral scientific measure. Polling is the art of framing issues for public evaluation. That's why in the Age of Polling, the pollster has replaced the party leader as the television commentator as well as the chief strategist. Pollsters are no less partisan than their party forebears were, but they do understand the limitations of what polls say and how wording affects national contests over political ideas. Pollsters have a nuance to their observations because they are aware of the dicey, shifting nature of the public's collected impressions, their conflicting values, and the lightning charge inherent in certain code words.

> In the Age of Polling, the pollster has replaced the party leader as the television commentator as well as the chief strategist.

Political pollsters are *more* sophisticated observers because they search for the gray areas as well the partisan differences that dominate the media's idea that politics is a zero-sum game of winners and losers.

For a campaign, the pollster's intelligence, cunning, and even recommendations are a qualitative testament to the quantitative limitation of polling information. Numbers are just the *beginning* of the debate. They are not the closing act in a political drama. The ability to persuade and the framing of the debate are the ways campaigns try to move adverse numbers. That's exactly what Morris knew, and he understood how to bring the two together to make Clinton politically viable once again.

The plan Clinton and Morris set in motion is well known by now but bears repeating. The White House would raise $25 to $30 million to finance a television campaign to attack the GOP and boost the Clinton-Gore reelection effort. Meanwhile, the White House would adopt a strategy of "triangulation"—neutralize GOP ideas by adopting them and ignore liberal Democrats, thereby standing above the partisan fray in Washington.

The Morris strategy worked well, because Republicans were demonized in the Medicare debate as enemies of the elderly. Meanwhile Clinton stole the GOP thunder by taking up the balanced budget and targeting "value" issues, such as school uniforms, stricter standards in Hollywood, and eventually welfare reform. Clinton's embrace of the balanced budget illustrates the power of the poll in the hands of the protean politician. The official who is willing to evolve with opinion can help ensure his or her survival, but such gamesmanship is not what we commonly associate with leadership. Both Stephanopoulos and Morris agree that they battled over Clinton's soul: Stephanopoulos vying for Clinton's liberal yearnings, Morris struggling to manipulate his lust for victory.

Years later, Stephanopoulos spared no words, expressing liberal rage at how the Democrat's ship of state was veering rightward in 1996 all because of gusts of public opinion wind. "[Clinton] wants to abandon our promises and piss on our friends," he writes of his thoughts at the time. "Why don't we go all the way and switch parties."[13]

Clinton embraced welfare reform (after two vetoes) because it robbed Republicans of a key election issue. Viewing his continual transformations, the *Nation* declared Clinton a "poll-guided, issues-tactical genius, stealing plans from allies and opponents alike and making them his own."[14]

So powerful was the influence of polls that they determined exactly when Clinton would address the nation on his balanced budget. Morris wanted the plan revealed in a way that challenged the Republican plan, so the GOP couldn't steal the mantle of budget balancers. Stephanopoulos and others opposed the balancing act and the speed required to get the plan to the public. Yet despite the objections of nearly every member of the White House staff, Morris's demands were met. So clear was Clinton's dedication to Morris's juggernaut of polling that Clinton's liberal staffers considered resigning in the midst of his strong tack to the center. The staff was horrified by the evolution of the fantastical monster: Government by Poll. "There was plenty of room for honest debate over budget policy," Stephanopoulos writes. "It was the assault on the integrity of our policy-making process, the fact that we were *beholden to polls* [my emphasis]" that upset the staff.[15]

In the end, however, no one resigned. Instead, the staff put together a speech unveiling a White House plan that purported to balance the budget in ten years.

In evaluating Clinton, few liberals or conservatives mistake the forty-second president's adeptness with polls for political courage. No one can argue that Clinton wasn't successful. He was reelected with 49 percent of the vote, even after striking out on his most liberal promises in his first administration. This fact raises the question: What exactly is it that we want from political leaders?

How Polls Shape Political Leadership

In our modern media climate, polling—whether public media surveys or internal campaign polls—undermines political leadership and the kind of debate that informs voters of stark contrasts in belief. For politicians, polling whittles down ideas. It leads to theme campaigning. It elevates tiny proposals over broad reforms. It favors spending and "targeted tax cuts" over serious reform, restructuring, across-the-board tax cuts, reduced government, and substantive debate.

The proliferation of polling has been so many nails in the coffin of issue-oriented campaigns. As journalists become more obsessed with gaffes, "positioning," and how a politician "comes off," the chances for political daring and heroism decrease. With polling, the opportunity costs of introducing new ideas become exorbitant. So, too, as donors, activists, pundits, and producers track a candidate's standing in the polls, rapidly falling support levels undercut the chance for enterprising thinkers to risk entering the arena. If a campaign begins to falter, even momentarily, chances are the policy proposals will get the blame.

As Daniel Casse, a former policy adviser to Republican presidential candidate Bob Dole and speechwriter for Ronald Reagan, writes, "Campaigns rarely make or propose policy these days. It is considered too risky an undertaking. Ideas still have consequences."[16] Those consequences are an albatross around the neck of a candidate in a media culture that delights in criticism and listens anxiously for opponent counterattack. Put forward a few ideas, and the political wolves smell blood. The media will pick up an opponent's cleverly worded countercharges and ram them down the throat of voters.

> In fact, the clearest sign that a campaign is "in trouble" is when it starts generating ideas or policy proposals.

In fact, the clearest sign that a campaign is "in trouble" is when it starts generating ideas or policy proposals. In the Age of Proliferating Polls, only underdog candidates and political dark horses dare talk about issues—otherwise, the softer and blander the themeless pudding, the better.

Casse describes this reality well. In 1996, he was one of those pushing for Dole to make a real campaign issue of 15-percent across-the-board tax cuts. During the Dole campaign, Casse and others talked about the success of Mike Harris, premier of Ontario, who resolutely pressed a tax-cutting plan, thus transforming the dynamics of his race and getting him elected. The response in the Dole campaign to Harris's success is a testimony to the power of pollsters:

But at the senior staff meetings and endless message meetings, these arguments [for the broad tax cuts] met with resistance from the core of pollsters. They cared little about
the benefits the tax plan would bring. They pointed out that
the tax cut was not selling in focus groups. . . . In the poker
game atmosphere of a campaign strategy debate, such focus
group data is the equivalent of a royal flush. [17]

The Dole campaign later opted for a platform based on
"moral issues," partly because polls indicated that this was a
concern of the public. It also gave the campaign a way to criticize Bill Clinton on the so-called character issue. It is unclear
what the public wanted the federal government to do about
"moral issues;" such a question was never posed. Pollsters,
whether they work with the media or campaigns, deal in impressions and gut feelings, not specifics. To ask specific questions seeking voter knowledge would be fatal, revealing
boundless ignorance and disinterest in thinking out policy issues. Better to remain in the abstract world of fuzzy logic and
warm sentiment.

For the politician, polling almost invariably works against
innovation. Americans distrust new ideas. What's more, because voters are so conflicted and ignorant, a new idea inevitably appears destabilizing, even dangerous. Throw in
media sensationalism and opponent hyperbole, and bids to reform health care or cut taxes are soon lost in a flurry of mad
attacks and big headlines.

Although large-scale reforms are suspect, voters find
small-scale spending initiatives nearly irresistible. So it is that
politicians are able to use polling to find those policy proposals that seem so popular with the public. In this sense, polling
makes it easier for politicians to win success through baby
steps. Americans are leery of political conflict. In a massive
system such as that in Washington, D.C., polling gives politi-

cians the insights into the small programs that will resonate with well-intentioned voters.

Bill Clinton used such small measures to send symbolic messages to voters that, despite his personal corruption and fallibility, he was the candidate of "values." Morris attributes Clinton's survival through various scandals to this headline-grabbing technique in which the president spoke up on issues such as teen tobacco use, drugs, drunk driving, gun control, education standards, family leave, health coverage, and school uniforms.[18] On the flip side, conscious adherence to polling has transformed Republican politics from the bold Reagan agenda into a cautious defense of tax credits, savings accounts, and other tax-code subsidies.

What Do We Expect of Political Leaders?

Whether on the left or the right, the conscientious citizen wants the representatives of the people to be the best and the brightest. Leaders, in the noblest American conception, should be committed to appealing to our best inclinations, using persuasive language and elevated oratory. To this extent, the American heart still pounds to the rhythm of constitutional republicanism. We are not Athens, randomly selecting our leaders by lots. We are not a Roman mob, screaming and shouting to push leaders in different directions. We still hold as an ideal the inspirational view of America put forward by John F. Kennedy and Ronald Reagan in their soaring rhetoric and grandest visions.

Americans have often upheld leaders who had the courage to lead even when public opinion was temporarily against them. Before the United States entered World War II,

Franklin Roosevelt armed merchant marines and pressed the Lend-Lease Act to help arm the British struggle against Nazi Germany. In the 1970s, Richard Nixon reopened diplomatic relations with China, in a move that cost him the support of some core members of his political base. In the 1980s, Ronald Reagan pressed for the deployment of Pershing-II missiles in Europe, despite initial public opposition, in an effort to balance the looming specter of the Soviet Union in Europe.

Americans look back on these actions with approval. But with the modern machinery of polling-fueled media coverage such acts become even more difficult to pursue. Polling can help politicians persuade citizens, but the media's use of polling shortens the time and depth of deliberation, often subjecting even careful appeals to the heated crucible of controversy before new ideas are communicated.

> Polling can help politicians persuade citizens, but the media's use of polling shortens the time and depth of deliberation.

What do the polls say about what voters want from their politicians? Even this question is dependent on the way it is asked. The Center on Policy Attitudes declared that "[e]ighty-four percent said the public should have far more influence on government decisions." COPA's poll, conducted January 26–31, 1999, asked a battery of more than seventy questions probing public discontent with the nonresponsiveness of Washington, D.C. Among the findings: Just over a third (33.8 percent) thought "[m]embers of Congress should not pay attention to polls that show their approval ratings, because this will just make them react to every little shift in their popularity." But 61.2 percent believe that "members of Congress should pay attention to polls that show their approval rating, because this gives them a measure of whether or not they are heading in the right direction."

COPA also asked:

If the leaders of the nation followed the views of the public more closely, do you think the nation would be better off, or worse off than today?
Fully 80.5 percent said the nation would be "better off." Only 9.5 percent said "worse," and 10 percent didn't know or refused to answer the question. What's more, two out of three respondents said a random sample of Americans informed on all sides of an issue would make better decisions than Congress. The broad frame of the nonresponsive nature of Washington politicians may have had an effect on the responses, however.

The Gallup Organization asked American adults, April 15–18, 1999:

In your opinion, would the country be better off if there was (1) More attention paid to the polls than now or (2) Less attention paid to the polls than now?[19]
The results were almost entirely the opposite, despite remarkably similar wording. Just 36 percent of Americans thought the nation would be better off if more attention was given to polls. A majority (52 percent) said the country would be better off if less attention was paid to the polls.

Narrowing the questions, Gallup focused on how the public feels about polls and their elected leaders:

In your own opinion, do political officeholders and public officials pay too much attention to the polls, or not enough attention to the polls?
A majority (54 percent) said political officeholders and public officials pay "too much" attention. Thirty-nine percent said not enough. Just 2 percent said the right amount.

More specifically, Gallup asked:

In your opinion, do President Clinton and administration officials pay too much attention to the polls, or not enough attention?
Slight fewer than one out of two Americans (49 percent) thought Clinton paid too much attention to the polls. Thirty-seven percent said not enough.

While the media use polls to hammer away at recalcitrant politicians, Gallup found (at least in this poll) that Americans are far more critical of the effect of polls *on the media.* Gallup asked:

In your opinion, do the news media pay too much attention to the polls, or not enough attention?
More than two-thirds of Americans (67 percent) think the media pay too much attention to polls. Just 25 percent answered "not enough."

Does the media obsession help Americans understand politics? Not according to the public:

Do you feel that polls help give you a better understanding of the news of the day, or not?
Fifty-one percent of the public said polls do not help. Forty-five percent thought they did help.

Even on the subject of the polls, the public is divided. Politicians are far more aware of the divided messages inherent in polls and endemic to the American electorate. Perhaps this is why special interests have so much power in Washington. Polls do not (and cannot) measure intensity because voters are too ignorant and too unreliable to give accurate answers about what will truly raise their ire. But special interests—from government workers unions and the AARP seeking to protect and expand entitlements for their members to business political action committees and the National Rifle Association trying to prevent further federal controls—represent voters and activists who will inflict pain on politicians. Polls are limited, and politicians know it.

CAN POLLS CONTRIBUTE TO DELIBERATION?

To some extent, polls already contribute to deliberation. When politicians use polls as a device to collect information about where the public stands, they are looking for areas of uncertainty and vulnerability, qualities absent from most media polls. Politicians then use these gray areas to persuade the public toward their positions. They craft their language using polls that test ideas and words and that challenge respondents to make tough choices. But can polls do more?

For some pollsters, public opinion polling is a way to get politicians to talk about issues. "Candidates don't talk about all the issues," said Michael W. Traugott, former president of the American Association of Public Opinion Researchers. "Candidates like to talk about a limited agenda—especially one favorable to them. Polls have the potential to give a voice to the people."[20] There is much truth to this. Politicians want to control as much of their message as possible, especially because in the Strategy Cult of modern journalism, a gaffe or tactical misstep can be punished with great severity.

> Politicians want to control as much of their message as possible, especially because a gaffe or tactical misstep can be punished with great severity.

The strength of Traugott's observation, however, depends on polling that is conducted using the careful strictures of a researcher, not the quick, often shallow methods of media polls. In most cases, media polls do not measure *intensity* of support, present the full costs of an idea, or word a question several ways to uncover response effects. More often media polls are cosmetic, meant to complement stories with colorful graphics and lend a thin veneer of science and fact.

Politicians have an incentive to make sure their sense of public opinion is more complete that what is offered by media polls. Their futures are dependent on the course of action they take. That's why politicians use other means to find out what constituents and citizen groups want. In addition to asking questions that frame the best argument for them, politicians will test vulnerabilities by making the best argument from the opposition. They present costs to citizens, ask follow-up questions, break down results, and cross-tabulate with as much detail as they can afford. But good politicians pay attention to constituent letters and questions in town hall meetings. They note the interests from phone calls. In the modern system, elected officials have to carefully balance the support of their strongest special interest backers with the overall feelings of the majority.

> The press tends to use polls as a kind of cudgel against politicians, blaring in headlines, "This Is What the People Want!"

They also have to avoid stumbling on issues that could be used against them in future electoral contests. Media polls *can* help bring some political issues to the forefront, but for candidates this is less important. Their own internal polls show where the fissures and seams are in the ever-shifting tectonic plates of opinion. Polling may be helpful in forcing political leaders to address a forgotten issue. But once again, we must ask: Who is conducting the poll? Who determines what the forgotten issue is? The average politician interacts with the public far more than any journalist does. The politician has resources in addition to polls to communicate issues of concern to the electorate. Journalists, on the other hand, use polls in conjunction with their own coverage, so it is doubtful that their media polls will contribute at all to public deliberation. The answer isn't more polling but rather a journalistic corps that will step back from its position as a modern praetorian guard and let the public and politicians interact with less commentary from the media and more respect.

Manipulating Polls and Politicians?

Obviously the relationship between polling and political leadership is a complicated one. Not every politician polls on where to go for a vacation or exactly what position to hold. But the feedback loop of media coverage, electoral challenge, and constituent outreach makes the role of polling all the more complicated. The press tends to use polls as a kind of cudgel against politicians, blaring in headlines, "THIS IS WHAT THE PEOPLE WANT!"

In America, most polling is in the hands of the media, so the questions and agendas set forth in polls are established by unelected editors, producers, and directors of media survey units. Those familiar with modern journalism know that this is hardly a representative sample of the diversity and differences of political opinion in America. The Freedom Forum found in 1996 that nearly nine in ten members of the Washington press corps voted for Bill Clinton. For the naïve there is the temptation to believe that this has no bearing on the product of a professional media establishment. But for those as skeptical as these journalists, such institutional claims are just a little too extravagant to believe.

Politicians, however, must respond to the powerful imperatives and interests of the Fourth Estate. Their leadership is dependent on public opinion. How that public opinion is measured is almost invariably in the hands of the media. The hydra-headed nature of this problem is not limited to America's public discourse. As French journalist Jean-Francois Revel writes:

> One is often surprised by the ignorance, the "holes," that certain leading politicians reveal in private conversations or even in public debates, simply because [of] what can be called "professional deformation"—the strains of overwork and the ever-increasing amount of time that has to be devoted to mediatic questions—leads them to interest themselves less in tackling specific issues and more and more in what public opinion, which is to say the press, thinks of them.[21]

But, as we've seen, elected leaders understand something missed by the Greek chorus in the media: The essence of political debate is the control and framing of the debate. Money makes a difference in political campaigns not because citizens are defenseless against slick brochures selling party propaganda. Rather, money lets politicians get out their "frame," or explanation for their actions. It also lets them frame their opponent's actions.

In a sense, if voters want politicians who look beyond polls and stand with the heroic stature of John F. Kennedy calling a nation to the better angels of its nature, then they in turn must know the limitations of polls. If voters want Ronald Reagans who deploy missiles that later bring totalitarians to disarmament talks, then they must show some patience for political officials.

The eternal challenge for political leaders in a democracy is how to cater to public sentiment as well as lead it. As the type and quality of public opinion measures proliferate, twenty-first-century America must come to understand the costs of polling as well as its benefits.

CHAPTER EIGHT

The Politics of Impeachment

If You Don't Have an Opinion, One Will Be Appointed to You

> *"But at this moment of maximum peril, the president chose to follow the pattern of his past. He called Dick Morris. Dick took a poll. The poll said lie. It was out of Clinton's hands."*
>
> —George Stephanopoulos,
> *former advisor to President Clinton*[1]

■ ■ ■

ALL THE PITFALLS AND PROBLEMS of polling came to a head in January 1998, when news broke that the independent counsel was investigating the allegations and legal actions of a former White House intern named Monica Lewinsky. Lewinsky was alleged to have had a sexual liaison with the president of the United States in a room adjacent to the Oval Office. For many Democrats, the news was only the most upsetting and recent example of unrelenting Republican efforts to hurt the president. For others, the Lewinsky saga was awful confirmation of Clinton's lifestyle—a sordid and self-serving pursuit of pleasure that many had suspected before, which inevitably culminated in the selfish use of power to protect his political viability.

When the story of Monica Lewinsky fell into the hands of the special prosecutors on Whitewater, Independent Counsel Kenneth Starr moved forward to investigate the allegations. The Lewinsky case was relevant to the independent counsel for reasons other than extramarital sex, Starr argued. Clinton's relationship with Lewinsky seemed to conform to other workplace liaisons, adding weight to a sexual harassment case against Bill Clinton for which he had recently testified. But what interested the independent counsel was that the Lewinsky case provided insight into the White House modus operandi for dealing with what one Clinton adviser called "bimbo eruptions." For Starr and his legal cohorts, the Lewinsky gambit carried allegations of lying under oath, abuse of power, obstruction of justice, witness tampering, and conspiracy.

Over the course of 1998, however, these grave issues, involving the power of the presidency and the rule of law, were submerged under a hurricane of rhetorical winds and wave after wave of public opinion polls. Polls soon became the most important ally in the White House effort to keep the president in the Oval Office. They vexed pundits, scared politicians, stunned average citizens, and emboldened Clinton's defenders. White House tactics fully exploited the power of polls, moving attention away from the legal issues into a morass of impugned motives, counterattack, and self-serving claims of public indifference.

To a certain extent, the Lewinsky scandal represented the standard Clinton damage-control operation: heavy on counterattack and merciless in partisanship. But it differed in one critical way from previous "bimbo eruptions" and scandal control. It announced, once and for all, the media's dependence on, and our Republic's vulnerability to, the public polling instruments that purport to represent the voice of the people. From the very beginning, polling played an integral role in the defense of Bill Clinton, even before the issue became public. Indeed, it *was* polling that set the president on the path to embracing one of the most well-planned and well-coordinated defenses of a political official this nation has ever seen. Just as the public was hit with the bombshell of Clinton's affair with Lewinsky, Clinton pollster Dick Morris called the president to sympathize. Morris had seen the *Washington Post*'s story on the Lewinsky allegations and was ready to help. The conversations that followed were an insight into the power of polling and how skillful politicians use that power.

> From the very beginning, polling played an integral role in the defense of Bill Clinton, even before the issue became public.

Morris's call found the president in a state of panic. "Oh, God. This is just awful," Clinton told Morris. "I didn't do what they said I did, but I did do something. I mean, with this girl, I didn't do what they said, but I did . . . do something. And I may have done enough so that I don't know if I can prove my innocence."

Morris tried to calm the president by telling him of America's enormous reservoir of forgiveness. But what Morris heard back were more worried pleadings from the president: "But what about the legal thing? You know, the legal thing? You know, Starr and perjury and all. You know, ever since the election, I've tried to shut myself down. I've tried to shut my body down, sexually, I mean. But sometimes I slipped up and with this girl I just slipped up."

In this moment of political crisis during which the president admitted a sexual affair, and the threat of perjury and even removal loomed, Morris suggested a poll. Clinton agreed. Later that day, Morris called the president to report the mixed results. Voters were "willing to forgive [the president] for adultery, but not for perjury or obstruction of justice." According to Morris, the results indicated that Clinton should *not* go forward with an explanation or confession. Clinton responded ominously, "Well, we just have to win, then."

Those were the words that let loose the White House dogs of war. The next day, Morris advocated a press conference to blast Lewinsky "out of the water." But that immediate retaliation never occurred. Clinton refused to green light this particular attack effort. He believed that she might *not* be cooperating with the independent counsel, and he didn't want to alienate her with a smear campaign. Nevertheless, the die had been cast, and the mind-set of counterattack would survive to strike others involved in the case.

For many American citizens, here was the real scandal of the Lewinsky affair: A president, who knew he lied, had orchestrated lying from others, and then poll-tested whether he should confess his wrongdoing. From any other citizen, this was legally unacceptable. But from a president who was master of the bully pulpit, who knew? With the prospect of losing his office and its protection always in the back of his mind, he worked hard to emphasize his political strength in order to preserve his job. The measure of that strength would be the polls.

Internally the poll would become an important part of the focus-group tested phrases, headlines, and policies presented to the public. As in the Medicare reform debates in 1995, polling would tell the president when he needed to shore up his job approval ratings with the right public policy spending initiative or headline-grabbing speech. What's more, polls would replace the debate about the rule of law and due process, making the battle a war of megaphones between the authority of the White House and a disparate and mostly silent band of political opponents. The only difference between 1995 and 1998 was that the stakes were much higher, and this time the gloves were off.

Just as Clinton was defining his strategy and polling to find the margin of error in his conscience, major media players deployed polls to determine the public reaction to the Lewinsky story. The Gallup Organization polled Americans just two days after the story broke. In a poll of January 23–24, Clinton's job approval rating fell slightly from 60 percent to 58 percent. But in the next poll (January 25–26), his job approval rating rose 1 percentage point. By January 28, following the State of the Union address, the rating soared to 67 percent, marking a new high for his presidency. (It is interesting to note that Kenneth Starr's approval rating hit its lowest point in Gallup's January 28 overnight poll, which lends some credence to an inverse relationship.)

The effect of these polls gave the Clinton administration the breathing room it needed, which inspired CNN's senior political analyst, Bill Schneider, to tell the president of the United States, "I think I saved you."

In the months that followed, polling was used to judge every step of the debate, relentlessly testing the question of job approval ratings and whether the president should be removed from office. The impact of polling went far beyond mere tactical use of private polls, however. Media polling also played a critical role—if not the decisive part—in ratifying the most brazen strokes of the Clinton defense. It was polling that breathed new life into the demoralized and disgusted Democratic allies in Congress. It gave pause to the media and then fed the debates among pundits. Polls were also used to show the disdain for Clinton critics. In the end, it was polling that would test, even reinforce, public apathy just hours after each new ripple in the Monica Lewinsky saga became glaringly clear.

> Media polling played a critical role—if not the decisive part—in ratifying the most brazen strokes of the Clinton defense.

Who was the real winner of 1998? It wasn't Bill Clinton. Although he overcame tremendous odds to survive impeachment, he was left crippled in office. His moral authority was permanently hindered, and his legacy stained. Republicans weren't winners either. The botched, last-minute case of the House and its fleeting consideration by the Senate were perfunctory, rather than honestly searching displays of Congressional oversight. There was a winner, however. One group walked away from 1998 with increased power and prestige: the pollsters. They had had their day, triumphantly stealing the debate about truth and the substance of outrage in the name of democratic rule.

In response to the Clinton-Lewinsky scandal, Michael Traugott, president of the American Association for Public Opinion Research, said, "I'm not sure we'll see soon another instance in which there was such highly focused polling activity on such a limited set of topics." He added that the pollsters showed quick public judgments—opposing Clinton's forced removal—that held throughout the entire scandal.[2]

It pays, then, to look closely once again at one of the most polled controversies in American history; how that subject affected public debate; and how it betrayed the ideals of the U.S. Constitution. The perils of methodology, question framing, media misuse of polls, public ignorance, and political cowardice combined to overturn the rule of law, limited government, and the simple question of truth.

Were the Polls Rigged? Methodology

Methodological rigor is what gives polling the appearance and feel of scientific truth and concrete fact. The methodology of a poll can have far-reaching ramifications in determining the final results, as was the case during the Lewinsky scandal. Perhaps the most critical methodological decision during the whole process came to pass in the first weekend of inquiry: Pollsters chose to use the sample of nationwide adults in almost every poll.

As we saw in chapter 3, such samples of nationwide adults tend to tap a more Democratic and liberal-leaning part of the electorate. Recall what a sample change can mean. One *USA Today*/CNN/Gallup poll switched from likely voters to registered voters in August 2000, leading to a seemingly momentous shift in support. With this simple stroke of the methodological pen, Governor George W. Bush's 17-point lead over Vice President Al Gore fell 15 percentage points— ostensibly in the wake of Gore's vice presidential selection. In explaining the new results, Gallup warned that registered voters shift results as much as 4 to 5 percentage points *away* from Republicans.

Could the choice of the even less accurate sample of American adults have had such a huge impact on the Lewinsky polls? Was the jury rigged from the start? It was never discussed during the Lewinsky scandal, but this choice of who to sample was a methodological shortcut probably intended to save the media conglomerates' money. The polls sponsored by ABC, CBS, NBC, the *Washington Post*, the *New York Times*, CNN, *Time, Newsweek, USA Today*, Gallup, Harris, the *Wall Street Journal*, and the Pew Research Center for the People and the Press all used the same inexpensive, shallow sample of American adults. In contrast, Fox News/Opinion Dynamics polls used registered voters.

Only one polling firm, Zogby International, insisted on using likely voters. It shouldn't be a surprise, then, to learn that Zogby's polls rendered far less positive results for the White House. Opinion was far more mixed and conflicted. While every other pollster produced quickie polls for media stories, Zogby's results showed a great deal more equivocation and concern about the scandal. Compare these two poll results:

On December 12–13, 1998, an ABC News/*Washington Post* poll asked 1,004 adults:

> The full House will vote on impeachment next week, and if the House impeaches Clinton, the Senate will decide whether he should be removed from office. Based on what you know, do you think Congress should or should not impeach Clinton and remove him from office?
> *Thirty-eight percent supported impeachment. Sixty-one percent opposed it.*

In a three-day poll on December 10–13, 1998, Zogby International interviewed 1,003 likely voters, asking:

> Should the House of Representatives vote "yes" or "no" to impeach the President and send him to trial in the Senate?
> *Forty-four percent said "yes," and 52 percent said "no."*

The margin of error on both polls was the same and the timing of the polls similar. But as these results show, a simple shift in the sample from registered to likely voters could have made a fundamental difference in the media coverage, the political debate, and perhaps even the outcome of the Lewinsky saga. For most Americans, the ABC News/*Washington Post* poll is the dominant memory. It seemed public support was decisively, unequivocally, and unquestionably against impeachment. But only selective measurement and the slanted presentation of polling results made support for Clinton seem so unambiguous. It was the idea that 60 percent of Americans opposed Clinton's removal that undermined each damaging blow to come throughout the saga.

Should media pollsters have used likely voters? When asking about Clinton and impeachment, would this have been fair? Or would likely voters just rig the polls for more conservative results? One might argue that a *broader* sample of adults or registered voters was warranted because the president's fate affected that of the whole nation. If Clinton were impeached and removed, the thinking goes, then the lives of every American would feel the constitutional ramifications. This seems to strengthen the argument for a broader sample. In addition, media stories began with a focus on what the average American on the street thought about Clinton's actions. Were Americans angry? Outraged? Accepting? If the mood of the nation was going to be the subject of debate, then the population of average Americans seemed to be the place to start.

In the end, however, the choices of methodology and the parameters of the debate about the Lewinsky scandal went undiscussed. Unlike the constitutional mechanisms spelled out in clear rules for the governance of the country, the nation was never allowed to debate these issues openly in public forum. Reporters wrote no stories questioning the sample used in the first polls. The decision to use adults nationwide as the dominant sample probably came down to an issue of money. Whatever the effect on democracy, it was cheaper to take the easy route and tap those whose only qualification was being a sentient life form 18 years or older who picked up the phone.

Of course, for nine out of ten Americans, the methodology would not matter. They would never detect the difference when journalists reported the final results. The polling units made a momentous decision for our democracy without even a modicum of debate. They did not even *poll* Americans on who should be polled. Instead they decided for themselves, choosing a polling methodology that guaranteed more Democratic-leaning results from a less informed, more suggestible sample.

There are arguments for using a sample of likely voters, as Zogby International did. As the allegations and stories about the Lewinsky affair progressed, media polls and stories began to focus on the possible electoral consequences of Clinton's moral choices and the ensuing partisan warfare. Americans were asked what they would do at the ballot box to those who voted for impeachment and those who voted against it. They were asked what they thought about the long-term consequences to the American political system. Meanwhile pundits attempted to calculate the damage to the two parties long before the House even began debating the independent counsel's report. Polls and media stories once again focused on the horse race. The combined force of polling and reportage carried subtle election-year messages of punishment and reward that no doubt pushed politicians toward political safety in their quest to survive to another term. More than one congressional player blamed these polls for shifting convictions on Capitol Hill.

Ironically it is the media's pressure on politicians that provides the best argument for using likely voters. Media polls often ask whether a political issue will make a citizen more or less likely to support a candidate. For just this reason, pollsters should attempt to find those who vote. Likely voters are an important segment to target in polls because they are the Americans who voluntarily do their duty on Election Day to ensure that their voices are heard. Of course it might be argued that just because likely voters show up at the ballot box doesn't give them the right to dominate political discussions. But, for a moment, turn this argument on its head.

> The combined force of polling and reportage carried subtle election-year messages of punishment and reward that pushed politicians toward political safety in their quest to survive to another term.

Should the polling units at the nation's largest media companies have the sole power to determine whose voices get heard before Election Day? This is in fact what happens. The media pit polls against the Constitution by using samples that vary markedly from a sample consisting of those people who on Election Day choose how they will be represented. Some citizens (upwards of 65 percent) opt *not* to be part of the pollsters' "random" sample. Instead, they make their opinions heard by choosing the nation's representatives inside the voting booth. One way or another, a sample is selected that has the power to shape America's future. One sample is determined by the Constitution and expressed at the ballot box. The other is a creature of media fiat, warping electoral politics before voters can show up at the voting booth—unless the media poll sample corresponds to those who actually select, reward, or punish their elected leaders on Election Day.

To a certain extent it is difficult to know just how much the polls are at variance with the voting electorate, because media polls refuse to report the declining response rates in their polls. Likely voters seem to become all the more important when one thinks harder on this niggling problem of refusal rates. Polls should "squeeze" likely voters to find out exactly who will show up, as Murray Edelman of Voter News Service puts it.[3] Polls of likely voters add a measure of accuracy that corrects some of the inherent bias stemming from high nonresponse rates. By trying to balance out the equation with likely voters, pollsters can control at least some of the problems of finding conservative voters who are more difficult to reach.

In any case, no matter what side the reader joins, it should be clear that the media's choice of methodology influenced the polling results that seemed so unassailable in the Lewinsky scandal. This polling methodology was never debated by the people for whom it presumed to speak. In an unrepresentative and elite debate, media operatives and polling specialists chose the cheapest, least accurate sample without public discussion or input in the matter.

Framing and Wording to Scare the People

Throughout the debate during the Lewinsky saga, another methodological artifact inherently biased polling in favor of Clinton. Returning to the earlier sample, in the ABC News/*Washington Post* poll of December 12–13, as noted above, the pollsters asked:

> The full House will vote on impeachment next week, and if the House impeaches Clinton, the Senate will decide whether he should be removed from office. Based on what you know, do you think Congress should or should not impeach Clinton and remove him from office?

Note how the ABC/*Post* poll stresses the seemingly extreme consequence—*removal* of Clinton—as the immediate retribution for Clinton's behavior. (The disturbing and destabilizing event is actually mentioned twice.) The Zogby question posed at the same time was more straightforward, presenting impeachment as a procedure on the way to trial. To repeat, Zogby International asked:

> Should the House of Representatives vote "yes" or "no" to impeach the President and send him to trial in the Senate?

This definition of impeachment and use of the word *trial* stresses the process of justice. It is more tentative and exploratory than the nation-shaking idea of removal of a president. And the word "trial" reinforces giving Clinton his day in court and giving the issue proper hearing. During the Lewinsky scandal, the journalistic drive for conflict and the lust to play hypothetical election games got ahead of the public—at least as presented in the polls. Long before an ignorant populace could grasp the full import of the Clinton case, his illegal actions (as determined by a Clinton-appointed federal judge), and the specifics of the allegations, polls were deployed that essentially asked: Should the leader of the free world in an era remarkable for its prosperity and peace be removed because of sexual dalliance? As we shall see, when the framing of questions omitted a jump to world-changing conclusions, there was much more support for the due process of law and institutional safeguards embodied in the separation of powers.

The framing of these impeachment questions turned upside down the usual procedure of media polling questions. As we saw earlier, Americans are tempted to say "yes" to small, reasonable sounding proposals, which is why specific, small spending programs do so well in poll after poll. Had voters been approached with such reasonable sounding steps along with a well-reported and well-debated process of inquiry, they would have been more likely to support the process. The polls in the Clinton case undercut the deliberative and educative process that works slowly through the minds of the voters.

Instead the media tended to emphasize the destabilizing impact of the case. The poll questions put a decision on the shoulders of the average adult respondents and pushed them to decide on impeachment when it wasn't clear they knew the process or even what the word meant. What was clear was that an opposing action would remove one of the few politicians they were familiar with, leaving the Oval Office in uncertain hands. As polling questions occasionally probed public reaction to specific charges or the need for hearings, or expressed tentative skepticism for White House claims, support for the constitutional process of impeachment would go up.

This same phenomenon occurred as the public digested the problems of Watergate, a case helped by the slow drip of new evidence seeping into the public consciousness.

In Gallup's first poll in June 1973, only 17 percent of Americans thought President Nixon should be impeached and removed by Congress. Seven months later, in January 1974, that number was still low, hovering at 37 percent—nearly identical to Clinton's percentage. In early May 1974, that number was still below 40 percent. Only in June 1974 did a Louis Harris poll break 50 percent.[4] Nixon resigned, but not because of the polls. The difference in his situation from Clinton's was a media and political elite that carried out the probe despite the public's misgivings.

Congress slowly thawed public opinion on the subject of Watergate. There was rising support for Nixon's removal from office, but it proceeded from congressional investigation and court inquiry into his corruption. Congressional Republicans in 1998 showed no such courage or skill for laying out their case to the people. And Democrats showed none of the honesty of their rivals in the 1970s in demanding an end to their leaders' shameful actions in the White House.

Clinton was also handed another gift in the way poll questions were worded. The media, after no discussion or explanation, assumed that Bill Clinton's job approval rating was the appropriate, nearly ultimate barometer for judging the public's reaction to the Lewinsky scandal. Using this broad measure, the media and Clinton defenders drew the conclusion that the public was behind the president. Not only was President Clinton's soaring job approval rating the final arbiter in many a political discussion, it also became the surrogate for public acceptance of the lurid or corrupt. The reason for this is partially a media phenomenon. The media are attracted to conflict and sharp ideological contrasts. Those questions that nuanced public disgust and concern about the scandal were repeatedly sidelined.

It should be clear by now that polling is not a surrogate for the debate and deliberation that can energize the public and educate the electorate. The forty to fifty words in a polling question are designed with few of the subtleties needed for useful political discussion, compromise, and problem solving. So it was with the job-approval questions asked during the Lewinsky scandal.

For years political scientists have attempted to define what exactly goes into shaping public approval for the presidency. Do public approval ratings mirror the nation's economic health or unemployment rate, or are they connected to some other complex formula? No one has been able to answer this question with a hard and fast mathematical relationship.

To many observers during the long, tawdry Clinton-Lewinsky tale, approval ratings were nothing more than a referendum on the economy in a time of peace and American prosperity. Rightly or wrongly, a president gets the credit or the blame for the economy's performance. For Clinton, there could be no better news. One pollster, Scott Rasmussen of Rasmussen Research, after looking at the job approval numbers, stated simply, "People are voting their wallets."[5]

The wording of the polling question on job approval ratings was simply too limited to answer deeper questions. What were voters thinking? While approval ratings became the *sine qua non* during the Clinton-Lewinsky saga, journalists blundered ahead with all manner of explanations, reasoning from effect (high approval ratings) to the cause (people didn't care). But questions lingered.

Did Americans oppose impeachment because it was simply too disruptive? Had they lowered their expectations of Clinton so the new revelations simply had little effect? Could Clinton's popularity be a measure of disgust with Republicans and the independent counsel? And was that disdain for Clinton's critics a product of White House smear campaigns and effectively managed partisanship?

As we have seen, how a question is framed has a profound effect on the answers respondents give. The reason for these response effects comes from the fact that Americans don't have deeply rooted or fixed ideological opinions. The polling question in most cases dictates what is "salient." The average American's political beliefs are a mixed jumble of values, bits of knowledge, and gross impressions. The often contradictory nature of American political beliefs became clearer in the Clinton scandal as polls asked more in-depth questions.

A pollster's first question was usually about how the president was doing in performing his job. In a sense this was a lead-in question. This is not to say it's wrong to begin with the job approval question, but it undoubtedly helped frame the issue in a way that the White House found easy to exploit.

The media reported the results of job approval polls as evidence that voters did not want the president removed. But as the evidence of abuse of power and obstruction mounted and the partisan body count grew, more specific polling questions showed a public more concerned about, than condoning of, Clinton. Still it was the job approval rating that gave Clinton defenders strength and often silenced his critics in Congress and the media.

> The average American's political beliefs are a mixed jumble of values, bits of knowledge, and gross impressions.

When polls did occasionally bring up the subject of charges and hearings, the public often warmed to the idea. The media's fixation on the most disruptive and extreme outcome of the case probably made respondents more cautious. That, combined with the frenzied and hysterical charges and hyperbole of the White House defenders, incited political upheaval. But the framing of poll questions made a difference, especially when an alternative frame, such as the rule of law, was pitted against removal for sexual dalliance. On December 10–11, 1998, *Newsweek* asked 806 adults:

> Which of the following do you think would be more damaging to our country and political system: having a

trial in the U.S. Senate over the charges in the Lewinsky matter, OR, allowing President Clinton to finish his term with no official punishment for his behavior in the Lewinsky matter?

The result was surprising. When phrased in this way, the question introduces a new frame, one ignored in most of the polling questions. By emphasizing the policing of the nation's highest official, this framing reflects more closely the purpose of impeachment as designed by the nation's founders. Americans were suddenly of two minds: 41 percent believed the greater damage would come from allowing President Clinton to go unpunished, while 39 percent feared a Senate trial more.[6] The point here is how *conflicted* voters were.

Asking about removal in a vacuum stressed a major change in government during a time of prosperity—all for an immoral act that didn't surprise most Americans. (When President Clinton finally admitted that he lied about his relationship with Lewinsky, 81 percent said they weren't surprised, according to an ABC News/*Washington Post* poll conducted August 19–21, 1998. Only 18 percent of the 1,015 adults polled nationwide said Clinton's confession was a shocker, presumably because they were the few who bought the February finger-wagging denial.)

Still for most Americans it was all too disgusting. They just wanted it to go away. In fact the White House tactics first heightened then exploited this sentiment, even as the Office of Independent Counsel continued with the mission mandated by Clinton's attorney general, Janet Reno. For instance, many Americans opposed release of the Starr Report. But was it because of the subject? Or were Americans just sick and tired of it all? Not if the question tested the trade-offs that included ignoring the constitutional process.

A Gallup/CNN/*USA Today* poll run September 14–15, 1998, asked 1,028 adults nationwide:

What do you think Congress should do with Ken Starr's report: hold hearings to investigate the charges contained in the report, OR, take no action on the report and end the investigation into these matters immediately?

Fifty percent supported hearings, and 44 percent opposed. Yet most Americans were exposed to media polling questions that tested the hypothetical results and the political end games of the Lewinsky scandal before the constitutional machinery went into action. A CNN/*Time* poll from October 14–15, 1998, asked 1,036 adults:

Which of the following possible outcomes of the investigation of Bill Clinton would you most like to see happen? Clinton is impeached and removed from office. Clinton resigns from office. Clinton is censured by Congress, and remains in office. Clinton remains in office, and Congress takes no action against him.

Phrased in this way, voters didn't support removal. But there was more to the story. If the media had chosen to parse voter sentiment then media reportage might have changed to preparing citizens for Congress' role and the issue would have been framed differently. Like the issue of abortion, the choice of answers in impeachment had to be as subtle and gradual as the respondents' beliefs. For instance, only 12 percent supported outright impeachment and removal. But 21 percent wanted Clinton to resign. Another 28 percent wanted Clinton to be censured and remain in office. And only 34 percent wanted Congress to take no action. When presented with more choices, the polls demand more careful reportage than often occurred throughout the case.

Public opinion showed all the signs of instability. While most pollsters point to the months of opposition to the removal of Clinton, there was still plenty of evidence for instability, especially as the case began to move through Congress and polling questions drifted to public appraisal of the facts. A *Newsweek* poll on December 10–11, 1998, asked 806 adults the following:

> The issue of impeachment is now before Congress. Do you think the House of Representatives should impeach President Clinton and make him stand trial in the U.S. Senate, or not?

Only 35 percent of those surveyed said the House should vote to impeach, while 60 percent opposed impeachment. Yet just one week later, the same question was asked of 753 adults, producing remarkably different results. Forty-two percent supported impeachment, and 55 percent opposed. This is a fairly significant shift in voter sentiment. Why?

Further evidence of media pollsters' intrusion on public debate came with the journalistic obsession of framing questions with reference to censure, in effect, creating a new unconstitutional middle-ground opinion. Reporters tended to emphasize the censure option response, but they could just as easily have stressed the American public's desire to see Clinton punished or focused on public opinion about Clinton's resignation. A CNN/*Time* poll conducted December 17–18, 1998, by Yankelovich Partners asked 1,031 adults nationwide:

> Thinking again about impeachment, if the vote goes through in the House of Representatives, an impeachment trial will be conducted in the Senate, where a two-thirds vote could remove Clinton from office. Which of these options do you think would be best for the country: for the Senate trial to go ahead in order to determine guilt or innocence, OR, for the Senate to end the trial immediately and

vote to censure, OR, for Clinton to end the trial immediately by resigning from office?

Again the results were surprising. Although only 16 percent said they wanted the case to go forward, 48 percent favored censure as a punishment, and 31 percent wanted Clinton to resign. Five percent weren't sure.

Then again, voters seemed to oppose abandoning the whole issue. Voters may have been against Clinton's removal by "Republicans in Congress," but they also tended to support Clinton's resignation if the charges were true. In a poll on October 8, 1998, Zogby International asked three questions, the results of which indicated that likely voters favored an honorable end to the unseemly saga:

> Now that the president has admitted to lying under oath in his testimony in the Paula Jones case, do you think he should consider leaving office?
> *A majority (52.4 percent) said yes, while 40.4 percent said no; 7.1 percent weren't sure.*

> If it turns out that the President encouraged anyone else to lie under oath, do you think he should consider leaving office?
> *More than six in ten (62.8 percent) said "yes," 29.9 percent said "no," and just over 7 percent weren't sure.*

> If it turns out that the President lied under oath in his testimony before the grand jury, do you think he should consider leaving office?
> *Nearly 60 percent (59.1 percent) said "yes," 33.3 percent said "no," and 7.8 percent weren't sure.*

By December 15, 1998, the share of likely voters supporting impeachment topped 60 percent when Zogby International pollsters asked whether the president should be impeached "if it turns out that the president lied under oath in his testimony before the grand jury." Obviously another story bubbled out there. But a conflicted public was difficult to cover with the limited questions in the polls.

Bombarded by reportage about high job approval ratings and with wording that emphasized removal, citizens retreated into a White House–manufactured position in the absence of an alternative. Every aspect of the Lewinsky saga reportage, polling,

> Every aspect of the Lewinsky saga reportage, polling, and Clinton spin had tiny influences on the public's perception.

and Clinton spin had tiny influences on the public's perception. In the end, these marginal biases had a decisive effect on public opposition to Clinton's removal.

Various theories have been put forward to explain what Frank Newport, president of the Gallup Organization, called the "popularity paradox." Among the theories was that the American public's low regard for the media helped boost support for the president. In January 1998, Gallup asked, "Overall, do you feel the news media have acted responsibly or irresponsibly in this matter?" Only 37 percent of the public thought the media were acting responsibly. Fully 55 percent thought the media were acting irresponsibly.[7]

What's more, Gallup asked:

> In general, which do you think the media are more concerned with in their coverage of the allegations about Bill Clinton and Monica Lewinsky: Being certain that a news story is accurate before they report it publicly, or, being the first media organization to report a news story?[8]

The public had little belief in the accuracy of the media sensationalism. Fully 77 percent said that journalists just wanted to be first. Fewer than one in five American adults (19 percent) thought the media cared about accuracy. What's interesting is that despite this smashing indictment by public opinion, the media, which ranked nearly as low as former House Speaker Newt Gingrich or Independent Counsel Kenneth Starr, soldiered on like Starr, choosing to serve their constitutionally protected mission instead of the polls.

Media Misuse of Polls and (Unwitting?) Complicity in Clinton Attacks

The media did little to help educate the public or clarify the issues involved in impeachment. From the very beginning, the Lewinsky scandal became an adventure in salacious reportage about sex, replete with partisan accusation and insults. In the midst of amplifying the sexual nature of the case, the media effectively downplayed the issues of constitutional procedure and the rule of law in cases of official crimes and wrongdoing. In the quest for conflict and color, the media unreflectively passed along White House criticisms of the independent counsel. Pundits, working as partisans in the cloak of the objective observer, debated among themselves the tactics of the White House. Meanwhile the media banged their own drum for congressional censure. The polls reinforced this unconstitutional answer to the charges of President Clinton's abuse of power.

Political scientist Thomas Peterson writes that "journalistic bias" plays a bigger role in coverage than liberal political bias. The journalistic lust for controversy, color, and conflict disposes the press corps to follow (and rebroadcast) accusations and attacks. The Clinton defense team and supposedly independent allies understood this and deployed every means to impugn the motives and credibility of those who dared to criticize the president's conduct. In some cases that meant resorting to private investigations, backdoor whisper campaigns, or outright attack.

These White House smear campaigns were designed to work hand in hand with the shallow and quickie world of public opinion polling. In fact the Clinton administration came to rely on the media polls as a measure of the effectiveness of its tactics.

> The journalistic lust for controversy, color, and conflict disposes the press corps to follow (and rebroadcast) accusations and attacks.

Left-leaning journalist Christopher Hitchens writes of his direct exposure to how media sensationalism and the gravity of poll numbers were manipulated to destroy Clinton's enemies.

Hitchens met with presidential aide Sidney Blumenthal shortly after Democratic volunteer Kathleen Willey appeared on *60 Minutes* accusing Clinton of sexual misconduct inside the White House. Willey, who had been an ardent supporter of Clinton, had sought solace from the chief executive after her husband killed himself. But while in the Oval Office to discuss her future with the Democratic Party, according to Willey, Clinton sexually accosted her, at one point taking her hand and placing it on his aroused member. Once her story was out, in the midst of the Lewinsky scandal, her charges created a stir. What's more, Willey was attractive, professional, and a one-time Clinton backer—not liable to the Carvillian line that Clinton accusers were motivated by hundred dollar bills dragged through trailer parks. Still the Clinton machine was confident it could deal with any adversity. Blumenthal informed Hitchens, "Her poll numbers look good now, but you watch. They'll be down by the end of the week."[9]

Later that week, the public learned of what Blumenthal meant. The White House released private correspondence

Willey had written to Clinton that showed her earlier support for him, her vulnerable state of mind, and her anger.[10] The smash-mouth tactics against Willey helped redirect the story back to the "sluts and nuts" theme of Clinton critics. Ultimately the White House didn't succeed in discrediting Willey. It didn't need to. In most cases, the Clinton counterattack failed in the long run, but it's short-run tactics and the media game that matter.

The Willey notes worked because they gave Clinton defenders and media allies an epiphenomenal debate topic to distract the public from the startling accusation that the president would go to the most extraordinary lengths to "feel someone's pain." In the environment White House noise, the primary questions of abuse of power and obstruction of justice, not to mention the predatory nature of the president, were lost in a farrago of counterattack and counterspin.

The biggest victim of Clinton's determination to fight wasn't Willey, however. She got off comparatively easy compared with the Office of Independent Counsel. Kenneth Starr and his subordinates were victims of a brutal takedown campaign that involved rumor and innuendo about their professional reputations, their sex lives, and their conduct during their legal inquiry. At one point, James Carville summed up the Clinton defense: "We have an out-of-control sex-crazed person that is running the [investigation], [who] has spent $40 million of taxpayers' money investigating people's sex lives."[11]

> The biggest victim of Clinton's determination to fight was the Office of Independent Counsel Kenneth Starr.

Aiding and abetting this effort was the irresistible media interest in partisan attack and bloodshed. At times it was difficult to see the difference between operatives such as Carville and the leading lights of the journalistic community. Both groups hammered Starr mercilessly. Dan Rather, as early as

August 12, 1994, reported, "New disclosures are fueling questions about whether or not Starr is an ambitious Republican
partisan backed by ideologically motivated anti-Clinton activists and judges from the Reagan, Bush, and Nixon years."[12]
Bryant Gumbel clearly sided with Susan McDougal when she
was imprisoned for contempt of court. He asked, "Have you
any doubt that Kenneth Starr and his deputies are pursuing an
agenda that is purely political?"[13]

Pro-Clinton pundits did their part to undermine the officer of the court. "By pandering to Clinton-haters, Mr. Starr
appears to be abandoning all pretenses of impartiality," said
Wall Street Journal Washington Bureau Chief Al Hunt. "He
now looks more like a political hit man desperately eager for a
future Supreme Court appointment."[14] *Newsweek*'s Jonathan
Alter charged in April 1998, "If [Starr] doesn't come forward
very soon with credible evidence of law-breaking, he will go
down in history as the Peeping Tom Prosecutor."[15]

ABC's Lisa McCree translated straight from the Clinton
defense book: "People are expecting detailed questions to leak
out of that grand jury testimony, questions that make Kenneth Starr and his attorneys look like zealots who are on some
sort of witch hunt."[16] The owner of *U.S. News & World Report* unloaded every round he could, accusing Starr of the
leaks that were often the work of Clinton lawyers trying to
diffuse the damage of allegations. Mortimer Zuckerman said,
"It is not the President who is assembling the dossiers and
leaking dirt on the intimate practices of an ideological opponent; it is the prosecutor. It is not the President who is involved in the politically motivated abuse of power. It is the
politically motivated counsel."[17] With such energy and evaluation coming from the journalistic community, it shouldn't be
a surprise that their polls once again walked hand in hand
with their biases.

The White House measured its success by its ability to
smash the approval ratings and credibility of the independent

counsel lawyers working with a mandate from the Department of Justice to investigate the executive branch. As *Washington Post* reporters Susan Schmidt and Michael Weiskopf later wrote:

> As allegations about Starr accumulated, it became more and more difficult for his supporters in Congress to come to his defense. And as his public image darkened, so did congressional prospects for action on his referral. The day after Marcia Lewis [Lewinsky's mother] collapsed at the grand jury, Clinton's pollster announced at the White House's morning staff meeting that Starr's public approval ratings had crashed. "He's down in Gingrich-land," Mark Penn said, referring to the House speaker's dismal poll ratings.[18]

Media polls helped raise doubts about Starr, increasing the sheer weight of pressure from supposedly objective stories. As of October 2000, there had been more than 516 polling questions involving Kenneth Starr—the vast preponderance focusing on public approval of Starr, according to the public opinion archives of the Roper Center. Most of the questions occurred over the nine-month period during which Starr was silent and before he appeared before Congress. It is interesting to note that Lawrence Walsh, the last high-profile independent counsel, never had to face this onslaught. The major public opinion polls only asked a total of eight questions about him and his work.

The few questions about Walsh tended to focus attention *away* from him personally and *toward* his investigation and allegations of his target's wrongdoing, lending his probe a more legitimate and positive feel. Several other factors also helped Walsh. He did not face the same strident public relations campaign from the White House, so there was no reason for the questions to focus on him so resolutely. Walsh also had one other critical advantage: He helped his own cause. He spoke out, allowing his words to frame the issues. This helped structure the frame of pollsters' questions. For instance, Louis Harris and Associates polled on the following:

> Let me read you some of the statements made by Independent Counsel Walsh [about the Iran-Contra affair]. For each, tell me if you agree or disagree. . . . Whether a person is popular or unpopular should not affect a criminal investigation or indictment.[19]

An amazing 90 percent agreed with this statement—one that put the rule of law above the popularity of a political figure. Only 9 percent disagreed! Such questions (and arguments) were absent during the Lewinsky scandal. Harris also asked:

> Let me read you some of the statements made by Independent Counsel Walsh [about the Iran-Contra affair]. [T]ell me if you agree or disagree. . . . Walsh also has said he will prosecute anyone who lied under oath in testimony before Congress, violated the Arms Export Control Act by shipping arms to Iran, or misused federal funds.

The answers were similarly lopsided. Eighty-three percent of 1,248 nationwide adults agreed that an independent counsel should press forward, whatever the consequences. Only 15 percent disagreed.

One phenomenon that was present in Whitewater and Watergate did appear in this high-profile investigation, however: the public's good feelings for the president. In January 1993, an ABC News/*Washington Post* poll asked 1,510 adults:

> Do you think the special prosecutor, Lawrence Walsh, should or should not investigate whether [George] Bush himself might have broken any laws in the Iran/Contra affair?

The support for Walsh had ebbed by this point after six years of investigation. Only 53 percent favored further investigation, while 42 percent opposed it.

What are the differences between Walsh and Starr? The questions about Walsh contained an alternate frame and invoked a separate set of American values: the rule of law, the prosecution of high-level offenders, and a fundamental commitment to see the justice system move forward. But these questions about Walsh differed in another critical way from those concerning Starr: They did not directly pit Walsh against the president. Americans were asked about specific aspects of the rule of law, not asked to choose in a game of personalities.

Even when Walsh faced setbacks, the media's polling shifted. For instance, in late 1992, the Gallup Organization asked 608 adults to choose President George Bush's motivations for pardoning former Secretary of Defense Caspar Weinberger:

> Which one of the following do you think is the main reason Bush decided to pardon Weinberger and other Iran-Contra defendants?
>
> To protect people he felt acted honorably and patriotically from unfair prosecution (15 percent)
>
> To put the Iran-Contra affair in the country's past (21 percent)
>
> To get back at Iran-Contra prosecutor Lawrence Walsh for bringing charges against Weinberger right before the election (2 percent)
>
> To protect himself from legal difficulties or embarrassment resulting from his own role in Iran-Contra (49 percent)

President Clinton wasn't hit with these kinds of questions and reportage that tested his motivations. This is all the more remarkable given his scorched-earth campaign against an officer of the court and every other person who threatened his public standing. True, Americans were asked about Clinton's bombing of a Sudanese pharmaceutical factory that coincidentally occurred as the House voted on impeachment procedures. But in the matchup between Starr and Clinton, the questions usually hinged on whether voters approved of Starr's "handling" of the Lewinsky scandal.

Starr was hamstrung from the beginning because the public's view of him was almost entirely one-sided. The public's introduction to him was decidedly negative and unwelcome. The Lewinsky news was distasteful and revolting. And Starr was pitted against President Clinton almost immediately with Clinton's assertion: "I did not have sexual relations with that woman, Miss Lewinsky." Then Hillary Clinton came forward to accuse the Office of Independent Counsel of being part of a "vast right-wing conspiracy." In the coming months, the circus antics of Lewinsky's first lawyer and family friend William Ginsberg threw the investigation off. And the story became all the more salacious and disconcerting: questions of love and obsession, secret notes, gifts, phone sex, answering machine messages, and finally a blue semen-stained Gap dress.

Starr resolutely adhered to the belief that facts and truth would see his office through the whole escapade, even as media reports and Clinton smear artists worked in the media-relations vacuum in which Starr was unable to respond publicly to Clinton accusations. Whereas Walsh had helped frame the debate, Starr believed that such a defense of the rule of law and the integrity of the justice

> In the matchup between Starr and Clinton, the questions usually hinged on whether voters approved of Starr's "handling" of the Lewinsky scandal.

system was the task of Congress. At the time, he believed his job was to execute the mission of the independent counsel law. He would later condemn his own silence.

Of course, when seen through the lens of media sensationalism, the Starr inquiry seemed to many Americans wildly out of control and unnecessarily intrusive. When Lewinsky's mother, Marcia Lewis, collapsed on the court steps after her testimony to the grand jury or when Starr sought verification of Lewinsky's testimony of gift purchases for the president by rooting through the receipts of a local bookstore, critics saw shadows of secret police tactics. The final blow, of course, was the Starr Report itself. It contained facts so detailed and intimate, it seemed to defeat itself; the weight of legal evidence turned an airtight case of perjury into a Freudian adventure of a lost intern and the most powerful ladies' man in the free world.

News broke so fast during this saga that the public was rarely asked about specifics. Instead the media turned to public opinion polls as judge, jury, and executioner. Would the latest revelation be the smoking gun, the killer blow, the coup de grace? The problem with the polling at the time is that it pitted the stability and economy of the country against what the public perceived as sexual allegations. The polling questions, media reportage, and the silence of key figures failed to make the kind of clear connections and present the ineluctable logic for prosecuting the wrongdoing of high-level officials in a constitutional republic.

Instead the polls worked like Carville to impugn the motives of Starr. On February 12, 1999, the *Los Angeles Times* asked 664 adults nationwide:[20]

Why do you think Starr is pursuing his investigation of President Clinton? Is it because he believes that Clinton committed perjury before the grand jury and obstructed justice, or is it just to hurt President Clinton politically?

Four in ten adults thought that Starr was investigating Clinton because Clinton was guilty. A majority (51 percent) said it was to "hurt Clinton politically." Nine percent didn't know.

Starr may also have fallen victim to the media's propensity to force ignorant or apathetic voters into making a decision. Gallup asked a sample of American adults on February 4, 1999:

> Next, I'd like to get your overall opinion of some people in the news. As I read each name, please say if you have a favorable or unfavorable opinion of this person—or if you have never heard of him or her. . . . How about . . . Kenneth Starr?[21]
> *Thirty percent ranked Starr favorably, and 61 percent ranked him unfavorably. In this case, just 4 percent admitted they'd never heard of him, and 6 percent had no opinion.*

But at nearly the same time, a CBS News/*New York Times* poll released on February 2, 1999, seemed to find softer results by slight changes in the choice of answers available:

> Is your opinion of Kenneth Starr favorable, not favorable, undecided, or haven't you heard enough about Kenneth Starr yet to have an opinion?
> *Twenty-two percent gave Starr a favorable rating. Only 48 percent ranked him unfavorably. In this poll, 17 percent of voters said they were undecided, and 12 percent—after a year of incessant coverage—said they hadn't heard enough (1 percent refused to give an answer).*

Both polls were measures of a national sample. Both were conducted by major pollsters, at nearly the same time. The differences are stark, however. In one poll, 12 percent—nearly one in eight Americans—didn't know enough about Starr. In the other, just 4 percent said they didn't know. In one poll,

17 percent were undecided. In the other, only 6 percent had no opinion. To put this in perspective: If a candidate were to surge eight points in a presidential race, the media would have all manner of explanations. If the use of the words "undecided" and "no opinion" results in an 11-point difference, and "haven't heard enough" influences results when compared with "never heard of," how accurate can these polls be? How can it possibly be a sound basis for democratic debate if such wording differences lead to radically different conclusions in print and in the corridors of power?

The CBS News/*New York Times* poll results bespeak a fundamental ignorance and conflicted thought. The Gallup results show a man loathed, distrusted, and thoroughly disliked by the majority. Was it possible that Gallup and others were pushing voters into making a decision about a figure who was the victim of a collective media and White House mugging?

Polling served to question motives, and in another sense diverted deliberation about the facts in the case. Congress, not just Starr, had to face such questions about baser motivations. Some of the polls helped to impugn the motives of those who sought to follow up on the independent counsel's report. For instance, on December 19–21, 1998, the Pew Research Center for the People and the Press asked 805 adults:

> Why do you think most members of Congress voted in favor of impeaching President Clinton: because they think what he has done is serious enough to end his presidency OR for political reasons?

Such a question plays off American suspicions about all politicians. Asking the American people whether they distrust the motives of those in power is a no-brainer. Sixty-seven percent said the members who voted for impeachment did so for "political reasons"—a strange outcome because the greater political risk would seem to be to vote impeachment when the polls and the media trumpet the people's opposition to it. If it was political, it was political suicide. It is notable that Pew did *not* ask a similar question about the political motives of those who voted *against* impeachment. The questions asked undeniably enabled the White House to advance, and the media to dwell on, the supposedly dark designs and lust for vengeance in Congress.

Some—notably left-leaning—people saw through the controversies and slowly made a career of being uniquely clearheaded about what was at issue in the impeachment. These included law professor Jonathan Turley, legal writer Stuart Taylor, and journalists Christopher Hitchens, Michael Kelly, and Chris Matthews. They soon became the most eloquent voices for the rule of law and the most persuasive voices on the outrageousness of the tactics plied by Clinton defenders.

For the most part, however, journalists were confused by the high job approval ratings and paid little attention to the more nuanced results of the polls. A typical example was Will Lester of the Associated Press, who felt compelled to write the story about the story: "Experts Baffled by Clinton's Approval Ratings." He interviewed a bevy of experts from polling, politics, and academia about the mysteriously high Clinton poll ratings. Lester's tone, unwitting or not, seemed to minimize the damage to the White House: "President Clinton's lofty job approval ratings seem far removed from the growing calls for his resignation and the talk in Congress of impeachment."[22]

Journalists proved to be just as susceptible to the crush of opinion as anyone else. A good example of this is Jean Bethke Elshtain, a writer for the prestigious magazine the *New Republic* and a professor of religion and ethics at the University of Chicago. She astonished one Washington, D.C., audience when she described the role of the polls during the Lewinsky drama. Speaking before the American Enterprise Institute in September 1999, Elshtain explained why she didn't support impeachment. "I didn't think the political will was there to make this a legitimate act, so that is why I did not call for impeachment," she said. Elshtain believed the polls did not show enough support for the removal of the president. Clinton's violations of the law and his actions to contain the scandal "disgusted" her, she admitted, but she feared removal would not seem legitimate to the American people.

In her view, the public was too ignorant, Clinton's defenders too cunning, and the media drumbeat too unanimous for removal to work. The polls showed that Americans believed the Clinton line that to remove the president would "overturn the election" and be a "coup d'etat." The problem, she felt, was that the polls indicated that the public believed Clinton was being prosecuted for a private sexual matter, not for obstruction of justice or lying under oath. "An honorable man would have resigned when the tapes came to light, given the revelation of how pervasive and voluble had been the lying, the prevarication, and to so many—from staff to cabinet officers to elected officials to the courts to his own spouse."

Asked to elaborate on why impeachment and removal would be illegitimate, she stated:

> I know you might say to me that we should not make assessments about behavior on the basis of opinion polls and so on. And I agree with that. Nevertheless, it strikes me that the well would have been so poisoned if the president had been removed from office. In part, because the people I am calling the president's most ardent defenders were busy poisoning it. And they argued in fact that it was a thinly disguised *coup d'etat* to de-legitimate or overturn the results of their democratic election. That's a position that enjoyed widespread currency. . . . [My position] was strictly a political judgment.

Elshtain's comments elicited two incredulous inquiries during the question-and-answer period. Her answer is worthy of the worst stereotypes of the poll-driven politician.

> Q: To clarify: I take it that if you had been polled in one of those early public measures of sentiment—Do you think the president should be removed from office?—before it was clear what public opinion was, do I take it that your answer would have been yes?

> A: Early on I wouldn't have made that kind of judgment. One needed some time for the full extent of all this to play out. Remember this went on for eleven months. The point I am making is that there needs to be a process of civic, public, and political debate the end point of which is the determination not the beginning. My preference would have been for pressure to have been built up for the president to resign as an honorable president would have done.

That a professor of religion and ethics would take a sounding of the polls to decide an issue of ethics and the rule of law is hard to believe. But there it is. Elshtain maintained that impeachment was ultimately a political judgment. "It's something that has to be arrived at after a certain period of intense civic discussion and debate," she said. "And it has to be because it is such a solemn and serious act. When that act is undertaken—when you have impeachment followed by conviction—it strikes me that in that interim between the impeachment and the debate concerning conviction that it is terribly important for what is being done to be accorded widespread legitimacy by the public."

Manipulating the Uninformed

Of course Elshtain may be right. From the position of practical politics, perhaps the American people weren't knowledgeable enough or mature enough to accept the constitutional removal of President Clinton and the "coup d'etat" swearing in of Vice President Al Gore. Perhaps the "well" was too poisoned. But if Elshtain and others in the opinion elite believe a point comes when the people aren't knowledgeable enough to accept certain courses of action, however proper, doesn't this line of argument undermine polling? Isn't the well-poisoning argument an open admission that polling is merely a test of who most effectively manipulates voter ignorance and conducts negative campaigns?

The fact that the well-poisoning argument worked, that people viewed a case about the rule of law as a scandalous incidence of mere sexual dalliance, is a measure of the media's failure to inform and Congress' inability to execute its duties. The pundits, whether observers such as Elshtain or willful Clinton hit men such as Geraldo Rivera, failed to execute the primary mission of the press to inform and educate and police. Poll-shocked musings and sensationalized accounts amplified the sex allegations and buried the questions about perjury, obstruction of justice, and abuse of power. A disconnected public was further conflicted by a process out of control and marching for seemingly no reason toward Senate trial. Where the media failed to inform and Republicans retreated, the White House filled in the vacuum.

The White House soon came to bank on public ignorance, disconnection, and apathy. Clinton's defenders took advantage of the public's distaste for partisan rancor and struggle. Allegations of sexual misconduct in both parties soon made it clear that political players were human beings with foibles, mistakes, and embarrassing secrets. What should make any civil libertarian blanch was the means by which those peccadilloes were unearthed, magnified, and broadcast. What should make any vigilant citizen worry is that all of the sexual allegations were irrelevant when compared with the abuse of power and contempt for the law in Clinton's case.

For Clinton's critics, the White House tactics were a bitter taste of Little Rock payback. For the public, the fighting attacked the motives of all those who dared attempt to question the veracity and conduct of the president. A whole host of code words and incendiary accusations were coined to scare the ignorant and deflect attention from the facts.

To dominate the twenty-four-hour-news cycle and drive up the numbers, Clinton's team came up with a few choice phrases smelted in the cauldron of focus groups. Soon talk shows, newspaper columns, and water-cooler debates were dominated by such evocative phrases as "the politics of personal destruction," "sexual McCarthyism," and "It's all about sex." Viewers and readers were warned about Independent Counsel Kenneth Starr's "prosecutorial zeal" and an ongoing "partisan witch hunt." All the while Clinton's defenders pleaded with Republicans to "just let the president do his job" and "get back to the business of the country."

> Poll-shocked musings and sensationalized accounts amplified the sex allegations and buried the questions about perjury, obstruction of justice, and abuse of power.

White House defenders threatened that removal of President Clinton would constitute a coup d'etat and would overturn the will of the American people. The polls dutifully tested the question, and the results were widely broadcast. The specious reasoning involved in this revolutionary argument is almost too ridiculous to be believed. The Constitution

provided for a lawful replacement in case of presidential removal—a man conveniently referred to as the *vice* president.
Since the ratification of the Twelfth Amendment, that candidate runs with the president, receiving the exact same number
of votes as his boss.

In Al Gore, voters had a well-qualified replacement who
did not appear on Clinton's re-election bumper stickers by ac-
cident. Further, to argue that the removal of Clinton for perjury, obstruction of justice, and the abuse of power
overturned the mandate of the people strains credulity. Clinton did not run on a ticket openly advocating illegal acts, so it
is hard to think the people willfully endorsed such actions.

This phrase "coup d'etat" in particular, writes Christopher Hitchens, was a red herring dragged out by Clinton's defenders in the press and could not be taken seriously by
knowledgeable journalists or politicians of either side. But
principle had nothing to with it. As Hitchens noted, "Their
outrage was directed not at any action of their commander in
chief but at any motion to depose him or even to impugn his
character."[23]

Coup d'etat and other phrases worked as code words, re-
orienting public debate and framing the investigation of the
whole affair. Every code word cleverly and cunningly portrayed Clinton as the victim of an invasive prosecution dreamt
up by a posse of malevolent partisans. Republicans, for whatever reason, bought into the meta-debate about the actual
case, arguing the relevance of an investigation instead of the
facts. (It is interesting to note that this mockery of debate carried into the House where Democrats attacked and Republicans defended Starr, with few discussing the actual details of
the report with the independent counsel when he testified.)

As wave after wave of polls crashed on the public and the
evocative phrases wrought by the spinmeisters in the White
House Legal Counsel's Office spread through the public con-

sciousness, the effect was the same: a highly charged partisan debate that missed the core issues involved. To put the Lewinsky saga in polling terms, the public was functioning almost entirely without any alternate frame of reference or values that could explain the rule of law, the constitutional importance of impeachment, and the role of the separation of powers in preserving the right of every citizen to equality under the law.

In the seven months following the story, Republican actions were marked by moral superiority, disgusting glee, and rank cowardice, but very few educational efforts to explain the American constitutional values on the line. By the time the case reached the House, Americans had graduated from the White House University with a degree in partisan prosecution with a minor in "It's all about sex."

While the defense of Clinton was honed and perfected, the White House succeeded in targeting the successive threats to the Clinton regime: Kenneth Starr, his fellow prosecutors, and Kathleen Willey. Republicans waited for Starr to do all their work for them. Starr, seeing his task in as limited a fashion as possible, continued to work in utter silence—expecting, one suspects, that one of the nation's elected "leaders" would defend the sanctity of the rule of law and field the ridiculous accusations against an officer of the court who worked under the auspices of Clinton's own Department of Justice. It seemed irrelevant at the time that Starr had the legal sanction of a law written by the attorney general and signed into law by the president himself.

> By the time the case reached the House, Americans had graduated from the White House University with a degree in partisan prosecution with a minor in "It's all about sex."

Story after story and leak after leak filled in the broad aspects of the sordid tale. But while Republicans squandered any opportunities for an eloquent and cautious defense, preparing the public for a critical test of equality under the law, Democrats marched in phalanx formation. Public attention was drawn almost exclusively to the salacious details of the Clinton-Lewinsky relationship, details that were quickly exploited to turn disgust into resentment against Starr.

The public's "frame," whether in polling questions or media reportage, wasn't the rule of law. For them, the scandal *was* all about sex and the disorder and embarrassment of a president's removal. The well was poisoned. The GOP never put forward a credible defense of equality under the law and of the long-term consequences of a system that lets the nation's highest officials oppress and silence lowly citizens.

By the time the Starr Report arrived to testify before the House, then, the painstaking details of his report were mostly old news. The stories about the semen-stained dress, the DNA, the recordings of phone sex, the fake pizza deliveries, the recorded messages, and the job at Revlon were all verified in the Starr Report. The Starr Report's excruciating detail—meant presumably to nail down all the discrepancies in the testimony of a president who could dispute what the definition of "is" is—was a grim reminder of just how disgusting the whole exhausting seven months had been. Members of Congress released the Starr Report wholesale onto the Internet in the vain hope that their jobs (once again) would be made painless and easy.

With the sex tale out in the public realm, Republicans hoped the polls would swing their way, and they could heroically run to the front of the mob that cried for Clinton's head. Once again, Republicans awoke to a harsh reality. The response to the Starr Report was anticlimactic. Absent any broader interpretive schema, the public yawned—or more correctly, retched—at the detail and prurient footnotes. They didn't see the Starr Report as a detailed case against a Houdini liar who could slip almost any legal knot. It wasn't about abuse of power, obstruction of justice, or the rule of law. These terms had only recently entered the public mind—a mind saturated by the code words of injustice coined by Clinton defenders and then ratified by polling questions that lent the tactics credibility.

But it *was* the rule of law that was ultimately at issue. When Starr left the independent counsel's office, his replacement, Robert Ray, stressed precisely this American ideal of equality under the law. "It is an open investigation," he said in April 2000. "There is a principle to be vindicated, and that principle is that no person is above the law, even the president of the United States."[24]

Even during the months of debate about the good or ill that would come from Clinton's removal, Democrats were careful to preserve the right of the justice system to move forward *after* Clinton left office. Politically, Democratic actions may have been self-serving, but legally, the ancient sinews of liberalism still existed. Many Democrats spoke out in favor of the eventual prosecution of the chief executive.

"President Clinton is not 'above the law.' His conduct should not be excused, nor will it," said Senator Herbert Kohl, D-Wisconsin. "The President can be criminally prosecuted, especially once he leaves office. In other words, his acts may not be 'removable' wrongs, but they could be 'convictable' crimes."[25]

Senator Joseph Lieberman, D-Connecticut, stated, "Whether any of his conduct constitutes a criminal offense such as perjury or obstruction of justice is not for me to decide. That, appropriately, should and must be left to the criminal justice system, which will uphold the rule of law in President Clinton's case as it would for any other American."[26]

Senator Kent Conrad, D-North Dakota: "Offensive as they were, the President's actions have nothing to do with his official duties, nor do they constitute the most serious of private crimes. In my judgment, these are matters best left to the criminal justice system."[27]

According to Representative Zoe Lofgren, D-California, "Punishment for alleged criminal law violations is not up to the United States Congress. That's up to the criminal justice system. After his term is up, less than two years from now, he is like any other American. He would have any other defenses that any other American has. That's the proper forum for that."[28]

Such quotes were common during the impeachment debate in Congress. Was this just political evasion? Were Democrats trying to find a way out of weighing the charges of perjury, obstruction of justice, and abuse of power? There is no need to question motives, because members of the Democratic Party specifically outlined the possibility, even the need, for the future prosecution of the president. Despite their misunderstandings of the function of impeachment, it is still clear that they embraced the need for some sort of criminal punishment, or at least a trial. Polling avoided exploring these issues, and in so doing undermined an important debate for a free people.

The Battle in Congress

Once the Starr Report was delivered to the House of Representatives, the polls became more frenetic and numerous. The constant refrain was that voters opposed impeachment and were not retreating from their opinion that Clinton should not be removed. The House managers had hoped that the facts of the case would change voter minds.

"We felt that when people saw for the first time all the deceitful, poisonous little details of what their President had done, the polls would change," wrote Democrat David P. Schippers, former mob prosecutor and majority counsel for the House Judiciary Committee. "Clinton's standing with the public would plummet, the Senate would follow the public's lead, and he would be convicted."[29]

But this never happened. Starr defended his investigation, for the first time giving the public a look at the mysterious man behind the probe of the president. But after Starr presented the facts, the two parties on the House Judiciary Committee split into two factions. The Democrats savaged Starr, attacking his handling of Lewinsky and the cost of his investigation. On the other side were the Republicans, who applauded Starr and threw softball questions to him about the difficulty of his task. The questions of evidence, truth, and fact in the case never became an issue for either side. To the public, Starr appeared to be less than the ogre of the past few months. But for public debate and deliberation, the facts remained on the back pages and insides of newspaper stories that sensationalized the sex and personalities involved.

> The questions of evidence, truth, and fact in the case never became an issue for either side.

Once again the polls leaped into action, seeking to declare a winner in the hearings. Through these polls, Starr was able to acquit himself in the public eye. An ABC News/*Washington Post* poll on December 12–13, 1998, asked 1,004 adults:

> Who do you think did a better job before the Judiciary Committee: the special prosecutor Kenneth Starr, presenting the case against Clinton, or Clinton's lawyers, presenting his defense?
>
> *Thirty-seven percent thought Clinton's lawyers did a better job. Forty-two percent thought Starr did a better job—a huge victory for a man as reviled as Starr.*

Further questions found that despite weeks of polls ratifying White House attacks, Americans thought the hearings were fair:

Do you think the House Judiciary Committee hearings were fair to Clinton, or unfair?
Fifty-seven percent thought they were fair. Thirty-eight percent thought they were unfair. This was the same public who thought Starr and the Republicans were politically targeting Clinton.

Only ten days before this poll, the ABC News/*Washington Post* poll short-circuited confidence in the process by a premature poll that lent suspicion to the system of justice:

As you may know, the House Judiciary Committee in Congress has been holding hearings on whether or not to impeach Bill Clinton. Do you approve or disapprove of the way the committee is handling its investigation?
Thirty-four percent approved of the hearings. Fully 59 percent opposed the hearings.

Starr's appearance and newfound respectability weren't enough to reverse the previous tide of media coverage or to extinguish the flaming-bandwagon impression that a vote for impeachment was a vote against democracy and the American people. Still it leads to a great hypothetical: What would have happened had the media focused on the integrity of the process, instead of on questions of ulterior motive, political plotting, and nation-shaking "what-ifs"?

For the House managers, the act of voting against Bill Clinton, a popular president with unprecedented job approval ratings, was not an easy one. The case scraped through and went on to the Senate—a body that wished above all things to contain and dispose quickly of the political hot potato.

The founders anticipated just such political battles fraught with emotion and bitterness. In writing about impeachment, Alexander Hamilton could not have come closer to predicting the spectacle of the Lewinsky debate than if he had lived to see it himself. In *Federalist* No. 65, he writes:

> The prosecution of them [public officials], for this reason, will seldom fail to agitate the passions of the whole community, and to divide it into parties more or less friendly or inimical to the accused. In many cases it will connect itself with the pre-existing factions, and will enlist all their animosities, partialities, influence, and interest on one side or on the other; and in such cases there will always be the greatest danger that the decision will be regulated more by the comparative strength of parties than by the real demonstrations of innocence or guilt.

To the founders, the power of impeachment was a critical mechanism by which the people could defend themselves against officials who used their offices for their own benefit and to the detriment of the people. Continuing, Hamilton describes the challenge of policing those with majority support:

> The difficulty of placing it rightly in a government resting entirely on the basis of periodical elections will as readily be perceived, when it is considered that the most conspicuous characters in it will, from that circumstance, be too often the leaders or the tools of the most cunning or the most numerous faction, and on this account can hardly be expected to possess the requisite neutrality towards those whose conduct may be the subject of scrutiny.

For Hamilton, popular rule, because of the influence of majorities and factions, can make it even *more* difficult for the impeachment power to be well disposed. The framers gave the final say in questions of impeachment and removal to the Senate, which at that time was more insulated from popular sentiment because senators were elected by state legislatures. It was hoped that senators would be more disposed to look closely at both the charges and the reputation of the man in power. As Hamilton puts it, "The delicacy and magnitude of a trust which so deeply concerns the political reputation and existence of every man engaged in the administration of public affairs speak for themselves."

> Polls became the last refuge for the senators, who were given the difficult case of determining the truth or falsity of the charges presented by their fellow elected leaders in the House.

The Senate, in the Lewinsky case, became the opposite of what the founders intended. The upper chamber kept a jealous eye on public opinion, instead of taking the often unpopular position as the anchor to the intemperate passions of the people who were hearing only part of the story. Polls became the last refuge for the senators, who were given the difficult case of determining the truth or falsity of the charges presented by their fellow elected leaders in the House.

David Schippers later wrote: "When people ask me what's the one thing Americans should know they don't already know about the impeachment process, it's that before we ever appeared on the floor of the United States Senate, the House impeachment managers and I knew we didn't have a shot to win. The bottom line was this: In the U.S. Senate, politics trumped principles, and polls trumped honor."[30]

Schippers wasn't the only member of the left to balk at the Senate's dependence on the polls. Christopher Hitchens wrote, "[I]t was most fascinating, in the early weeks of the century's closing year, to witness the open collusion between constitutional obscurantism [of the Senate] and the hucksterism of the polls; between antique ritual and shrewdly calculated advice on short-term media advantage; between . . . the elitist style and the populist style."[31]

The Senate sought to dispose of the case quickly. Senate leaders, both Democrat and Republican, forced the House to make its case in fewer than twenty-four hours. With only three days of hearings of eight hours each, the House managers became part of a sham trial. There would be no witnesses and nothing permitted outside the articles of impeachment passed by the House.

When the case was being heard in the lower chamber, additional evidence from Starr was made available for members in an adjacent room filled with nonpublic supplemental materials. Included in that evidence was a rape accusation by Juanita Brodderick. At the time, not one House Democrat went to see any of the supplemental evidence to judge for him- or herself. When the case reached the Senate, an evidence room was opened holding other information collected by the independent counsel. Not one senator, Democrat or Republican, bothered to look at it.[32]

In the Senate, the battle to frame the debate and mold the language about the Lewinsky scandal continued unabated. Perhaps the greatest example of the Democrats' fine-tuned effort to control the "code words" of debate came during the Senate trial. As House Manager Lindsey Graham made his case on the Senate floor, he referred to the senators of the chamber as jurors. Senator Tom Harkin, D-Iowa, stood up and objected to the use of the word "jurors." The Constitution, Harkin said, made no reference to those hearing an impeachment case in the Senate as jurors. In fact, the model for impeachment, with the trial in the two chambers, was based on the form of a grand jury and a petit jury. Chief Justice William Rehnquist swore in the one hundred members of the Senate. Their oath was to impartially hear the case against the president. In this sense, they *were* jurors. Rehnquist agreed with Harkin, however, and Graham beat a hasty retreat, inserting the word "triers of fact" for "jurors" in his presentation.

Harkin's move showed a Democratic attention to detail that sought at every stage of the process to minimize the damage and reframe the issues heard by the public. There is little doubt for those familiar with the power of words to shape public opinion that such efforts added up.

The Senate Defies the People?

In the end, however, it was the Senate that "went against the polls." The public may not have favored the president's impeachment. But if the public had been sitting in the Senate chamber, they would have been forced to vote for removal because the majority of them believed Clinton guilty on nearly every count.

On December 10, 1998, a *USA Today*/CNN/Gallup poll asked 550 adults about the four charges against the president:

> Now I am going to read you four charges that have been made against Bill Clinton related to the current impeachment hearings. Regardless of whether you think Clinton should be impeached on any of the charges, please indicate if you think the charge against Clinton is or is not true. . . .

The charge that Clinton committed perjury by providing false and misleading testimony to Ken Starr's grand jury. *Yes: 71 percent. No: 23 percent.*

The charge that Clinton committed perjury by providing false and misleading testimony as part of the Paula Jones lawsuit. *Yes: 64 percent. No: 27 percent.*

The charge that Clinton obstructed justice by trying to influence the testimony of Monica Lewinsky, his secretary, and others in the Paula Jones lawsuit.
Yes: 50 percent. No: 43 percent.

The charge that Clinton misused and abused his office and impaired the administration of justice by making false and misleading statements to the public, his aides, and Congress.
Yes: 63 percent. No: 35 percent.

A similar poll by ABC News and the *Washington Post* yielded roughly the same results. Eighty percent thought Clinton lied under oath, and 59 percent thought he obstructed justice. Just before the Senate vote, Gallup found that 73 percent believed the perjury charge, and 49 percent believed the obstruction of justice charge. The polls may have varied, but the unanimous view was that Clinton had committed criminal acts to cover up his relationship with Lewinsky and to erode the court's inquiry in the civil case.

Thus only by invoking a kind of jury nullification would Clinton have survived to finish his term. Under the strict rules of truth, evidence, and due process of law, the Senate trial should have—according to polls of the American people—ended in a conviction. Whether the average voter would have set aside his or her conscience, as did so many senators, isn't clear.

CHAPTER NINE

Accountability, Openness, and Other Absurd Reform Ideas

Improving polls requires a citizenry willing to hold media polls to a higher standard.

■ ■ ■

IN 1786, THOMAS JEFFERSON CONFRONTED the eternal challenge that faces the friends of freedom. He advised a friend on the mind-set that the thoughtful citizen should possess when working for the good of the people: "Cherish therefore the spirit of our people, and keep alive their attention." Jefferson's words remain both an invitation and a challenge. Then, as now, education was the first and primary step in preparing for self-rule and individual liberty.

Jefferson warned against being "too severe" on the errors of the people. He did not ignore the fact that the people may be misled or may withdraw from their civic duty. But after confronting such a reality, he offered his prescription for the preservation of freedom: "[R]eclaim them by enlightening them." Jefferson understood how deeply connected the cause of freedom was to an educated, informed, and alert citizenry. Should the most vigilant citizens fail to reach out to their fellows, the results would be dismal, and the future of freedom would assuredly turn dark. "If once [the people] become inattentive to public affairs, you and I, and Congress, and Assemblies, judges and governors shall all become wolves," he warned.

Unfortunately, that is where we stand. Conscientious and involved citizens across the nation are growing skeptical of the media's manipulation of polling and their selective reportage. We now see pundits who warn against premature polling. Many Americans are beginning to grasp the differences between using likely voters and registered voters. And even some media organizations, such as MSNBC and others, are turning to focus groups to enrich their stories and explore how independent or undecided voters view campaigns and the electoral process.

But whatever tentative steps there are, the power of the polls is still potent and far-reaching. Skepticism, in even a few informed members of the opinion elite, will never be able to muster the unwavering voices needed to cast doubt on the legions of polls released on the front pages of newspapers and on television. The problem, as we've seen, is deeper. The media imperative to be the first to run polling results on important races has pushed up the "virtual primaries" of polls. In many cases, the lust for the story tests ideas and candidates long before they've had a chance to be fully presented to the very people being polled. And even if one believes that polling is more advanced than ever, most reporting on those polls is still unreflective and gives only cursory warnings about the limitations inherent in public opinion measures.

What's to Be Done?

This book was written for the citizen who cherishes America's tradition of limited government. Point by point, we've seen the shortcomings of polls in the methodology, from sample selection to question framing. We've seen how media coverage can bias results. We've learned how polls are abused to advance agendas, not to challenge media prejudices. We've seen how the architecture of polling is built on the sandy foundations of a public largely apathetic and ignorant about politics and issues.

None of these criticisms of polling should be perceived as an elitist's attack on constitutional self-rule, however. This is not a plea for central planning by Ivy League professors or Beltway bureaucrats. If we truly believe in the broadest conception of self-determination, the apathy and ignorance of the American public should move us to reconsider the virtues of limited government.

> It is an oddity of the Age of Polling to think that the carefully scripted words of polling units best represent the "voice of the commoners."

Those who push polling as the definitive tool of democratic expression still hold the majority in political and journalistic discussions. That is because they have also been largely unquestioned except in the odd academic journal or self-congratulatory media seminars that purport to be media criticism.

America has embraced polling as the voice of the commoners, but the voice of the individual is best expressed by freely chosen actions and words. It is an oddity of the Age of Polling to think that the carefully scripted words of polling units—funded by the media conglomerates in America and presented in language that mirrors their agenda—best represent the "voice of the commoners."

To truly reclaim the political process and to bring back the educational power of political debate and deliberation, we must reform our understanding and the standards of that process. But the prospects for media reform are never inspiring. In his 1998 book *No-Fault Politics: Modern Presidents, The Press, and Reformers,* Democratic presidential candidate Eugene McCarthy wrote sardonically:

> The process of press self-examination can do little harm and very little good. The inevitable conclusion will always be that the press, under difficult circumstances, has done as well as could have been expected. The situation is similar to what happens when monkeys at the zoo get involved with examining each other. The work is serious. There is a lot of scratching and scrutiny. Something is usually found, or appears to be found. Sometimes it is merely tasted; sometimes it is eaten after careful consideration; sometimes it is shared with the others. In the end, the monkeys appear to be deeply satisfied. Life in the zoo goes on as before.[1]

It is tempting to agree with McCarthy, because in the end the monkeys are still monkeys. Deadlines, twenty-four-hour news services, and the competitive imperative may create tremendous pressure for the media to air their stories with little thought. But for anyone who has seen journalists gather after an election to discuss their frenzied coverage of "issues" during a past election contest, McCarthy's observation is all too accurate. Inevitably journalists let themselves off the hook with a sense of mercy and understanding that they rarely show for elected leaders, institutions, or political parties.

This lack of self-scrutiny should not prevent concerned citizens from questioning the media and the way the press handles polls. The advocates of media polling are right: Polling measures of public opinion have become "players in the political process." Yet this truism should elicit more concern about what kind of standards and improvements can be brought to the arena of public dialogue and deliberation in our nation. Life in the monkey cage can be changed—as long as the changes aren't entirely left up to the monkey.

When forced by outside considerations of democracy and fair play, the Fourth Estate has, at times, backed down in the face of public opinion and Congressional action. For instance, in the 2000 primaries, *Slate* and *National Review* both threatened to release exit polling onto the Internet as it came to them instead of holding the results. Voter News Service, which is the combined polling efforts of major media, responded with a barrage of threats of legal action. Eventually both backed off, and the media agreed not to release the results of exit polls on Election Day until the process of voting was officially over.

Slate and *National Review* were acting in the interest of readers and responding to their journalistic imperative to report the news. But even the media and Congress have come to see premature exit polling as a threat to open democracy. The two magazines argued, rightly, that the Voter News Service embargo doesn't keep anchormen and television correspondents from giving on-air hints and making insinuations about the exit poll information before the polls close. In the competition to "call" a race for a candidate, news anchors do everything *except* deliver the official exit polling that comes across their desks. Yet despite the imperfections of the system, there is at least some sense (or fear of Congressional retaliation) that an election should not be made a charade for the citizenry.

The media stood firm and agreed to keep a lid on election results until every voter had a say. And they were able to cast social onus (if not actual legal retribution) on those who would destroy the system. The media can show restraint when the good of democracy is at issue. Reform is possible. (Unfortunately, this restraint was forgotten when the networks created the Election Night debacle in November of 2000.)

Of course we must distinguish between what is ideal and what is possible. The embargo on exit polling from Voter News Service is successful not only because of pressure from Congress, but also because the rules are clear and unequivocal. No news organization gets the upper hand, which is what exacerbates the rush to call states for presidential candidates on Election Night. In the 2000 election, Florida was called at 8:02 p.m. EST for Vice President Al Gore, even though election officials in the Sunshine State specifically warned the media that not all voting precincts were closed at that time. The key to any reform is that it reaches across all media and that rule breakers can be easily identified. Let's look at some specific reforms that seem to embrace these criteria.

End Overnight Polls

We've already seen innumerable examples of how the overnight poll can mislead. Such quickie polls risk a host of methodological errors. They are shallow, miss key groups, and pollute the environment for higher quality polls. Most seriously, these polls undermine debate—in some cases deliberately, as media pollsters attempt to bludgeon politicians with the appearance of unequivocal public opinion at key points of public opinion formation.

The advantage of eliminating the quickie, overnight poll is that it targets the most inaccurate and misleading polls. Eliminating this poll would allow politicians to make their policy cases and let voters learn before they respond. Further it would expose the absurdity of polling people before anyone but journalists have had a chance to recognize an issue. Given the level of ignorance about political issues, it is important for public opinion to be given time to settle, for voters to hear both sides, even just to get the facts, before being asked to render judgment.

This kind of reform is not a pipe dream. We know the media can show backbone and walk away from unscientific measures of public opinion. In 1995, NBC refused to report on the Iowa straw poll because it was not methodologically valid. Such a decision *should* be a simple and unarguable one for editors and producers. The straw polls of Florida, Iowa, and Louisiana are paid events masquerading as public opinion. Journalists cover these events because they are "tests" of the financial and organizational muscle of campaigns. Fine. This is not to say that they are unimportant measures of organization, money, and manpower. But it is most important in the early stages of political debates

> Overnight polls are shallow, miss key groups, and pollute the environment for higher quality polls.

to give *more* hearing to issues and less focus on the numbers. When candidates are numerous, public opinion divided, and primary voters looking to hear new ideas, that is the time for journalists to report with substantive attention to facts; that is the time to look at innovative ideas and novel arguments.

Use Only Likely Voters

The first and most promising step toward reform would be to conduct polls that screen, and screen tightly, for *likely voters*. This concept won't make most media pollsters or journalists happy, but as long as polls are used as the judge, jury, and executioner in partisan debates, they must be fair. Otherwise, they distort our public debate and institutions. Because the ultimate measure of our representative democracy is determined by the *sample* that goes to the polls and the *representative sample* that ends up in office, we should make the polls the servant of our Constitution—not make the Constitution the handmaiden of the apathetic and disconnected. If polling is as important to America as the media claim it to be, then we must demand that polls be as accurate as possible.

In the 2000 presidential race, it should have been clear to media sources that using registered voters is simply unacceptable; likely voters are a far better measure. Yet several media organizations continued to tap registered voters. Going into Labor Day weekend, television pundits and reporters covering the presidential election were shocked, appalled, and thoroughly baffled by this. For weeks leading up to the three-day weekend, nearly every media outlet had hyped the importance of a Labor Day lead in the polls. But three polls (by Research 2000, ICR, and Gallup) put the race between Vice President Al Gore and Texas Governor George W. Bush at a near dead heat just days before the Labor Day weekend. Research 2000 put Gore up by only 4 percentage points.[2] ICR gave the vice president a 3-point edge. Gallup had Bush ahead by 1 point. For anyone familiar with the race, public opinion was obviously soft and support constantly shifting.

Unfortunately the media's own imperatives for conflict, controversy, and color make such subtleties nearly impossible to report. The horse-race reporters need winners and losers. They need the ecstasy of victory and the agony of defeat.

Enter *Newsweek*, coming to the rescue of the working press. In a fourth poll conducted August 31, *Newsweek* discovered a tremendous 10-point lead for Gore. Although this poll gave the apoplectic talking heads desperately needed material, it also severely deceived the public. A week later, a Reuters/Zogby poll gave Gore a more modest 6-point edge.[3]

Newsweek's poll was deceptive because it employed sloppy methods. It was even more misleading because of its immediate results. It gave journalists exactly what they wanted: a massive Gore shift that foreshadowed a campaign of conflict and exciting swings in voter support. The *Newsweek* results were appended to an article that focused on the nearly unbeaten track record of candidates who were ahead on Labor Day weekend.

Every one of the Sunday morning talk shows that weekend cited the *Newsweek* poll.[4] The new numbers became the subject for debate. Anxious pundits used the data to offer their explanations for why Gore was up and Bush was down. The explanations ranged from the success of Gore's convention speech, to his choice of Lieberman, to missteps by Bush and Cheney.

Newsweek's polls consistently gave Gore the highest support among the dozens of polls over the months prior to Labor Day weekend. Due to *Newsweek*'s consistent use of registered voters and low samples (fewer than six hundred people in one case), the magazine stupidly or cunningly set itself up as a propaganda mill for the Gore campaign, sacrificing accuracy and objectivity, to join the mad dash for polls.

On August 18, *Newsweek* had Gore leading Bush by 6 points (48 to 42 percent). A Voter.com poll had Bush *up* by 5 points just two days earlier. And on August 19, a *USA Today*/CNN/Gallup poll had Gore leading by only 1 point (47 to 46 percent). In early August, a Reuters/Zogby poll (August 6) had Bush up by 17 points, while *Newsweek* (August 4) had Bush up by just 11 points. Even after weeks of results that cast doubt on the *Newsweek* numbers, journalists were still eager to glom onto the new data, although they should have known better.

The *Newsweek* poll was like a fiery car wreck or tragic plane disaster. The sheer drama and grotesque implications of the results made them irresistible to reporters. Journalists see the wild gyrations and comment, in part because they know that other journalists will comment.

The best way to prevent such misuse of polling is to improve the sample. Simply put, *Newsweek* and other media organizations should cease to use registered voters for political

Fox *News Sunday's* Brit Hume quipped that *Newsweek* would have shown a Gore lead if it were polling the Bush family.

polling. Those papers and networks that do violate this stricture would be easily identifiable. Other media organs could simply sanction the irresponsible work of those, like *Newsweek,* who cut corners and endanger democratic debate—discounting their work and refusing to report it until their methodology improves. As it stands now, a pollster is only subject to the occasional criticism of someone like Fox *News Sunday's* Brit Hume, who quipped that *Newsweek* would have shown a Gore lead if it were polling the Bush family.[5]

Sample One Thousand Voters

Sampling a thousand voters is another simple methodological reform that would allow citizens—whether journalists or just vigilant members of the body politic—to evaluate quickly the accuracy of a poll. Expert pollsters are almost unanimous that overnight polls yield erroneous or misleading results. Yet the media continue to use them. The chances are very slim, of course, that the media will retreat from the use of overnight polling, because those polls offer immediate evaluation and instant news for television segments and newspaper copy. But when it comes to horse-race polls, the quick and sloppy polls would be reduced if all media organizations used the simple standard of a thousand-person sample. A sample consisting of 1,000 people has a margin of error of ±3.1 percent. Typically overnight samples are much smaller than this, often dropping below 750 people.

What makes this a critical reform is that it provides an easy-to-understand measure and puts media organizations on the same competitive plane. Citizens could understand a

"1,000 or worthless rule." Reducing the margin of error becomes especially important in close races. Media polling isn't disposed to finding the most accurate poll and then dwelling on the many facets of its results. The proprietary nature of many polls and the selfishness of rivals prevent media organs from finding the best polls. Instead attention to horse-race polls is widespread, and the latest polling results are reported with little regard for accuracy. In such an environment, the worst polls are essentially equal to the very best. And the slightest shift of a few points, even when it is a sloppy poll of less than six hundred registered voters, can steal headlines, affect coverage, and squelch debate.

Release All the Information Related to Public Polls

Media pollsters and many journalists deflect criticism of the polling process, claiming that polling augments democracy. "News polls are a mirror to the public, permitting individuals to understand where they fit into the political system," says Kathleen Frankovic, director of surveys for CBS News. "Reporting public-opinion polls tells readers and viewers that their opinions are important, and can be even sometimes more important than the opinions of the elite."

While these descriptions praise polling as an extension of the democratic process, the track record of pollsters opening their results to public scrutiny is lamentable at best. Democratic institutions ought to be open and accountable to the public. But for most readers and viewers, the techniques used by media pollsters aren't just technically mysterious, they are deliberately hidden from scrutiny. For instance, the *New York Times*/CBS polls refuse to report nonresponse rates—the share of voters refusing to participate in the polls. (They do claim, however, they will hand over the information to other reporters on request.)[6] While Frankovic says polls are a reminder that all information in a democracy is free, CBS holds back the controversial and critical nonresponse data.

It's not hard to imagine the furor that would occur should some government official decide to do the same with government data. Section III of the American Association of Public Opinion Research Code states: "Good professional practice imposes the obligation upon all public opinion researchers to include, in any report of research results, or to make available when that report is released certain essential information about how the research was conducted."

As we saw earlier, GOP pollster Frank Luntz's refusal to abide by these rules resulted in professional censure. And some pollsters have attacked John Zogby of Zogby International for his proprietary methodology that re-weights results to correct for the Democratic biases of polls. In both of these cases, polling insiders have sought a more open and public process.

These efforts at disclosure should be applauded. They should also be applied more consistently. In chapter 3, we saw that full disclosure of polling conducted by the *New York Times* would have cast doubt on some of the editorial conclusions of the writers. The *Times* claimed in a front-page story, just a day before a critical vote on Medicare, that the public opposed Republican reforms. But in the full ninety-six-question survey, many of the GOP ideas were viewed far more favorably when actually explained to the public. In this case, the truths omitted by the paper would have led to a richer and far more accurate portrayal of public opinion.

Businesses that attempt to influence the public discourse about the direction and policies of government are subject to laws intended to minimize the manipulation of the system. When a newspaper times the release of its big news about public opinion on an issue just before a specific vote on that issue, it has the appearance of manipulation. Of course, an editor might plead that the newsworthiness of the event makes such polls not just inevitable, but helpful. When debate is compressed by a critical event, such as a vote, all aspects of a poll should contribute to public debate, not just those results that please the editorial board and ideological journalists.

As more and more polls come out, citizens need to conduct their own due diligence. The biggest problem with polls isn't in the sample used. The more serious problem is found in the way questions are worded. Media polls have become the sorry replacement for the debate that once took place among party leaders and the public. If polls are truly going to contribute to democratic debate, every question and all relevant details should be made public.

"Polls are accurate. The problem is that the media give polls out without essential information which would allow people to dispassionately judge," said Arnold Steinberg, author of *Political Campaign Management.* "Sometimes you can read an entire media report and never see what the questions were. It's like reading an article about union strikes and never finding out what the wages are and what the union wants."[7]

> Media polls have become the sorry replacement for the debate that once took place among party leaders and the public.

The media would do well, even in a routine matter, to provide the source of a poll. Take, for instance, the *Washington Post* article "Democrats' Takeover Dreams Take Shape." That report of September 20, 1999, focused on a possible changeover in Congress. The reporter quoted confident House Democrats and fearful Republican operatives about the close contest going into the 2000 election. One factor that favored Democrats was the high turnover of Republican incumbents. The reporter speculated on another factor: "Polls suggest that the issues on the current congressional agenda—HMOs, campaign reform,

gun control, Social Security, Medicare—tend to favor Democrats as well."[8] This kind of story is repeated hundreds of
times during an election year.

But the public's concern for these issues depends almost
entirely on how professional pollsters frame their questions.
It is critical that readers and viewers get a chance to judge for
themselves. A common media interest is the "priority poll,"
which presumes to rank exactly what voters want and where
they stand on basic issues. Journalists use such polls, as in the
2000 election, to report that some candidates, such as Vice
President Al Gore, back the most popular measures. The implication is that over time the (usually liberal) candidate will
begin to rise in the polls as voters figure out where the candidate stands on the issues. But most of these polls are highly
suspect because they demand nothing of the respondent. Unlike the daily task of weighing the costs and benefits on an individual level, the respondent is asked to give an opinion on a
question that rarely compares and contrasts the various costs
of a given course of action.

Today's newspapers make use of their Web sites to expand
and improve coverage. A hyperlink to the exact polls being
used by reporters would help bring some facts and subtlety to
deliberation in the public square. The *Washington Post* already discloses the questions and even demographic break-
downs of its issue polling. This is an example that should be
followed by more newspapers and networks.

Media pollsters should simply apply journalistic logic to
the "democratic devices" they call the voice of the people.
Journalists, being the guardians of the public trust, aggressively ferret out stories that are in the public interest. They report secrets, scoops, and use sources to report what the public
doesn't know—on the theory that the people have a "right to
know." The objective reporter tells the story, gets the facts,
and lets the chips fall where they may.

Politicians and concerned citizens have long complained about the media's double standards when it comes to criticizing their errant comrades. The fact is that journalists and editors are afraid of having the power of polling taken out of their hands. Polling provides them with a way to ratify their agenda-setting and then pummel those politicians who dare to contradict the public opinion polls they commission.

If polls are truly going to democratize information, then voters should have access to all the questions, their wording, and the order in which they were asked. Let the public judge the substance of the survey, who is being polled, and the relevance of the nonresponse rate.

> If polls are truly going to democratize information, then voters should have access to all the questions, their wording, and the order in which they were asked.

Television pundits, of course, are another matter. Most are mouthpieces for ideology or party, and it is naïve to expect them to hedge their claims of majority support for their ideas with public confessions about the gray areas from polls that they claim are the *vox dei*. But most television shows now have Web sites that can reveal the full results of polls used by participants and hosts.

In the model of John Stuart Mill's marketplace of ideas, pundits making claims from polls should take a step toward clarity. Like reporters, they should talk in terms of real numbers with sources and samples, disclosing exactly where they got their data. Pundits representing differing segments of the ideological spectrum could then hold each other accountable for the interpretation of the results. This isn't impossible. On many of the most famous political talk shows, participants discuss their topics before appearing in front of the camera. During those prep sessions, it is quite conceivable that journalists could turn over their polling data to their colleagues so voters could hear them challenged on the air.

Finally, in the interests of the public, media pollsters should learn from pollster Daniel Yankelovich, who believes that his job goes beyond merely recording answers to public opinion questions. He sees the main challenge of polling to be finding when polls will fall short because public attitudes haven't yet formed. "The missing concept [of American democracy] is a set of terms to describe the quality of public opinion and to distinguish 'good' public opinion from 'bad.'"[9]

> It is critical in a democracy to know the function of public opinion as well as when it is reliable enough to be a part of public debate.

Yankelovich believes so deeply in trying to distinguish between good and bad opinion that he has developed a "mushiness" index for *Time* magazine—a reform that could bring needed honesty and admissions of humility. The idea behind the mushiness index is to identify those cases of "bad" public opinion, when feelings are mixed, contradictory, or ill-formed. *Time* decided against using the measure. This, by itself, is a profound statement about media arrogance.

Yet such a reform—a way to make polls serve the people—helps demark the limitations of polling by fully disclosing those times when public opinion measures are going to be misleading. Polls *cannot* speak for the people and should not be accorded currency in the national dialogue if Americans are of two minds—and in far too many cases, the public is of two, three, or four different contradictory beliefs.

Media pollsters may not want to admit it, but the facts are still there: Americans are disconnected, apathetic, and ignorant. Most media organizations won't want to implement any type of reform. But it is critical in a democracy to know the function of public opinion as well as when it is reliable enough to be a part of public debate. If public opinion isn't formed, then this should prompt elected leaders and journalists to continue the debate until the American people understand and can come to some sort of judgment. To report public opinion before it settles (if it settles at all) is misleading and is a profound betrayal of the public trust.

Ask Content-Oriented Questions

What do people actually know? When a poll is conducted, we have no idea what information, facts, or illusions created public opinion. In this information vacuum, journalists too often assume an informed public and presume explanations for why the majority believes or supports a certain course of political action.

The next step in polling reform is to increase the number of nuts-and-bolts questions that are usually glossed over in the average poll. Before asking questions about vouchers, opportunity scholarships, or school choice, early questions should test what the public knows. Can the citizen define what a voucher is? Does a citizen know that "voucher," "opportunity scholarship," and "school choice" are the same thing? Do voters know how much is being spent on a given initiative? Do voters know what state governments are doing? In short, polls must ask fundamental questions if public opinion surveys are going to be something more than mere word recognition or reflex.

By knowing the results of content questions, vigilant citizens can more easily detect mushy opinion or shaky impressions. This is especially important because very few media polls ask the same question in several different ways. When pollsters do ask the same question in different ways, however, readers are better able to see how wording affects the out-come. If results differ radically from question to question, it is safe to assume that voters don't have strong opinions. Unfortunately most media organizations are unwilling to spend the money on such careful questioning.

Simple content questions, however, can give us some insight into voter apathy, alienation, or ignorance.

Of course, many polls already ask, "How closely have you followed . . . ?" This requires self-analysis and implies some degree of embarrassment or guilt for those who say they aren't following a public policy controversy closely. Assuming that voters have knowledge or have paid attention to the news turns polls into a measure of media stories and saturation rather than of opinion. This assumption means that questions will force voters to give answers for topics to which they have given little thought.

The Vanishing Voter Project routinely found at election time that voters were *not* nearly as settled on their choice for president as media polls showed. By asking voters an open-ended question—such as "Which presidential candidate do you support at this time, or haven't you picked a candidate yet?"—the Project discovered the number of undecided voters was much higher than in questions that simply supplied the names and parties of the rival candidates. Three weeks before the 2000 election—after three presidential debates, two party conventions, a vice presidential debate, and several million dollars in ads—14 percent of voters selected no candidate. One in seven registered voters still couldn't decide. This result was anywhere from three to four times as many undecided voters as were found in major

> When journalists report rough prejudices, gut feelings, or momentary passions, and then walk away, they undermine democracy.

media polls that pushed voters into making a partisan choice. Such results may undermine the horse-race polls, but they are critical to understanding the level of ignorance or indecision in the populace.

If knowledge is low and a voter does not understand basic definitions or cannot properly identify the institutional roles played by political actors, we know that such respondents are more likely to be tripped up or unduly influenced by question bias. Polling, therefore, should investigate not just what voters feel and believe, but also the knowledge and facts relied upon to reach a given conclusion.

When journalists report rough prejudices, gut feelings, or momentary passions, and then walk away, they undermine democracy. They are betraying the trust given to a free press, our primary marketplace for the exchange of ideas. Our liberal belief in democracy is predicated on the principle that all ideas and opinions will receive a fair hearing and compete against one another for the support of the public. Open debate requires that polls test exactly what voters know, however discouraging the results are for the media and pollsters who are eager to report on what the people "think."

Quality Debate Is Needed for Quality Opinion

A representative democracy rises or falls on the rhetoric used in the public square, because rhetoric frames the way we look at the world. Peace, prosperity, and public policy come from the meeting of minds and the deliberation of political leaders. Our finest moments as a nation are defined in the words and eloquence that persuade the nation to follow a new course and take up new challenges.

Thomas Jefferson is remembered first and foremost for his eloquence in writing the Declaration of Independence. Abraham Lincoln's Gettysburg Address reminded the nation in a scant few words of the sacrifices undertaken by soldiers who fought for the Union. Franklin Delano Roosevelt's words were the inspiration for many during the Depression and World War II. And Martin Luther King Jr. spoke with an eloquence that made people look deeply into their hearts to transform a nation.

These speeches weren't just verbal finery. They signaled the ideas and direction that leaders would take. Their polish and clarity gave Americans an insight into their leaders' minds and into the American purpose. Hearing how something is reasoned is as important to a democracy as the conclusion. Reasoned discourse allows every citizen to listen and decide. The leadership of these men would not have been possible if they were limited to a few sound bites—no matter how well they competed for the palm of eloquence.

If polling is to serve democracy through the dissemination of information, then, it must contribute to this process. Too often voters are asked to decide on issues for which they may have little or no information. As polls have become players in the political process, we must rethink what they are communicating.

Merely broadcasting the whims of voters, even those in a majority, truncates debate. This tends to make the lives of political leaders more difficult, and it pollutes the public square. Politicians tend to dumb down their message if voters express their beliefs with little reference to reality or politics. As polls continue to "represent" the direct voice of the people via an impatient media, we will continue to have politicians skilled in the art of pandering or manipulating the brute manifestations of emotive expression. They will use shortcuts and public relation devices that cater to the lowest common denominator of emotion with little respect for a well-argued or direct appeal to citizens.

Such a phenomenon is already in motion. This may be one reason that campaigns have become softer, conventions fuzzier, and candidates less open and daring in the presentation of their vision of reform—except in their rapacity to launch negative campaigns against opponents. By asking voters what knowledge they possess and what reasoning they may be using to make their decisions, we expand public debate to include something more than manipulation of the horse race through negative ads. We can then deepen the knowledge of voters so they can make informed decisions, not just respond to applause lines.

Some pollsters will object, of course. The prospect of exposing the sandy foundations of public opinion threatens their influence on the democratic process. But citizens need transparency if America is to tackle those real-world challenges that go beyond the fifty-word questions plied by a young interviewer rushing through a survey while a harried citizen tentatively answers in one or two words after a hard day of work.

Polling citizen knowledge about institutions or resources involved in solving problems lets us know more than merely what our fellow citizens think. It tells us *how* they think about critical issues, or even whether they are thinking at all. Polls, even content-based polls, are an imperfect surrogate for the debate and deliberation of the people's representatives, however. The give and take of candidates and officeholders has intrinsic value beyond the outcomes in elections and legislation. It is educational. When our fellow citizens are "winging it" on public policy questions, the media must have the moral courage to take responsibility and report the ignorance or apathy of the public.

The People's Ignorance Is a Report Card on the Press

Ultimately journalists must come to realize that much of the citizenry's ignorance flows from frivolous and nutrient-deficient reportage. The perilous state of the nation's government-run schools is partly to blame. But journalists should understand that just as they have imposed themselves on the process and television has become such a powerful force, so have voters tuned out. Over the past three decades, politicians and parties have struggled to reach voters, while the time given to anchors, correspondents, and journalists has skyrocketed.

> Journalists need to change their tune and remember whom they serve.

Journalists and pundits often lament the choice of candidates in the election cycle. Their jaded and cynical view of political candidates fans the flames of distrust and undermines the ability of elected officials to lead. The traditional press' bias for the horse race and their tendency to dissect the strategy of the campaigns are as destructive as any negative campaign ad paid for by voters.

Journalists need to change their tune and remember whom they serve. By stressing issues, journalists would not only inform voters and help battle the appalling gaps in voter knowledge; some experts think issue coverage could also help reinvigorate interest in politics.

Political scientist John D. Anderson writes, "[E]xposure to strategy . . . informed people about the candidates' standing in the horse race. Exposure to issue coverage encouraged learning about the issues."[10] Such issue coverage might help diffuse the power of polling. Polls have gained power because a candidate's electoral viability and leadership are wrapped up in the health of his or her campaign as measured by the trends and gaps between rivals. Journalists consciously—and citizens subconsciously—have come to see polls as harbingers of coming coverage and the apparent strength of candidates. But this does little to excite voters. The constant chorus of coming defeat or eventual coronation is what gives polls their hypnotic effect.

The prospects for reform aren't good. Journalists, as a class, want to have an impact. It is a peculiar feature of the profession that journalists work with ideas but usually only in a shallow and indirect way. Journalist Eric Sevareid once compared journalists to alcoholics. They make bold and impassioned promises to improve themselves and avoid the cause of their ruin. In this case, it is common for the press to hold conferences and seminars about how to improve issue coverage in the next election. But once the new election cycle begins and that wine touches their lips, they can't help themselves. Perhaps the reason is hidden deep in the psychology of the journalist, a creature prone to talking about trends, not ideas; strategy, not issues; blunders and gaffes, not speeches and policy. In such an issue-poor news environment, the herd mentality and personality hazing of the media lead not just to a trivialization of the news but to a more ignorant public as well.

Pollsters Must Object to Sloppy Polling

Some pollsters have objected to some media polling, in the abstract. These critiques are usually expressed in seminars, at conventions, in books, or on scholarly panels. And like media criticism, it is rare for one pollster to criticize another and even more rare to criticize a poll in the media on which the pollster depends to have his or her own polls made public. Most such critiques appear too late and in too protected a sphere to rise into public consciousness, balance the debates, and critique the enormities of the worst manipulations of public opinion. Yet journalists can be held accountable when experts try hard enough. This could be extremely helpful for reforming media treatment of polls. As Tom Rosenstiel writes:

> The press, in a sense, is engaged in a continuing three-way conversation, between its sources, its audience, and itself. If any of the participants no longer seem interested—if, for instance, the press writes about something but experts consider it insignificant—the story will soon die. If the press believes people no longer want to hear about a story, or that its coverage has gotten too far ahead of its audience, it similarly tends to stop.[11]

Unfortunately such a process is slow. When a poll comes out essentially attacking one party's ideas on Medicare reform the day of a vote, the need for vigilant and informed critics of polling rises exponentially. It is a sad fact that media is probably the most unaccountable profession in America. Rarely are the withering lights of the cameras or the reporter's clever interrogatories turned on other journalists. It is a common complaint from elected leaders—voiced under the breath or long after they are out of office—that the press exists on a privileged and untouchable plane.

Every polling story must include caveats, especially if the poll being cited is an advocacy poll.

Still, even if the monkeys can't reform themselves, other creatures on the media landscape can respond. If polling experts can talk about the limitations of polls, then there is the possibility for reform. Of course many pollsters are dependent on the media to get out their observations and critiques. Therefore many are no doubt reticent about voicing any strong criticism of when public opinion is soft or when polls are misleading. But the point here is to realize that every polling story must include caveats, especially if the poll being cited is an advocacy poll.

Eliminate Pseudo-Polls from Web Sites

Polling experts and media polling advocates can complain all they want about pseudo-polls, but ultimately they have failed to make any inroads against the proliferation of unscientific and methodologically unsound measures of public opinion. The attraction of polling is simply too psychologically irresistible. Every one of the major media Web sites—*Newsweek, Time, U.S. News & World Report,* the *Washington Post,* the *New York Times,* CNN—uses pseudo-polls to test what Internet users think and feel about the most trivial of questions.

This should remind us of the power that polls exercise over our lives. That influence does not come from the role of public opinion in a democracy, as media pollsters would have us believe. It comes about because polls provide a statistical denouement in media stories, a curiosity marker, or a distraction for cyberslackers at work. Many polling experts see plenty of examples of the misuse of polls. Web pseudo-polls undermine the critical appraisal of polling results, which is necessary for good debate, an accountable press, and a vigilant citizenry.

Polling Should Challenge Journalists

Washington Post columnist E. J. Dionne recommends two uses for polls: "First, polls are most valuable in challenging and overturning preconceptions; second, polls should be used to describe the complexity of public opinion, not oversimplify what citizens think."[12] As we've seen, polling too often mirrors the prejudices of reporters and editors. They schedule when polls are conducted and determine what frame of reference and narrative will contextualize the results. But such tactics lead to a self-reinforcing process in which media pollsters learn whether the media's own stories and schema have sunk in.

For instance, in the middle of the 2000 presidential race, an NBC poll asked on *Nightline:* Whom do you trust more on gun control? George W. Bush or Al Gore? How different the question would be if it asked: Whom do you trust to protect the Second Amendment? The same kind of question-baiting occurs on such topics as campaign finance "reform," pitting one candidate or party for a government regulation against another candidate or party opposing a government restriction. Almost invariably, in a liberal media culture, Democrats are allies in the quest for government activism, with Republicans acting as unfeeling reactionaries who stand in the way of journalists and their polls.

The 2000 presidential primaries are an excellent example of how polling can challenge journalists and keep them accountable. As media support for the insurgent campaign of Senator John McCain gathered momentum in the press, journalists began to suspect that McCain was being propelled by his advocacy of campaign finance reform. For reporters it was the perfect story, providing the opportunity to push McCain and campaign finance reform, which was an idea dear to their hearts. But as polling at the time indicated—in one of the few unequivocal instances—voters were not that concerned, were even unaware of, campaign finance reform.

For years, voters routinely ranked campaign finance last or next to last on the list of their priorities. Such priority polls can be equivocal when several issues have roughly equally divided support, but it is fairly unequivocal when voters put the same idea at the bottom. This type of polling did help check journalistic excess in turning the appeal of McCain's personal heroism during Vietnam and his crusading rhetoric about the need for reform in Washington into a specific endorsement of campaign finance spending restrictions.

Recognize the Limitations of Polls

Polls are not and can never be a surrogate for debate. The length of questions, the portrayal of issues, and the ignorance of the sample can never replace the rich and full deliberation needed to answer policy questions. And the clear record is that polling reportage similarly fails as a substitute for substantive issue coverage. Polls cannot uncover new and relevant facts as quickly as congressional hearings can. They cannot compete with the nuance of a House debate or a Senate speech. "Rarely, if ever, do polls give us thoughtful, considered answers to truly important questions," observes Larry Sabato, political science professor at the University of Virginia. "Polls are inherently superficial. They are constructed on the lowest common denominator of society—both in terms of language and in terms of ideas."[13]

> Polls are not and can never be a surrogate for debate.

Polls are particularly dependent on the old computer slogan "Garbage in, garbage out." Public opinion polling is only as good as the work that goes into the questions. Complex, nuanced questions yield a more subtle and profound final result. Asking respondents about trade-offs, challenging them to rank what they believe, and asking the same question in different ways can help uncover weaknesses and inaccuracies resulting from the way questions are worded.

The French political philosopher Alexis de Tocqueville worried about how public opinion could come to dominate debate and erode reason in a democracy: "[Democratic public opinion] uses no persuasion to forward its beliefs, but by some mighty pressure of the mind of all upon the intelligence of each it imposes its ideas and makes them penetrate men's very souls."[14] It is this self-destructive aspect of democracy that should lead us to be careful with polling results. Because polls ostensibly speak for the people, they have a unique power in political debate. They also drive government power and intervention more than they restrain it. When our political system moves slowly and an idea loses support (such as nationalized health care or campaign finance reform), we should remember that our Constitution does this for a reason. With reflection and education, we can come to see that a "crisis" is often just an excuse for some elites to increase the power of the state. Tocqueville lamented that the formalities of institution and law that slow the execution of democratic measures are exactly what democracies need most:

> Men living in democratic centuries do not readily understand the importance of formalities and have an instinctive contempt for them. . . . Formalities arouse their disdain and often their hatred. . . . [T]heir chief merit is to serve as a barrier between the strong and the weak, the government and the governed, and to hold back the one while the other has time to take its bearings. Formalities become more important in proportion as the sovereign is more active and powerful and private individuals more indolent and feeble. Thus democracies by their nature need formalities more than other peoples and by their nature have less respect for them.[15]

Public opinion is difficult to discern exactly. But as Tocqueville and the American framers understood, it doesn't always translate directly into the good of the people. "Formalities" such as the Bill of Rights, the separation of powers, the veto power of the presidency, or the filibuster in the Senate may be annoyances to those enamored of plebiscitary democracy and polling tyranny. But neither journalists nor media pollsters would endorse suspension of the First, Fifth, or Sixth Amendments, even if such moves polled well. America is, after all, a constitutional republic that specifically limits government power in certain spheres. The majority, even backed by government force, is restricted from certain invasions of personal freedoms.

Let Political Leaders Frame Questions

If journalists understand the limitations of polling and the importance of deliberation, then it follows that they should search for some way to increase the knowledge of voters and educate them. When the framers wrote the Constitution, they sought a process that would lead to rich and wise discourse among all the participants in government. During the past forty years, the power of television and polling and the decline of parties have reduced the educational function of political leaders and party outreach. Journalists have imposed themselves on the political process. As a result, politicians have less time to persuade voters and deliberate for public benefit.

> During the past forty years, the power of television and polling and the decline of parties have reduced the educational function of political leaders and party outreach.

It is interesting to note that the Center for Media and Public Affairs found in a 3,000-person survey conducted by Louis Harris and Associates that 65 percent of Americans do not believe that "journalists should point out what they believe are inaccuracies and distortions in the statements of public figures." That's a sharp break from what the framers intended, but a rather unequivocal statement about the resentment many Americans feel toward a press that dominates America's political process.

But the media can give some measure of influence back to political leaders to educate, persuade, and deliberate. In the current system, candidates must find ways to get their campaign messages through the cynical critiques and armchair strategizing of the media. The media should step aside and give voters more time to judge candidates for themselves. The best way to do this is to hold more debates. Instead of two or three debates, politicians should be put into the position of defending their ideas in a series of debates, as many as ten or twenty per election season. Debates can be popular modes of generating candidate and public interest, and such forums can force candidates to differentiate themselves from one another.

It is a sad fact that there is more interaction between rivals in the carefully scripted world of wrestling than there is between those men and women who ostensibly represent the ideas and factions seeking to shape the future of America. For the Bob Doles of the world who must square off against the Bill Clintons, it will be a painful change. Like dinosaurs, some politicians may become extinct. But debates do give voters an opportunity to make up their minds based on what candidates say.

If debates were more frequent, they could also be more focused. A debate on a single issue would enable candidates to prepare specific answers, and questions for the other candidate. If candidates could challenge one another more closely, answers could be more effectively challenged than in the current system of questions from journalists. In addition, a freer format would allow voters to see how candidates think through the policies they support.

In late 1999, Vice President Al Gore challenged his Democratic rival for the presidential nomination to a series of debates, even though Gore was the front-runner. For much of the media, the story wasn't what could be gained from such debates, rather it was Gore's political motivation, the strategy behind Gore's tactics, that garnered their interest. Whatever his motives for the challenge, Gore deserved praise for his courage to put his position as front-runner on the line.

The value of debates, especially at moments of controversy when polls are most popular, is even more apparent after a study of soft public opinion. As we've seen, a polling question isn't just influenced by the wording. Most journalists and citizens already have a sense that biased words can throw results. From polling we soon learn that how a question is framed is more difficult to detect, but just as consequential. Most voters don't have anything approaching the political consciousness to hazard the strong, unequivocal positions demanded by public opinion polls. They decide questions based on how the poll primes their minds. For example, in a poll about taxes, are they being asked about tax cuts or more spending? Are they being asked about spending for specific programs, or does the question imply more government pork barrel? Are they being given any information about the efficiency of current government programs, or are they being asked to judge a new, well-intentioned program without comparison to existing programs?

> Public exploration of ideas in which two parties frame the language of debate would help energize the electorate and take some of the power from the one voice of an ideological press.

All these factors frame and influence the mind-set of the respondent. The importance of framing is a good reminder of why debates can play such a big role in educating and improving American representative democracy. Candidates from the two parties can be forced into taking concrete positions; and they can show in a debate the trade-offs, considerations, compromises, and nuances that form their worldview. Such a public discussion can help voters understand the complexities that go into making decisions in the grit and grime of politics. Such a public exploration of ideas in which two parties frame the language of debate would surely help energize the electorate and take some of the power from the one voice of an ideological press.

Provide a More Partisan Press

America would be a better place if press and television sources were *more* partisan, not less. Journalists now struggle with an impossible standard: objectivity. Some have dismissed it altogether. As Tom Rosenstiel writes, many journalists do not believe in objectivity, what they seek is fairness. They want a balance to their reporting. Anyone who has attended a symposium on journalism or polling is struck by just how limp-wristed criticism is. Rarely do journalists subject one another to the kind of withering scorn to which they subject politicians. And pollsters are loathe to criticize other pollsters, and then only in the most roundabout ways.

The notion of objectivity shields the press from accountability. In the more partisan model of the past, media presented their opinions openly and were forced to defend their ideas with clear and decisive reportage. Americans already believe that journalists are biased. In the polls that dare to ask the question, most Americans indicate they believe the media are left-leaning. It would be healthier for public debate, especially in light of the decline in party power and the concomitant rise in media influence, to honestly put forward these biases. Journalists would be required to reason more clearly, do more research, and present more facts to defend their work. Slapping a "news analysis" label on those pieces that step over the edge into noticeable news editorializing is simply not enough.

As we've seen, polling depends on media imperatives and reportage. The subtlest change in wording or presentation of questions can vastly alter the results. The weak, fluid, often ignorant opinions of citizens make the framing of public policy questions critical. This is a reminder of the power of words and their importance to public discourse. In the past, political leaders were the representatives of the collected opinion of the nation. But their role in the political drama went far beyond mere transmission of local opinion. They were empowered to advance ideas, negotiate, discuss, and deliberate.

The relationship between political ideas and the rhetoric we use to explain our values isn't value neutral. Our language and the way we discuss freedom, responsibility, and government action vary with our opinions about what government ought to do. Journalists should learn from these meta-issues of public opinion polling. The vigilant citizen should rethink the idea that journalism is an objective practice.

> Journalists are attracted to the idea of objectivity because it helps them escape scrutiny.

Journalists are attracted to the idea of objectivity because it helps them escape scrutiny. The media now play such a powerful role in American society that we ought to reexamine the schema, the imperatives, and the political biases of the Fourth Estate.

To consider a writer, producer, or editor's bias does not mean that the reader or viewer is a right-wing nut or left-wing conspiracy theorist. It merely means that we recognize the value-laden worldviews of our fellow human beings, even in a professional pursuit that seeks truth, fact, and knowledge. As political science professor Richard H. Reeb Jr. writes, "A healthy political journalism should not suppress its major premises or implied conclusions but assume the honorable burden of stating and defending them, in open and honest debate, to other members of the media, to politicians, and to other citizens."[16]

Right now, political discussions struggle to *seem* objective. Pundits talk in clichés and journalistic shorthand with a jejune detachment better fitted to Oscar Wilde than to democratic citizens. Debate is basically nonexistent as they talk about a politician's problems, how he or she "comes off," or other ephemera. Objectivity is a fig leaf that does little to conceal. Instead it has led to an absurd situation in which journalists strike the pose of outside observers in a representative democracy that lives or dies by the quality of debate and vigilance of a participating citizenry.

By elevating the idea of objectivity, journalists are really accomplishing two things. First, the notion of objectivity distracts citizens from being critical and the press from being accountable. The objectivity myth creates a guaranteed point of contention in every debate about journalistic partisanship or error. Journalists are programmed early on to defend the entire profession with the Pavlovian reflex "Bias is in the eye of the beholder." Such claims are a smoke-and-mirrors tactic.

Second, the idea of objectivity saps the energy of reportage and contributes to the herd mentality. Journalists are usually intelligent professionals, and they soon figure out the power relationships in their career. The highest aspiration of most reporters, if they cover politics, is to attain a position with the *New York Times,* the *Washington Post,* or some other big city daily. Journalists understand that the journalistic establishment is overwhelmingly liberal. Individual stories may be fair with a lead that emphasizes the liberal take and ends with a few odd conservative or Republican responses. So one endangers one's claim to being an objective journalistic by slipping outside these well-defined boundaries. PBS's *Washington Week in Review* is stocked with journalists, nearly every one disposed to liberal ideas. It is also the most boring program on television, as the leftists strain to cloak their partisan positions in the gray prose of "objectivity."

It is a poor reader, indeed, who cannot detect the bias of writers by their work. Sometimes it comes out in the reporting. In most cases, however, the objectivity campaign hides bias by making press coverage univocal. The same schema and narratives pervade story after story. As we saw in the case of Dick Cheney, the media report on a beleaguered politico's defensive responses to an "objective" media's blitzkrieg of questions.

> Whether left or right politically, Americans have fears of government power and political intrigue.

But there is always bias. When the *New York Times* decides to do a story on divisions in the Republican Party or waste at the Pentagon, editors have chosen (perhaps unconsciously) *not* to pursue a story on divisions in the Democratic Party or waste at the Department of Education, Housing and Urban Development, or the IRS.

In the current climate, biases are cloaked—sometimes very well—but they still exist. In the vain quest for objectivity, readers and viewers are subjected to safe reportage that hammers away at how politicians appear, what campaign strategists are doing, or what is going on in the polls. It is poor news coverage. The idea of objectivity has led to a kind of colorless, empty, and ridiculously contrived reportage of little interest to Americans (particularly those in many of

Bush's red states) and, in many cases, of interest only to other reporters.

Whether left or right politically, Americans have fears of government power and political intrigue. In the early years of American nationhood, the press was a vigilant and vigorous *partisan* in policing the power of parties and protecting the people. Today's press may be more intelligent, better informed, and more skeptical of politicians, but it has little of the energy necessary to engage the public. In the past three to four decades of rising "objectivity," government has grown astronomically as voters increasingly stare into space. The professionalism of the media and its claims of objectivity have become an excuse to cozy up to those in power to catch a few bread crumbs of a breaking story or get an unsourced account for the horse race. Only by tracking the drama of such political races is it possible to delude oneself into thinking it is interesting or substantive.

The First Amendment was written to hold government accountable, keep officials in check, and spread education and ideas. We can do this best through strong, unrelenting, and tough coverage that challenges the citizenry—and other reporters—to think deeply about the future of America. For polling, we should take as our reform model the work of Celinda Lake and Ed Goeas. These pollsters, one democrat and the other republican, combine forces to write questions and then give separate analysis. What a different world polling would be if it were given such in-depth partisan scrutiny.

Remember the Role of the Constitution

In *Federalist* No. 52, Alexander Hamilton argues for the limited government established by the new written constitution.

"With less power, therefore, to abuse, the federal representatives can be less tempted on one side, and will be doubly watched on the other."[17] Unfortunately, today we have forgotten the wisdom of these words. Voters are tuning out even as government grows in power and gains more control over American lives. By inverting Hamilton's argument, the people have become less vigilant and the government more tempted to expand the power of the state.

For the most part, the framing of polling issues creates forty-point shifts in policy questions, because citizens still value limited government, however popular individual spending proposals may be. Today our political debates and polling questions are caught between two parties and ideologies: one that advocates a vast bureaucracy and regulatory state with power and authority over even the smallest parts of life, which are run for the benefit of all; and another that advocates a small government with reduced federal powers, which presumably trusts the individual to make his or her own moral and economic choices.

Depending on how media pollsters frame the questions, limited constitutional government can be stressed or minimized. In most cases, polling questions test controversies over how to spend more money on things the public "needs." The results naturally tend to favor the well-intentioned, nice-sounding proposals. But the wording and results bias democratic debate against the limited government, separation of powers, and accountability so treasured by the framers of the Constitution. Polling, especially in the hands of a media that are more disposed to trust government than the people, leads to this paradox: a constant stream of polls testing the public's disposition to increase the power of government at the expense of the individual.

For those who wish to portray the state as the compassionate vehicle for the attainment of a painless utopia, the poll is the perfect weapon. The media still work from the progressive model: They identify a wrong and hint at (or sometimes suggest) a government regulation, law, or increased spending. They rarely question or police government programs, but rather operate from the presumption that the federal bureaucracy could do so much more if given just a little more money. Few questions probe cuts, corruption, or the waste in government agencies.

Polling fits in with this progressive, crusading, and liberal model because it automatically undercuts any debate about limited government. Polling isn't disposed to asking fundamental questions that animated our founders. Are there certain things we simply don't want government to do? Are there powers we don't want officials to have? Can we limit government and keep those in government accountable? This frame of liberty is absent from most polls. Polling and media coverage have combined to make the media the true agenda setters. Despite the evident distrust of government in polls and the near hatred of media in other polls, government continues to expand. Like the feared mob of old, we simply don't know what the crowd will do. It is almost guaranteed, however, that the public will embrace the most shallow and seemingly easiest answers at the expense of in-depth discussion and debate. In *Federalist* No. 55, James Madison writes: "In all very numerous assemblies, of whatever character composed, passion never fails to wrest the scepter from reason. Had every Athenian been a Socrates, every Athenian assembly would still have been a mob."

> For those who wish to portray the state as the compassionate vehicle for the attainment of a painless utopia, the poll is the perfect weapon.

Pollsters continue to ask voters to back policies that expand government, while expecting the mob of polls to provide the deliberation and education that make for a healthy Republic. For the most part, Americans don't want to be hard-hearted or selfish, so they endorse government-expanding plans because the economic cost isn't real to them. They can rule their pocketbook but, with shallow media reportage, reasoning about $2 trillion budgets quickly becomes childlike in its simplicity.

Rarely, if ever, do voters get to consider the reform or alteration of government programs already in place. Voters aren't asked questions that call into question or fundamentally debate the role of government in America, because media pollsters work in conjunction with editors and journalists. The media simply create a defensive phalanx that questions the motives of those who would "gut the social safety net," "rob seniors," and so forth.

"Draconian cuts" or "savage spending reductions" are the code words and incendiary language that will alarm a populace largely ignorant of the passing political scene and the vast sums and legions of programs already in place. What is most odd in the current media-polling regime is that media pollsters still insist that polls are a democratic good, in and of themselves. Why is the mere expression of opinion in a poll an important part of democracy?

While the media are championing the opinion of the American Everyman in polls, his economic and political liberty continues to be curtailed. As the state expands, the ability of Everyman to enjoy the wages and rewards of freedom shrinks. Eventually it won't matter what polls ask because the regulatory state will be so unlimited and unrestrained that a voter's opinion won't really matter. Voters will only be free to emotionally grunt their daily opinions by Internet or to automated phone dialers, unable to lower the level of government that restricts their lives and takes more and more of their earnings to pay for ill-conceived and corrupt spending.

We must remember that ultimately human beings are creatures capable of choice and liberty. We must remember the promise of America is a trust in the people—or more precisely in the right of each citizen to life, liberty, and the pursuit of happiness. It is not a trust in government. It is a trust in the liberty that animates and excites innovation, experiment, and intellectual adventure. Human beings can reason and deliberate in their private lives far more effectively than any bureaucracy or polling majority can. The noblest expression of liberty and self-rule isn't found in the questions written by a pollster working in New York for a newspaper story about a Washington controversy and then tested on a busy and uninformed citizen. Liberty values action and rewards individual decisions in every life where the margin of error is contained by personal responsibility and government is limited to allow the full expression of every belief and private opinion.

NOTES

Chapter 1

1. Laurence McQuillan, "Poll: Public Changes Its Mind on Impeachment," *USA Today*, 17 December 1999.
2. William Schneider, interview with the author, 4 November 1999.
3. George Gallup, "Polls and the Political Process—Past, Present, and Future," *Public Opinion Quarterly* (Winter 1965–1966), 549.
4. http://www.cbsnews.com/now/story/0,1597,275048-412,00.shtml.
5. Richard Morin and Dana Milbank, "Poll Shows New Doubts On Economy," *Washington Post*, 27 March 2001.
6. Richard L. Berke and Janet Elder, "60 Percent Favor Bush, But Economy Is Major Concern," *New York Times*, 14 March 2001.
7. "Poll: Taxes Replace Education As Top Issue for Americans," Reuters, 14 March 2001.
8. Will Lester, "Poll: Bush Tax Plan Lacks Support," Associated Press, 10 April 2001.
9. http://www.foxnews.com/story/0,2933,5055,00.html.
10. Michael Traugott, interview with the author.
11. Richard Benedetto and Jim Drinkard, "As Political Polls Grow, So Does Their Influence," *USA Today*, 13 September 2000.
12. Richard Morin, "What Monica Taught Me About Polling in the 2000 Presidential Election" (Election Polling: Nebraska Symposium on Survey Research, 1999).
13. Paul J. Lavrakas and Michael W. Traugott, in press.
14. Kathleen A. Frankovic, speech to the Fifth Latin American Marketing Research Conference, Santiago, Chile, April 25–28, 1999.
15. "Polls and Scandal, from Nixon to Clinton: A Resource for Journalists," *Media Studies Center* (1998), 5
16. Sander Vanocur, "Impact of Presidential Debates," National Communication Association, 2000.
17. "Poll Says Americans Ignore Polls," The Joan Shorenstein Center on the Press, Politics, and Public Policy, June 8, 2000.

18. Kellyanne Fitzpatrick, speech to the Fifth Annual Conservative Leadership Seminar, Washington, D.C., June 14, 1999.
19. John Zogby, speech to the National Press Club, Washington, D.C., March 10, 1999.
20. *The Simpsons*, "Two Cars in Every Garage, Three Eyes on Every Fish."
21. William Safire, "The Wild Poll Pendulum," *New York Times*, 28 September 2000.
22. *CNN Talkback Live*, October 24, 2000.
23. Ariana Huffington, "Some Democracy: Hang Up on Pollsters," *Chicago Sun-Times*, May 24, 1998.
24. Alison Mitchell, "A Modest Poll Proposal," *New York Times*, 8 October 2000.
25. Peter Jennings, "How Polling Has Trampled the Constitution, and Other Mild Observations," *Civilization*, September 1999.
26. Mitchell, "A Modest Poll Proposal."
27. Steve Holland, "Bill Maher Unbound at Democratic Fund-Raiser," Reuters, 24 June 2000
28. "Poll Numbers Don't Deter Dems," *USA Today*, 14 August 2000.
29. Dan Lewerenz, "Forbes: Polls Are 'Writing in Sand,'" Associated Press, 19 October 1999.
30. George W. Bush, Prepared Remarks to the National Center for Policy Analysis, March 31, 1998, Dallas, Texas.
31. Ramesh Ponnuru and John J. Miller, "McCain Gets Acheson Wrong," *National Review Internet Update*, 8 December 1999.
32. Alexander Hamilton, James Madison, and John Jay, *The Federalist* (Washington, D.C.: Regnery Publishing, 1998), 110.
33. Camillus, no. 5, 1795.
34. Alexander Hamilton to Robert Morris, August 13, 1782, Quoted in *Alexander Hamilton and American Foreign Policy*.
35. Larry Sabato, National Press Club, Washington, D.C., March 10,1999.
36. James Madison (Papers of Madison: 14 178–179) *National Gazette*, January 2, 1792.

Chapter 2

1. Peter Jennings, "How Polling Has Trampled the Constitution, and Other Mild Observations," *Civilization*, September 1999.
2. Susan Herbst, *Numbered Voices: How Opinion Polling Has Shaped American Politics* (Chicago: University of Chicago Press, 1993), 42.
3. Sandra L. Bauman and Paul J. Lavrakas, "Reporter's Use of Causal Explanation in Interpreting Election Polls," 3.
4. Howard Kurtz, "For Gore, This Buss Was Right on Time," *Washington Post*, 22 August 2000.

5. Richard Morin and Claudia Deane, "Gore Leads in Poll," *Washington Post*, 22 August 2000.
6. Media Research Center, *MediaWatch*, 1 September 1988, 1.
7. Barbara Ehrenreich, "Whose Gap Is It Anyway," *Time*, 6 May 1996.
8. Steven Stark, "Gap Politics," *Atlantic Monthly*, July 1996.
9. Laurence McQuillan, "First Jewish VP Pick Lifts Dems' Standing in Poll," *USA Today*, 8 August 2000.
10. David W. Moore, "Positive Public Reaction to Gore's Choice of Lieberman As VP," Gallup News Service, 8 August 2000.
11. Kathy Kiely, "Poll: Gore Trails by 16 Points," *USA Today*, 14 August 2000.
12. Richard Morin, "Telling Polls Apart," *Washington Post*, 16 August 2000.
13. Murray Edelman, interview with the author, 22 March 2000.
14. Paul J. Lavrakas and Michael Traugott, in press, chap. 14.
15. Daniel Yankelovich, *Coming to Public Judgment: Making Complex Democracy Work in a Complex World* (Syracuse, N.Y.: Syracuse University Press, 1991), 22.
16. Alison Mitchell, "The Politics of Guns: Tilting Toward the Democrats," *New York Times*, 14 May 1999.
17. Ceci Connolly, "Littleton Alters the Landscape of Debate on Guns," *Washington Post*, 5 May 1999.
18. David Jackson, "Gun Lobby Faces First Congressional Test After Littleton," *Dallas Morning News*, 12 May 1999.
19. Associated Press, "Gun Control Bolstered: Americans Want Tougher Laws, Poll Shows," *Newsday*, 6 May 1999.
20. Geoffrey Dickens, "Outgunned: How the Network News Media Are Spinning the Gun Control Debate," Media Research Center, 5 January 2000.
21. Roger Rosenblatt, "Get Rid of the Damned Things," *Time*, 9 August 1999.
22. Gwen Ifill, *NBC Nightly News*, May 18, 1999.
23. Roger Rosenblatt, "The Killing of Kayla," *Time*, 13 March 2000.
24. Jerry Adler and Karen Springen, "How to Fight Back," *Newsweek*, 3 May 1999.
25. James Dao, "New Gun Control Politics: A Whimper, Not a Bang," *New York Times*, 11 March 2000.
26. Matthew Robinson, "Polls Aplenty, But More Is Less," *Investor's Business Daily*, 12 July 1996.
27. Adam Clymer, "Americans Reject Big Medicare Cuts, New Poll Finds," *New York Times*, 26 October 1995.
28. Ian Fisher, "Battle Over the Budget: The Polls," *New York Times*, 27 October 1995.
29. Ibid.
30. John Merline, "The Dems' Medicare Flip-Flop," *Slate*, 28 June 1997.

31. Analisa Nazareno, "Majority of Voters Flunk Idea of Schools Vouchers," *Miami Herald,* 8 November 1999.
32. Randy Lewis, interview with the author.
33. Yankelovich, *Coming to Public Judgment,* 22.
34. John Zogby, speech to the National Press Club, Washington, D.C., March 10, 1999.
35. Robinson, "Polls Aplenty."
36. Yankelovich, *Coming to Public Judgment,* 170.
37. Thomas E. Patterson, *Out of Order* (New York: Vintage Books, 1994), 212.
38. Alexis de Tocqueville, *Democracy in America,* vol. 1, chap. 11, 186–187.
39. Jeremy Torobin, "Dole Falls to Horse-Race Campaign Coverage," *Newswatch* (http://www.newswatch.org/electionwatch.htm), 20 October 1999.
40. S. Robert Lichter and Jeremy Torobin, "Is Media Attraction Fatal?" *Newswatch* (http://www.newswatch.org/electionwatch.htm), 21 January 2000.
41. Charles W. Roll Jr. and Albert H. Cantril, *Polls: Their Misuses in Politics* (New York: Basic Books, 1972), 29.
42. Thomas Patterson, *Out of Order,* 74.
43. E. J. Dionne, "Impact of Polls on Reporters and Democracy," *Media Polls in American Politics* (Washington, D.C.: Brookings, 1992), 153.
44. Tom Rosenstiel, *Strange Bedfellows: How Television and the Presidential Candidates Changed American Politics, 1992* (New York: Hyperion, 1993), 45.
45. William Raspberry, "A Little Knowledge Can Be a Meaningless Thing," *Washington Post,* 29 November 1999.
46. Mike Allen, "A Shift in Bush's Footing," *Washington Post,* 23 August 2000.
47. Frank Bruni, "Bush Stumbles, and Questions Are Raised Anew," *New York Times,* 24 August 2000.
48. Maria L. La Ganga, "Bush Tallies Up the Trillions, Trips," *Los Angeles Times,* 23 August 2000.
49. Linda Feldmann, "In a First, Gore Forces Bush to Play Defense," *Christian Science Monitor,* 24 August 2000.
50. Terence Hunt, "Gore Trying To Connect to Voters," Associated Press, 17 August 2000.
51. Susan Milligan, "Gore Campaign Picks Up Speed on Friendly Turf," *Boston Globe,* 21 August 2000.
52. Tom Raum, "Gore Bounces Back After Convention," Associated Press, 24 August 2000.
53. Ceci Connolly, "Gore Warms Up to Clinton (Iowa)," *Washington Post,* 21 August 2000.
54. Robinson, "Polls Aplenty."

55. Paul Singer and Shaun Waterman, "Focus Group Raises Concerns About Cheney," UPI, 30 July 2000.

56. Gary Langer, "Bounces and Bumps: Americans Give Bush Bounce, Worry About Cheney," ABCNews.com, 31 July 2000.

57. Electionline, "Polling Flap," *USA Today,* 21 January 2000.

58. Jim Yardley, "Call to Voters at Center Stage in GOP Race: Clashing Over Whether a Smear Is the Goal," *New York Times,* 15 February 2000.

59. Paul J. Lavrakas and Michael W. Traugott, in press, chap. 14.

60. Cheryl Arvidson, "Be Wary of Poll Numbers, Reporters Warned" (http://47.freedomforum.org/professional./2000/1/6pollsters.asp), 6 January 2000.

61. Ibid.

Chapter 3

1. Harry O'Neill, "Polling Pitfalls: 10 Cautions," *Campaigns and Elections,* September 1998.

2. Humphrey Taylor, "Myth and Reality in Reporting Sampling Error," *The Polling Report,* 4 May 1998.

3. Michael Kagay, "How the 'Typical' Respondent Is Found," *New York Times,* 4 November 1999.

4. Herbert Asher, *Polling and the Public* (Washington, D.C.: CQ Press, 1992), 39.

5. Kevin Phillips, "Can Dole Pull a Truman? In His Dreams, but It's Not All His Fault," *Washington Post,* 19 May 1996.

6. Susan Yoachum, "Smugness Worries Top Democrats, Big Lead Holding Up at Labor Day Milepost," *San Francisco Chronicle,* 2 September 1996.

7. Mitofsky's preferred method for assessing the accuracy of polls is the "difference between two differences." The first difference is a poll's prediction of the election results for the two leading candidates. The second difference is the actual election results for those same two candidates.

8. Warren J. Mitofsky, "Poll Review: Was 1996 Worse Than 1948?" *Public Opinion Quarterly* (Spring 1998), 245.

9. Paul J. Lavrakas, interview with the author, 14 November 1999.

10. Peter Cleary, "Just What Are Polls Good For?" *Investor's Business Daily,* 25 January 2000.

11. Albert H. Cantril, *The Opinion Connection: Polling, Politics, and the Press* (Washington, D.C.: CQ Press, 1991), 4.

12. Tony Fabrizio, interview with the author, 1 June 2000.

13. Don Van Natta Jr., "Polling's 'Dirty Secret': No Response," *New York Times,* 21 November 1999.

14. Larry Sabato, interview with the author, 13 November 1999.

15. Lavrakas, interview.

16. Charles Cook, "Here a Poll, There a Poll," *Christian Science Monitor,* 19 January 1996.
17. Matthew Robinson, "Polls Aplenty, but More Is Less," *Investor's Business Daily,* 12 July 1996.
18. Sarah Simmons, interview with the author, 24 March 2000.
19. Cheryl Arvidson, "Be Wary of Poll Numbers, Reporters Warned," (www.freedomforum.org/professional./2000/1/6pollsters.asp), 6 January 2000.
20. Lloyd Grove, "New Hampshire Confounded Most Pollsters; Voters Were a Step Ahead of 'Tracking' Measurements," *Washington Post,* 18 February 1988.
21. Murray Edelman, interview with the author, 22 March 2000.
22. Michael R. Kagay, "Poll Results Show Vulnerability in Calling Primaries Accurately," *New York Times,* 3 February 2000.
23. Mitofsky, "Poll Review," 232.
24. Philip Meyer, "Why Do Pollsters Flub Election Results?" *USA Today,* 9 February 2000.

Chapter 4

1. Matthew Robinson, "Polls Aplenty, but More Is Less," *Investor's Business Daily,* 12 July 1996.
2. Michael W. Traugott and Paul J. Lavrakas, *The Voter's Guide to Election Polls* (Chatham, N.J.: Chatham House Publishers, 1996), 106.
3. Matthew Robinson, "Is 'Voucher' Now a Bad Word?" *Investor's Business Daily,* 30 October 1997.
4. Daniel Yankelovich, *Coming to Public Judgment: Making Complex Democracy Work in a Complex World* (Syracuse, N.Y.: Syracuse University Press, 1991), 32.
5. Richard Noyes, interview with the author.
6. Richard Noyes, "When Bigger Isn't Better," Media Research Center *Special Report,* March 6, 2000.
7. Matthew Robinson, "Reform Advocate Steve Forbes on Lower, Simpler Tax Code," *Investor's Business Daily,* 27 February 1999.
8. Herbert Asher, *Polling and the Public* (Washington, D.C.: CQ Press, 1992), 39.
9. Everett Carll Ladd and Karlyn H. Bowman, *Public Opinion About Abortion* (Washington, D.C.: AEI Press, 1999), 32.
10. Kellyanne Fitzpatrick, "A Guide to Polling," speech to the Clare Booth Luce Institute, July 1999.
11. Greg Schneiders and Jo Ellen Livingston, "Can You Trust the Polls? Well, Sometimes," *Wall Street Journal,* 8 February 1999.

12. Yankelovich, *Coming to Public Judgment*, 32.
13. John R. Zaller, *The Nature and Origins of Mass Opinion* (New York: Cambridge University Press, 1992), 95.
14. Donald Kinder and Lynn Sanders, "Mimicking Political Debate with Survey Questions: The Case of White Opinion on Affirmative Action for Blacks," *Social Cognition* (August 1990), 99.
15. Zaller, *The Nature and Origins of Mass Opinion*, 93.
16. Alexander Hamilton, James Madison, and John Jay, *The Federalist* (Washington, D.C.: Regnery Publishing, 1998), 287.
17. George Santayana, *Dominions and Powers: Reflections on Liberty, Society, and Government* (New York: Charles Scribner's Sons, 1951), 140.

Chapter 5

1. Public Agenda, *On Thin Ice*, December 1999, 10.
2. Alexander Hamilton, James Madison, and John Jay, *The Federalist* (Washington, D.C.: Regnery Publishing, 1998), 110.
3. Kathleen Frankovic, speech to the American Association of Public Opinion Research, August 1999.
4. Michael X. Delli Carpini and Scott Keeter, *What Americans Know About Politics* (New Haven, CT: Yale University Press, 1996), 98.
5. Ibid.
6. Opinion Research Corporation, survey of 1,008 adults, June 29, 1999.
7. Ibid.
8. International Communications Research Poll for National Public Radio, 1,557 adults, May 26–June 25, 2000.
9. Gallup Organization Poll, 1,018 adults, March 7–10, 1991.
10. Princeton Survey Research Associates Poll for *Times Mirror*, 1,500 adults, June 8–11, 1995
11. Pew Research Center for the People and the Press, September 1998.
12. Delli Carpini and Keeter, *What Americans Know*, 101.
13. John R. Zaller, *The Nature and Origins of Mass Opinion* (New York: Cambridge University Press, 1992), 16.
14. Delli Carpini and Keeter, *What Americans Know*, 43.
15. Christopher Shea, "Is Voter Ignorance Killing Democracy?" *Salon* (www.salon.com/book/it/1999/11/22/voter/index.html), 22 November 1999.
16. Delli Carpini and Keeter, *What Americans Know*, 100–101.
17. James D. Reschovsky and J. Lee Hargraves, "Health Care Perceptions and Experiences: It's Not Whether You Are in an HMO, It's Whether You Think You Are," Issue Brief No. 30, September 2000.
18. James L. Payne, *The Culture of Spending* (San Francisco: ICS Press, 1991), 118.

19. Matthew Robinson, "Polls Aplenty, but More Is Less," *Investor's Business Daily,* 12 July 1996.
20. Rogan Kersh, "Anti-Democratic Demos: The Dubious Basis of Congressional Approval," *Critical Review* (Fall 1998), 581.

Chapter 6

1. Rogan Kersh, "Anti-Democratic Demos: The Dubious Basis of Congressional Approval," *Critical Review* (Fall 1998), 581.
2. John R. Zaller, *The Nature and Origins of Mass Opinion* (New York: Cambridge University Press, 1992), 29.
3. Daniel Yankelovich, *Coming to Public Judgment: Making Complex Democracy Work in a Complex World* (Syracuse, N.Y.: Syracuse University Press, 1991), 21.
4. Ibid., 16.
5. George Gallup, "The Quintamensional Plan of Question Design," *Public Opinion Quarterly* 11, no. 3 (Fall 1947), 386.
6. Yankelovich, *Coming to Public Judgment,* 42.
7. Ibid., 42.
8. Ibid., 44.
9. Ibid., 43.
10. James Bovard, *Freedom in Chains* (New York: St. Martin's Press, 1999), 107.
11. Thomas Jefferson to William C. Jarvis, 1820.
12. Alexander Hamilton, James Madison, and John Jay, *The Federalist* (Washington, D.C.: Regnery Publishing, 1998), 49.
13. Thomas Jefferson to Charles Yancey, 1816.
14. Charles S. Hyneman and Donald S. Lutz, *American Political Writing During the Founding Era, 1760–1805, Vol. 1* (Indianapolis: Liberty Fund, 1983), 700.
15. Ibid.
16. Ibid.
17. Ibid.
18. John Adams, *Political Writings of John Adams* (Washington, D.C.: Regnery Publishing, 2000), 4.
19. Ibid., 6.
20. Ibid., 13.
21. Richard D. Brown, *The Strength of a People: The Idea of an Informed Citizenry in America, 1650–1870* (Chapel Hill: University of North Carolina Press, 1996), 40.
22. Madison to William T. Barry, August 4, 1822.

23. Colleen A. Sheehan and Gary L. McDowell, *Friends of the Constitution: Writings of the Other Federalists 1787–1788* (Indianapolis: Liberty Fund, 1998), 197.

24. Bovard, *Freedom in Chains,* 108.

25. Michael X. Delli Carpini and Scott Keeter, *What Americans Know About Politics and Why It Matters* (New Haven, CT: Yale University Press, 1996), 59.

26. Ibid., 49.

27. Fred Yang, interviewed by Mark Helperin, *ABC News,* 27 August 1999.

28. Margaret Stimman Branson, "What Does Research on Political Attitudes and Behavior Tells Us About the Need for Improving Education for Democracy?" Paper delivered to The International Conference on Education for Democracy, October 3, 1994.

29. Todd G. Buchholz, "Hope and Danger for Economic Literacy," *The Region* (December 1998).

30. William B. Walstad, "Why It's Important to Understand Economics," *The Region* (December 1998).

31. Ibid.

32. Stephen Ansolabehere and Shanto Iyengar, *Going Negative: How Negative Advertisements Shrink & Polarize the Electorate* (New York: Free Press, 1995), 37.

33. Frank Luntz, "Focus Group Research in American Politics," *The Polling Report,* 16 May 1994.

34. Ibid.

35. Thomas Patterson, "Election 2000: How Voters 'See' a Presidential Debate" (http://www.vanishingvoter.org/releases/10-03-00debate-1.shtml).

36. Hamilton, Madison, and Jay, *The Federalist,* 576.

37. James Madison, *Journal of the Federal Convention* (American Freedom Library CD-ROM), vol. 1, 93–94.

38. Hamilton, Madison, and Jay, *The Federalist,* 104.

39. Ibid., 109.

40. Ibid., 110.

41. Ibid., 476.

42. Ibid., 533–534.

43. Ibid.

44. Sheehan and McDowell, *Friends of the Constitution,* 196–197.

45. Hamilton, Madison, and Jay, *The Federalist,* 533–534.

46. Ibid., 477.

47. Ibid., 477, 478.

48. Ibid., 476.

49. Sheehan and McDowell, *Friends of the Constitution,* xii.

50. Hamilton, Madison, and Jay, *The Federalist,* 49.

Chapter 7

1. Christopher Hitchens, *No One Left to Lie To: The Triangulations of William Jefferson Clinton* (New York: Verso, 1999), 35.
2. Herbert Asher, *Polling and the Public* (Washington, D.C.: Congressional Quarterly Press, 1992), 17.
3. Lawrence R. Jacobs and Robert Y. Shapiro, *Politicians Don't Pander* (Chicago: University of Chicago Press, 2000), 125–126.
4. Ibid., 11.
5. Tom Rosenstiel, *Strange Bedfellows: How Television and the Presidential Candidates Changed American Politics, 1992* (New York: Hyperion, 1993), 54.
6. William A. Henry III, *In Defense of Elitism* (New York: Bantam, 1994), 1999.
7. John R. Zaller, *The Nature and Origins of Mass Opinion* (New York: Cambridge University Press, 1992), 96.
8. Will Marshall, speech to the Heritage Foundation, Washington, D.C., 30 September 1999.
9. Dick Morris, *Behind the Oval Office* (Los Angeles: Renaissance Books, 1999), 10.
10. George Stephanopoulos, *All Too Human: A Political Education* (Boston: Little, Brown and Company, 1999), 332.
11. Morris, *Behind the Oval Office*, 11.
12. Stephanopoulos, *All Too Human*, 335.
13. Ibid., 336.
14. The Editors, "And Now—Social Security," *The Nation*, 15 March 1999.
15. Stephanopoulos, *All Too Human*, 351.
16. Daniel Casse, "The Quadrennial Fear of Ideas: Policy and Presidential Campaigns," *Policy Review* (August/September 1999).
17. Ibid.
18. Dick Morris, *The New Prince* (Los Angeles: Renaissance Books, 1999), 129.
19. Question order rotated.
20. Michael W. Traugott, interview with the author.
21. Jean Francois-Revel, *The Flight from Truth: The Reign of Deceit in the Age of Information* (New York: Random House, 1991), 250.

Chapter 8

1. George Stephanopoulos, *All Too Human: A Political Education* (Boston: Little, Brown and Company, 1999), 436.
2. Michael W. Traugott, interview with the author.

3. Murray Edelman, interview with the author.
4. Everett Carll Ladd, "The Approval-Score Trap," *IntellectualCapital .com*, 1 October 1998.
5. Scott Rasmussen, interview with the author, 1998.
6. Six percent thought "both equally" damaging; 6 percent said "neither" would be damaging; and 8 percent said "don't know."
7. Frank Newport and Alec Gallup, "The Popularity Paradox," *Gallup Poll Releases*, 31 January 1998.
8. Rotated by half samples.
9. Christopher Hitchens, *No One Left to Lie To: The Triangulations of William Jefferson Clinton* (New York: Verso, 1999), 109–110.
10. It is amazing it took only a few for the White House to uncover Willey's letters after the damage done on *60 Minutes* given the White House's history of losing critical e-mail on national defense, misplacing billing records on million-dollar land deals, forgetting the details of million-dollar fund-raising plans, and repeatedly bungling subpoenas from Congress.
11. James Carville, to ABC's *Good Morning America*, February 26, 1998.
12. Dan Rather, *CBS Evening News*, August 12, 1994.
13. Bryant Gumbel, to Susan McDougal and her attorney on *Today*, September 17, 1996.
14. Al Hunt, on CNN, October 5, 1996.
15. *Newsweek*'s Jonathan Alter, on MSNBC, April 1, 1998.
16. ABC's Lisa McRee, August 19, 1998.
17. Mortimer Zuckerman, April 6, 1998.
18. Susan Schmidt and Michael Weisskopf, *Truth at Any Cost: Ken Starr and the Unmaking of Bill Clinton* (New York: HarperCollins, 2000), 151.
19. Louis Harris and Associates, 1,248 adults nationwide, August 14–19, 1987.
20. *Los Angeles Times*, 12 February 1999.
21. Question rotated through other figures including Bill Clinton
22. Will Lester, "Experts Baffled by Clinton's Approval Ratings," Associated Press, 14 September 1998.
23. Hitchens, *No One Left to Lie To*, 70.
24. David A. Vise, "Counsel Keep Clinton Investigation 'Open,'" *Washington Post*, 11 April 2000.
25. Congressional Record, February 12, 1999.
26. Ibid.
27. Ibid.
28. Bill O'Reilly, "The O'Reilly Factor," Fox News Channel, February 3, 1999.
29. David P. Schippers with Alan P. Henry, "Senate Leaders Rigged Impeachment Trial," *Human Events*, 25 August 2000.

30. Ibid.
31. Hitchens, *No One Left to Lie To*, 106.
32. David P. Schippers with Alan P. Henry, *Sell Out: The Inside Story of President Clinton's Impeachment* (Washington, D.C.: Regnery Publishing, 2000), 254, 266.

Chapter 9

1. Eugene McCarthy, *No-Fault Politics: Modern Presidents, The Press, and Reformers* (New York: Random House, 1998), 197.
2. Research 2000, 810 likely voters; Bush: 42 percent, Gore: 46 percent. ICR, 784 registered voters; Bush: 41 percent, Gore: 44 percent. Gallup, Bush: 46 percent, Gore: 45 percent.
3. Alan Elsner, "Gore Leads by 6 Points in New Reuters Poll," Reuters, 7 September 2000.
4. Michael Brus, "Sunday Morning with God and Joe," *Slate*, 3 September 2000.
5. *Fox News Sunday*, September 10, 2000.
6. Don Van Atta, "Silent Majorities; Polling's 'Dirty Secret': No Response," *New York Times*, 21 November 1999.
7. Matthew Robinson, "Polls Aplenty, But More Is Less," *Investor's Business Daily*, 12 July 1996.
8. Michael Grunwald, "Democrats' Takeover Dreams Take Shape," *Washington Post*, 20 September 1999.
9. Daniel Yankelovich, *Coming to Public Judgment: Making Complex Democracy Work in a Complex World* (Syracuse, N.Y.: Syracuse University Press, 1991), 15.
10. John D. Anderson, "The Place of the Media," *Critical Review* 12, no. 4 (Fall 1998), 489.
11. Tom Rosenstiel, *Strange Bedfellows: How Television and the Presidential Candidates Changed American Politics, 1992* (New York: Hyperion, 1993), 70.
12. Quoted in Thomas E. Mann and Gary R. Orren, *Media Polls in American Politics* (Washington, D.C.: The Brookings Institution, 1992), 14.
13. Larry Sabato, speech to the National Press Club, 10 March 1999.
14. Alexis de Tocqueville, *Democracy in America* (New York: Harper & Row, 1969), 435.
15. Ibid., 698–699.
16. Richard H. Reeb Jr., *Taking Journalism Seriously: "Objectivity" As a Partisan Cause* (Lanham, Md.: University Press of America, 1999), 4.
17. Alexander Hamilton, James Madison, and John Jay, *The Federalist* (Washington, D.C.: Regnery Publishing, 1998), 408.

INDEX

Abortion issues, 161–163
Accountability: First Amendment and, 356; objectivity and, 352; as policing by informed citizens, 224, 225, 315; of politicians, 233; reform ideas for, 343–345, 346–347
Adams, John, 220–222, 225, 230, 238
Advocacy polls, 136–137
Agenda, setting, 68–69, 76, 85
Alienation: distrust of government and, 25–26; ignorance as result of, 81; need for debate and, 40; public opinion and, 142; reasons for, 216, 233; sampling and, 142–143, 327
Anecdotal quotes, 16
Apathy: ignorance and, 207–208, 230; negative ads and, 231; polling and, 27, 31, 142–143, 206, 208, 212, 327; reasons for, 26, 212–214, 216; oward politics, 24, 26, 138, 248
Ashcroft, John, 4–6, 7, 8–10, 12

Bandwagon effect, 120, 122–126, 143, 249
Bias: effect on measuring public opinion, 22; of the media, 352, 353; of media news coverage, 62–64, 215, 354–355; of media polls, 7, 10, 18, 22, 57–68, 132–135, 159; objectivity vs., 354–355. See also Objectivity; Partisan press; Wording.
Bill of Rights, 4, 42, 200, 214, 349
Bush, George W.: appealing to voters, 252–253; criticism of polls, 37–38; education issues and, 18–19; gender gap and, 55; pardoning Weinberger, 298; polls on, 7, 27, 49, 57, 76–77, 86–87, 88, 93, 94, 100, 110, 118, 156, 251, 277, 328–330; position on issues, 192–193; tax cut debate and, 11–17; voter ignorance about, 186, 192–193; welfare policy of, 20

Campaign finance reform, 10, 76–79
Campaign polls, accuracy of, 135–136
Causal analysis, using polls for, 49–50
Cheney, Dick, 13, 95–97, 98–99, 101
Churchill, Winston, 245
Civics, ignorance of, 189–192, 208
Clinton, William: allegations/charges against, 272, 306–307, 311–312, 317; appealing to voters, 252–253, 263; election campaign, 119–120; gender gap and, 55, 56; job approval rating of, 284, 285, 286, 303; Medicare issues and, 69, 72–73; on the NRA, 68; polls on, 23, 36, 83, 86, 101, 109, 118, 129, 250–251, 275; public approval ratings, 285; sexual harassment suit against, 272, 293–294; use of focus groups, 232–233; use of polls, 30, 83, 136, 255–256, 271, 273–274, 275. See also Impeachment crisis.
Confidence interval, 112, 113, 114
Constitution: as context for understanding public opinion, 40–43; deliberation supported by, 239, 242–244; ignorance about, 189–190; ignoring, 287, 292, 309; impeachment and, 287, 307–308, 309; role of, 217–218, 220, 239, 356–360; undermined by polls, 34
Controversy: creating, 6; media craving for, 53, 85, 282, 293, 328; polling during, 2, 5, 7–8, 61, 62, 64, 67, 80; topics of, 152. See also Crises.
Crises, polling during, 2, 61, 62, 64, 67, 80

Debate: agenda set by media, 68–69, 76, 85; avoiding issues during, 29, 84, 260–262, 268; bias in media polls and, 57–68; framing of, 270; gender gap assumptions and, 54–57; honing and channeling of, 38; ignorance's

during, 293, 299. *See also* Starr, Kenneth; Starr Report.
Impeachment process: Constitution and, 287, 307–308, 309; described, 315; public's ignorance about, 184–185; role of the Senate in, 316
Impression democracy, 12, 39, 42, 124, 156, 237
Impressions of voters, 19, 27–28, 244, 252
Information. *See* Education of voters
Instant media polls. *See* Quick polling
Internet. *See* Web sites
Issues: avoiding, 29, 84, 260–262, 267, 268–269, 272, 306, 309, 311; framing, 152–156, 159, 183, 258, 270, 357; ignorance about, 150, 181, 184, 192–195, 197; issue polls, 102–103, 104, 236, 268–269; lack of reports about, 73, 89–91, 159, 215; polls' contributions to, 267. *See also* New ideas; specific issues.

Jefferson, Thomas, 218, 219, 224–225, 238, 321–322, 340

Kennedy, John F., 23, 270
Knowledge: illusion of, 195–200. *See also* Ignorance.

Landslide leads, 119–120
Language. *See* Questions; Wording
Leadership: polls' undermining of, 94–97, 260–263, 264; as protection of liberty, 40–41; voter expectations for, 263–266, 270. *See also* Politicians
Liberty: beginnings of, 21; education and, 219–225, 321, 322; protecting, 40–41, 42, 130–131, 219–225, 242; threatened by ignorance, 200; threatened by mob rule, 42, 239–240; trust in, 360
Lincoln, Abraham, 21, 340

Madison, James, 39, 42–43, 142, 174–175, 225, 239, 358
Mail surveys, 143–144
Majority rule, 35
Margin of error, 112, 113, 114, 330
Media: misuse of polling data by, 74; need for accountability by, 343–345; polling influenced by, 141, 269; polls' catering to stories, 68–79; polls' effect on, 27, 34, 47; polls ignored by, 75–76; as public agenda setters, 68–69, 76, 85; reform needed in, 324–325, 342–343, 346–347; shallow news coverage by, 86, 175,

253–254, 341. *See also* Bias; Media polls.
Media polls: academic polls vs., 60; bias in, 7, 10, 18, 22, 57–68, 132–135; private polls vs., 136; quickness of, 59, 133; reasons for creating, 46–48. *See also* Quick polling.
Medicare issues, 69–70, 71–73, 133–134, 198, 232–233, 248, 332
Methodology of polling: as art vs. science, 36, 173–174; during impeachment crisis, 276–292; representative democracy and, 144–145; voter refusal and, 126–127, 128, 129–130. *See also* Framing; Sampling; Wording.
Missile defense issues, 18
Mob mentality: deliberations vs., 42, 240; encouraged by polling, 143, 203, 205; manipulation of, 230; as threat to freedom, 239–240
Mobocracy, defined, 42
Moynihan, Daniel Patrick, 34–36

Negative advertisement, 231–232, 250–251
New ideas: effect of polling on, 28; public distrust of, 262; undermined by polls, 28, 83–84, 105, 261
Nixon, Richard, 23, 283–284

Objectivity, 17, 20, 101, 173, 352, 354
Overnight polls: deliberation undermined by, 81, 82–83, 326; inaccuracies in, 31, 80, 128–129, 330; need to eliminate, 326–327; sampling for, 330

Partisan press, 352–356
Patriotism vs. popularity, 40
Policy issues. *See* Issues
Political leaders. *See* Leadership; Politicians
Political parties, 21, 357
Politicians, 245–270; accountability needed for, 233; appealing to ignorant voters, 252–254; avoiding issues, 267, 268–269; contemptuous media coverage of, 253; dislike of polls by, 36–38; landslide leads of, 119–120; nomination process for, 84–85; poll-driven, 305; polls' effect on, 81, 85–89, 177; polls' undermining of, 4–5, 94–95; polls used by, 245–247, 248–250, 267, 268; public distrust of, 45–46, 302; shallow media coverage on, 90, 91, 92, 124, 203; terms of office, 240–241, 242; view of public opinion, 38, 253;

on, 112, 117–118, 129–130, 142–143;
undermined by voter ignorance,
196. *See also* Framing; Questions;
Sampling; Wording.
Rule of law, 42, 221, 272, 274, 292, 311

Sampling: alienated voters and,
142–143, 327; during impeachment
crisis, 277–281; margin of error in,
112, 113, 114, 330; number of people
used in, 329, 330; random, 80,
114–116, 126–127, 141, 142, 144,
145; registered vs. "likely" voters,
58, 116–122, 131, 277–279, 280–281,
327–330; results effected by, 112,
117–118, 129–130, 142–143; voter
nonresponse/refusal rates, 31,
126–127, 128, 129–130, 281, 331;
weighing the sample, 130–131
School voucher polls, 18–19, 73–75,
152–156, 179–181
Science of polling. *See* Methodology of
polling
Special interest groups, 267
Starr, Kenneth, 7, 272, 294–296,
298–301, 309–311, 313, 314
Starr Report, 287, 300, 310, 313

Tax cut issues, 11–17, 156–160, 197, 351
Television, 33, 85, 86, 231, 247, 254, 335,
341
Tyranny, 221, 237–238, 239, 242

Underdog effect, 123

Virtual primary, 86, 87, 88, 89, 322
Voters , 27–40; distrust of government
by, 25, 217; impressions of, 19,
27–28, 244, 252; "likely" vs. registered, 58, 116–122, 131, 277–279,
280–281, 327–330; lying to pollsters
by, 33, 126; new trends of, 112; non-
response/refusal rates of, 31,
126–127, 128, 129–130, 281, 331;
power and importance of, 227;
turnout for elections by, 116,
119–120, 121, 125, 138, 143,
216–217; "unlikely," 117; virtue and
intelligence needed in, 42–43, 220.
See also Alienation; Apathy; Education; Ignorance.

Walsh, Lawrence, 296–299
Washington, George, 189, 218, 223
Web sites: newspaper reports on, 334;
pseudo-polls on, 4, 345; for researching candidates, 253
Wording: biased, 7, 8–9; clarity of,
164–167; code words, 147, 167–170,
307, 308, 317, 359; framing issues by,
152–156, 159, 183, 282–291, 310;
public opinion pushed by, 17, 25,
167; response manipulated by, 7,
8–10, 50, 52, 70, 73–75, 147–148,
150–151, 152, 168, 170–174, 180,
183. *See also* Push polling; Questions; Results of polls.

Year-round campaign, 30

ABOUT THE AUTHOR

Matthew Robinson is the 1999 Philips Foundation Fellow. Before that, he worked for four years as a writer and editor with *Investor's Business Daily*. In addition, he has written for the *Los Angeles Times, Wall Street Journal, National Review, City Journal, Cincinnati Enquirer, Human Events, Baltimore Sun, Consumers Research,* American Spectator Online, and IntellectualCapital.Com. He is currently the managing editor at *Human Events* magazine.

He and his stories have been featured on Fox News Channel, CBN, News Talk Television, The Rush Limbaugh Show, and others. His work has also been used and quoted by Bob Dole, Newt Gingrich, Bill Bennett, and Rush Limbaugh.

Mr. Robinson is also an award-winning education writer. He has spoken to the American Political Science Association about the media and polling, and he is an adjunct fellow with the Claremont Institute, where he frequently writes on the history and ideas of the American Revolution.

In college, Robinson majored in philosophy, graduating *summa cum laude* from the University of California at San Diego. He grew up in Southern California with two younger brothers where he enjoyed surfing—a sport more difficult to pursue in his new home of Alexandria, Virginia. He can be reached at msrob53@aol.com.